The Archaeology of the

Clay Tobacco Pipe

XII. Chesapeake Bay

edited by

Peter Davey and Dennis J. Pogue

Liverpool Monographs in Archaeology and Oriental Studies No. 14

BAR International Series 566

1991

B.A.R.

122, Banbury Road, Oxford, OX2 7BP, England

GENERAL EDITOR

A.R. Hands, B.Sc., M.A., D.Phil.

BAR 566, 1991: 'The Archaeology of the Clay Tobacco Pipe. XII. Chesapeake Bay'
Liverpool Monographs in Archaeology and Oriental Studies No. 14

© The Individual Authors, 1991

The authors' moral rights under the 1988 UK Copyright,
Designs and Patents Act are hereby expressly asserted.

All rights reserved. No part of this work may be copied, reproduced, stored,
sold, distributed, scanned, saved in any form of digital format or transmitted
in any form digitally, without the written permission of the Publisher.

ISBN 9780860547150 paperback
ISBN 9781407348636 e-book
DOI https://doi.org/10.30861/9780860547150
A catalogue record for this book is available from the British Library
This book is available at www.barpublishing.com

CONTENTS

	Page
List of illustrations	ii
Foreword	
Peter Davey	iii
Introduction	
Dennis J. Pogue	1
Clay Tobacco pipes from four 17th century domestic sites in the Lower Patuxent Valley of Maryland.	
Dennis J. Pogue	3
An analysis of Clay Tobacco Pipes from Harmony Hall, Maryland.	
Stephen R. Potter and Robert C. Sonderman	27
A Descriptive Analysis of the White Clay Tobacco Pipes from the St. John's Site in St. Mary's City, Maryland.	
Silas D. Hurry and Robert W. Keeler	37
Tobacco Pipes from Pope's Fort, St. Mary's City, Maryland: an English Civil War Site on the American Frontier.	
Henry M. Miller	73
Seventeenth Century Clay Tobacco Pipes from Smith's Townland, St. Mary City, Maryland.	
Timothy B. Riordan	89
Tobacco Pipes from the Abell's Wharf Site (18 ST 53), St. Mary's County, Maryland.	
Michael E. Humphries	99
Clay Tobacco Pipes from Two Early Colonial Sites at St. Inigoes Manor, Maryland.	
Julia A. King	105

LIST OF ILLUSTRATIONS

Frontispiece: Chesapeake Bay location map   iv

Pogue:
1. Lower Patuxent Valley, Maryland, site locations.   2
2. King's Reach Site plan.   4
3. Distribution map of total pipe stem fragments, King's Reach.   7
4. Distribution map of early pipes (9-8-7/64th").   7
5. Distribution map of middle pipes (6/64th").   7
6. Distribution map of late pipes (4-5/64th").   7
7. Maker's marks, King's Reach.   8
8. Representative pipe bowls recovered from plowzone, King's Reach.   11
9. Representative pipe bowls from features, King's Reach.   13
10. Representative pipe bowls from King's Reach; rouletted decoration from 18 Cv 232.   15
11. Pipes from Mattapany-Sewall (18 St 390).   19
12. Pipes from 18 Cv 169.   21
13. Decorated pipe stems from 18 Cv 169, and pipes from 18 Cv 232.   23

Potter:
1. Area map of Harmony Hall (18PR305), Prince Georges County, Maryland.   28
2. Plan view of the main block of excavations at the site of the earthfast house, Feature 17.   29
3. Clay tobacco pipes from Feature 17, the burned, earthfast house midden. Scale 1:1.   31
4. Clay tobacco pipes A and B from Feature 22, a trash pit. Pipes C-F from stratum above Feature 17. Pipe G from Feature 14, a trash pit. Scale 1:1.   33

Hurry
1. Type A Bowls: Variety 1 a-c; Variety 2 d-f; Variety 3 g-o.   39
2. Type A Bowls: Variety 4 a-f. Type B Bowls: Variety 1 h-i; Variety 2 j-k.   40
3. Type C Bowls: Variety 1 a-c; Variety 2 d-f. Type D Bowls: g-h. Type E Bowls i-j.   41
4. Type F Bowls: a-b. Type G Bowls: c-k.   43
5. Type Bowls: Type H a; Type I b; Type J c; Type K d-g; Type L h-i.   45
6. Type M Bowls: Variety 1 a-n.   46
7. Type M Bowls: Varieties 2 a-g and 3 h-m.   47
8. Type M Bowls: Variety 4 a-n.   48
9. Type M Bowls: Variety 4 a-d; Variety 5 e-f; Vareity 6 g.   50
10. Type M Bowls: Vareity 7 a-c; Variety 8 d-g.   51
11. Makers' Marks: Heels a-k; Bowl Marks l-aa.   52
12. Stem Marks a-k.   58
13. Stem Marks: a-b; Mould Imparted Bowl Base Marks: c-h.   60
14. Decorated pipe bowls and stems: Relief Moulded Bowls a-f.   62
15. Decorated Pipes: Rouletted and Impressed Stem Decoration a-k.   64
16. Decorated Stems: Rouletted and Impressed Decoration a-f; Mold decorated g-h.   66

Miller:
1. Location of St. Mary's City and Pope's Fort (18ST1-13).   74
2. Plan view of Pope's Fort, built in 1645.   75
3. White clay tobacco pipes with maker's marks (bowls 1x, Marks 2x).   77
4. Unmarked white clay pipes from Pope's Fort.   79
5. White clay funnel pipes and stem decorations of likely Dutch origin.   81
6. Molded terra cotta pipes.   83
7. Molded terra cotta pipes from Pope's Fort.   85
8. Handmade terra cotta pipes from Pope's Fort; probably of American Indian manufacture.   86

Riordan:
1. Distribution of Excavation Squares on Smith's Townland and the Major Structures found there.   89
2. Pipes by Country of Origin.   90
3. Graph of Bowl Shape types.   91
4. Stem Bore Diameter from Plowzone.   91
5. Bore Stem Diameter by Country of Origins.   91
6. Smith's Townland Pipes, identified and marked Bowls A-F.   95
7. Smith's Townland Pipes, Identified and Marked Bowls A-I, Marked Stem J.   96
8. Smith's Townland Pipes, Marked Stems A-J.   97

Humphries:
1. Location of Abell's Wharf Site (18 St 53), St Mary's County, Maryland.   99
2. Representative pipes from Abell's Wharf.   101

King:
1. Project Location.   104
2. NESEA facility map showing location of Antenna Field.   106
3. The Fort Point (18 ST 386) and the Spence (18 ST 41) sites in the Antenna Field.   107
4. Relative frequency of tobacco pipe bore diameters at the Fort Point site.   108
5. White clay tobacco pipes from the Spence collection.   109
6. Temporal range of dated pipe marks and decorations from the Spence collection.   110
7. Relative frequency of tobacco pipe bore diameters in the Spence collection.   111
8. Isolated clay pipe stems, marked "JOHN LEWIS" and "D.R.".   112
9. Isolated clay pipe stems, marked "1666" (reverse of "JOHN LEWIS") and "D.R.".   112

FOREWORD

The contents have much to say to the European as well as to the American reader. It is rare to be able to consider clay pipe evidence from such a series of well excavated, stratified and closely dated sites from a relatively small geographical area. In England we have a Civil War horizon at many castle sites which provides a datum point for clay pipe research, particularly in the assessment of the development of regional styles and the fixing of local chronologies. Apart from this, such sites as are presented here, focussed on Chesapeake Bay, are rare and isolated in the British Isles.

I am very grateful to my co-editor Dennis Pogue for much assistance and forebearance in the lengthy process of producing this volume and to his co-authors. Anthony Hands of BAR has been most helpful and encouraging. Without his support it would have been impossible to proceed with the remaining numbers in the series. I am grateful too, to Professors Davies and Shore for their agreement to include a new subject area in the Liverpool Monograph series. Finally, I would like to thank Viv Proctor who typed up the text, Jane Lawrence who drew the frontispiece and Philippa Tomlinson who did all of the technical editing and set the text and figures for the printer.

Peter Davey
Department of Archaeology
University of Liverpool
March 1990

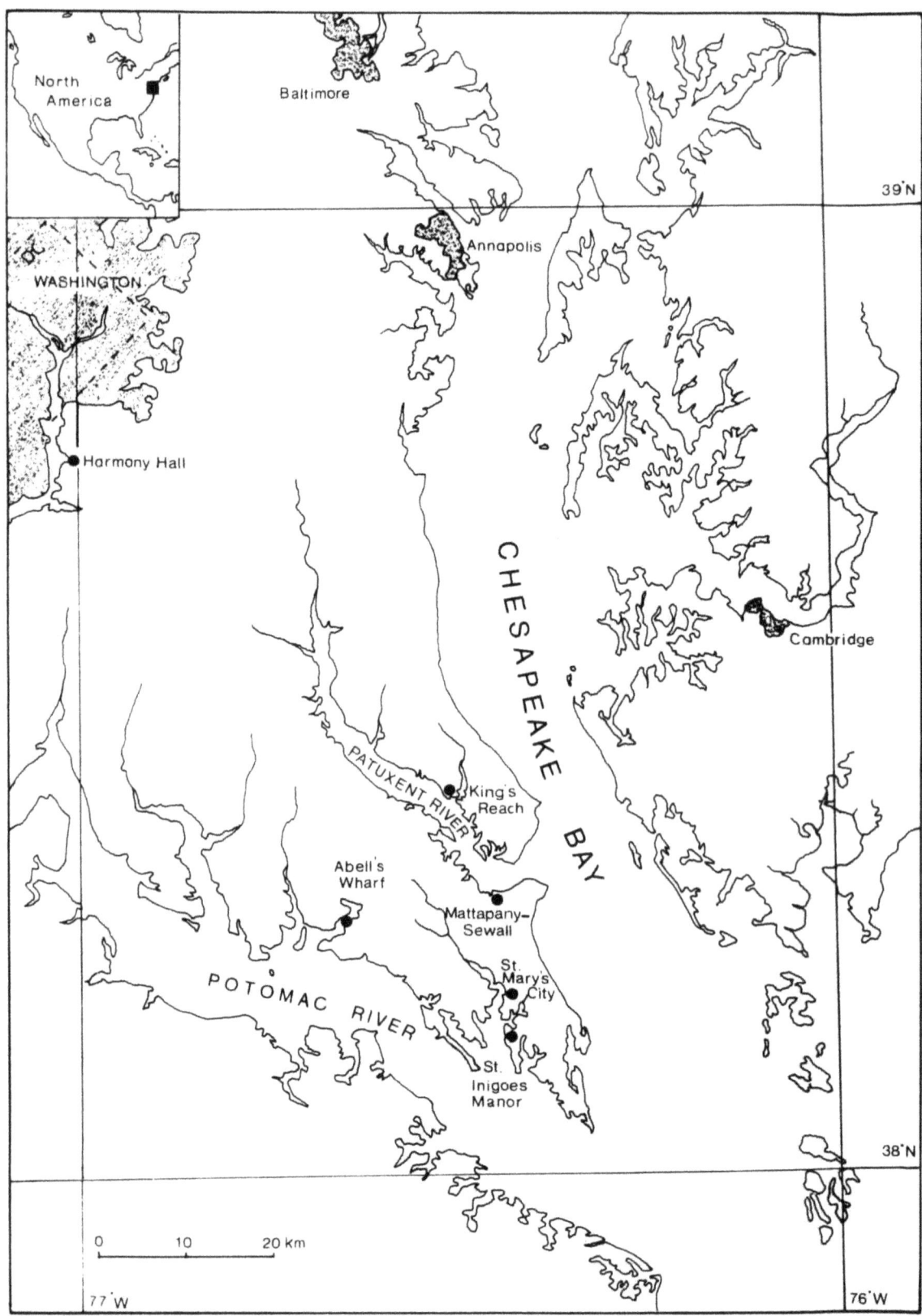

Frontispiece: Chesapeake Bay location map.

INTRODUCTION

It has been ten years since publication of the previous BAR International Series volume that focused on analysis of tobacco pipes recovered from North American archaeological excavations. Since then, a great many domestic sites dating to the Colonial period have been excavated, yielding untold thousands of pipe fragments. The seven articles contained herein certainly do not remotely approximate the total research that has been conducted on those collections. But it is hoped that these selections will add significantly to the available literature, especially for pipes recovered from 17th-century contexts, and will serve as a primary reference for anyone conducting similar studies. As such, an overall emphasis has been placed on providing basic descriptive data for the pipes, so that their comparative value to other scholars will be optimized.

The Editorial prefacing the 1979 volume succinctly discussed the reasons why the study of tobacco pipes recovered in the trans-Atlantic colonies is relevant to the BAR and to its English audience. Tobacco pipe research is an important aspect of the analysis of all sites from this period, and is especially helpful in assigning temporal ranges of occupation. In this undertaking, American scholars are indebted to the numerous English pipe studies that have appeared over the years, and intensively study those volumes for clues to identify maker's marks, to compare pipe bowl shapes, and for other identifiable characteristics. On the other hand, pipes excavated in America often derive from extremely closely dated contexts, providing invaluable comparative data for English researchers. Therefore, the English and American evidence comprise a complementary body of data with which to examine the English pipe industry from two interrelated perspectives.

Ever since the 1954 publication of J.C. Harrington's provocative study proposing the use of pipe bore diameter size as a general dating tool, American archaeologists in particular have focused on the uses of this idea. Harrington's bar charts representing percentages of the bore sizes for successive 30-year time periods have stood the test of time and remain an important research tool. The development in 1962 by Lewis Binford of a formulation by which a mean date may be calculated for any given pipe collection has proven similarly important, if more controversial. After almost three decades and numerous attempts to "refine" the technique, Binford's formula remains in common use. Both dating techniques have been utilized in many of the papers to follow, but always as components within a broader study and with care to take into account their well documented limitations.

In addition to those methods of analysis, Pogue analyzes the spatial distributions of measurable pipes as a tool in interpreting the layout and functional uses of the King's Reach plantation homelot. This technique, using the distributions of a variety of artifact types in addition to pipes, has become a useful and increasingly popular tool in this type of analysis. That paper also attempts to use other pipe data to study the temporal relationships of pipe assemblages retrieved from subsurface features at the site. This includes inter-assemblage comparison of the percentages of rouletted pipe bowls and of the mean bore diameters and standard deviations from the means. Finally, Pogue interprets the combined patterns from the four collections studied as a preliminary model for pipe use in the Patuxent River valley over the second half of the 17th century and first quarter of the 18th century.

Potter and Sonderman present the pipe data from Harmony Hall, another late 17th-early-18th-century site, this one located along the Potomac River in Prince Georges County, Maryland. This evidence serves as a valuable source of comparison with the pipes from the other sites dating to that period contained herein. Interestingly, while Harmony Hall and King's Reach appear to have been occupied for almost the identical period, in general the maker's marks recovered are not the same. Pipes from Bristol do make up the great majority of diagnostic pipes from both sites, as well as at the remainder of the late-17th-century sites studied here.

Three articles in this volume derive from extensive and intensive excavations carried out at St. Mary's City in far southern St. Mary's County, Maryland. St. Mary's City was the site of the colonial capital from 1634 to 1695 and is the closest to an urban context to have existed in 17th-century Maryland. Between them, the articles present evidence from three sites that overlap in time, but which represent very different site histories. Hurry and Keeler analyze pipes from the St. John's Site, occupied over an unusually broad span, circa 1638 to 1720. As such, this provides a rare opportunity to chronicle long-term patterns in pipe use at a single site. In contrast, the other two articles present pipe assemblages retrieved from very narrowly dated contexts. Miller studies the pipes recovered from a ditch associated with Pope's Fort, built during the "time of troubles" in Maryland occasioned by the English Civil War, and dating to the period 1645-1655. Riordan analyzes a pipe collection recovered from a similarly temporally circumscribed context, but which dates to the circa 1666-1678 period. Together, the St. Mary's City data comprise an unusually complete record of the tobacco pipes used in one locality, spanning almost an entire century of occupation.

The final two papers derive from outlying plantation sites in St. Mary's County. The Abell's Wharf Site is another late 17th century plantation and, as such, provides valuable comparative data to the others presented. The pipes studied by Humphries derive almost completely from excavation of a single large, artifact-rich pit, and therefore represents a temporally restricted deposit. King's article examines an unusually rich collection of pipes recovered from two similar sites spanning the second half of the 17th century, believed to have been occupied by tenants at the Jesuit's St. Inigoes Manor. The results of these studies provide a particularly interesting source of comparison with the St. Mary's City data.

All but one of the collections studied in this volume derived from intensive excavations, with the great majority recovered from tightly datable contexts. As such, they provide the control required to allow the detailed study of diachronic patterns in pipe use in 17th century Maryland. These data, in turn, then may be compared with similar studies from other areas, such as the Virginia portion of the Chesapeake region, to allow the interpretation of regional patterns in pipe use.

D. J. Pogue
February 1989
Mount Vernon, Virginia

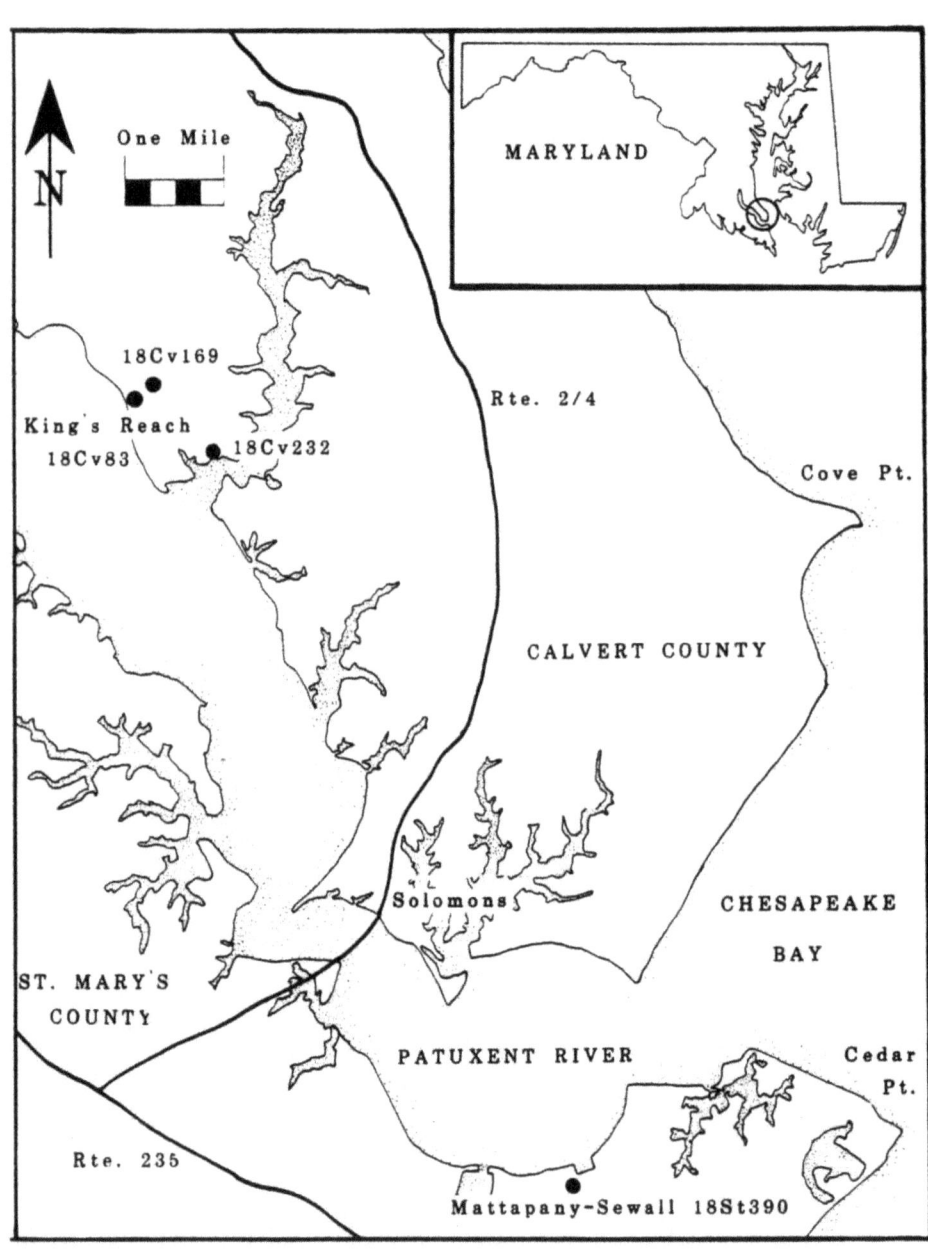

Figure 1: Lower Patuxent Valley, Maryland: site locations.

Clay Tobacco Pipes from four 17th century Domestic Sites in the Lower Patuxent River Valley of Maryland.

Dennis J. Pogue

INTRODUCTION

Over a six-year period (1981-1987), the author conducted archaeological investigations at four separate domestic sites located in Maryland's lower Patuxent River valley (Figure 1, opposite). The investigations included a long-term and intensive excavation (18 Cv 83), limited subsurface testing (18 St 390 and 18 Cv 169), and surface collecting (18 Cv 232). Together the sites span the period *circa* 1660-1715. The excavation of the King's Reach Site (18 Cv 83) revealed an extensive complex of features relating to a residence, associated quarter, and fence lines, borrow pits, etc. That excavation generated a total of several thousand tobacco pipe fragments, analysis of which has been instrumental in assigning a range of occupation as *circa* 1690-1715. The more limited investigations at Mattapany-Sewall (18 St 390) yielded 540 total pipe fragments, with 421 fragments recovered from 18 Cv 169. Only 11 tobacco pipe fragments were recovered from 18 Cv 232, temporally the earliest of the four assemblances.

The overwhelming majority of these pipes are English in origin, with a small percentage being local products, made both by Colonists using imported molds and by American Indians. While Dutch pipes often are found on Maryland sites dating from before *circa* 1660, none of the recovered pipe maker's marks, nor any decorated fragments, from these sites have been positively identified as Dutch. The great majority of marked pipes appear to be of Bristol manufacture, lending support for the contention that the Bristol pipe industry had come to dominate the pipe trade in the Patuxent, if not all of the Chesapeake, in the second half of the 17th century.

The four collections are analyzed separately, then compared with each other and examined as a whole assemblage representing tobacco pipes from the Patuxent for the period 1660-1715. Each collection has been analyzed via examination of a number of characteristics, i.e. stem bore size, bowl shapes, maker's marks, and bowl and stem decorations, and in reference to the substantial body of literature pertaining to English tobacco pipes that has been generated by English and North American scholars over the last several decades. The American evidence consists largely of archaeologically retrieved pipe collections and their accompanying analyses. English research not only has provided a number of such studies, but also includes extensive documentary evidence pertaining to the English tobacco pipe industry, which has yielded invaluable data to link pipe marks with their makers. Finally, two other 17th-century sites have yielded large pipe collections, which are discussed briefly.

In addition to the standard analyses of tobacco pipes generally found in articles of this type, a portion of the study of the King's Reach pipes will entail discussion of the results of the analysis of the patterns in the spatial distributions of pipe stems according to bore diameter. This type of study has been carried out at a number of sites in the Chesapeake region, and has proven extremely helpful in identifying diachronic shifts in intrasite refuse disposal (*cf.* Keeler 1978, Neiman 1980, King and Miller 1987, and King 1988). Those patterns, in turn, have been combined with distributions of other artifact types to allow interpretation of the spatial arrangement and functional uses of the homelot.

KING'S REACH (18 Cv 83)

Over the course of two summers in 1984-85, the Maryland Historical Trust/Jefferson Patterson Park and Museum conducted intensive excavations at the King's Reach Site. The site is located at the Jefferson Patterson Park and Museum, a 512-acre archaeological preserve in lower Calvert County, Maryland (Figure 1). Systematic collection of artifacts from the plowed field surface in a 50-by-60-meter area delineated the general site boundaries. A total of 144 two-by-two-meter-square quadrats were excavated over the ensuing two summers' field work, with 116 of those concentrated in the site core and the remaining 28 systematically distributed in the outlying zone. The plowed stratum of each square was hand-screened through 3/8-inch hardware cloth for uniform artifact retention. Numerous substantial subsurface features were revealed below plowzone and were selectively excavated.

The plantation core appears to have been completely exposed, revealing remains of a relatively large post-supported frame dwelling measuring 30 by 30 feet, and a smaller, 20-by-10-foot quarter, with a connecting fenced foreyard (Figure 2). The combination of the architectural and artifact evidence suggests a relatively wealthy household and a short-term occupation, dating to the *circa* 1690-1715 period. Unfortunately, no documentary data pertaining to the site have survived, largely due to a series of courthouse fires that destroyed most of the early county land records.

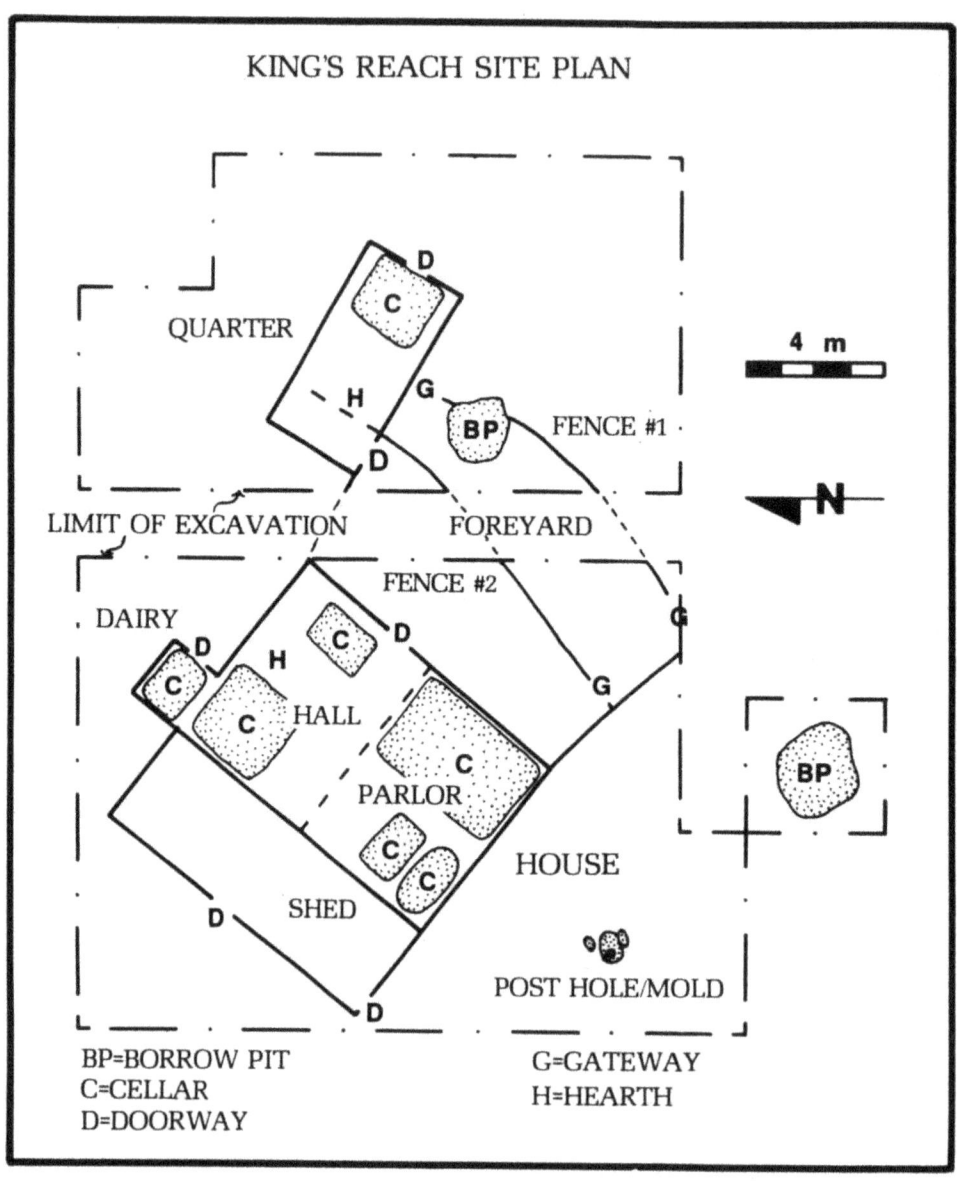

Figure 2: King's Reach site plan

The site has been interpreted with reference to evidence provided by previously excavated sites in the region from this period (cf. Keeler 1978, Neiman 1980, Kelso 1984, King and Miller 1987, and King 1988), and to the results of extensive research using surviving probate inventories in Maryland for the period 1650-1720 (Main 1982). In many respects King's Reach appears similar to other excavated plantation sites from the period. The structures are representative of the dominant type of dwelling that evolved in the region, known as the "Virginia House" (cf. Carson et al. 1981). Tobacco cultivation was the economic underpinning of the colony, and dispersed plantations like King's Reach came to dominate the landscape.

PIPE STEM DISTRIBUTIONS

Plotting the distributions of various types of artifacts recovered from the 144 plowzone quadrats has proven especially useful in interpreting the layout and use of the structures and the surrounding homelot. Such analyses are possible since it has been demonstrated that even though plowing destroys stratigraphic relationships, the horizontal distributions of plowzone artifacts remain generally intact (cf. Lewarch and O'Brien 1981). In addition, it has been found that during this period refuse was commonly dumped in surface middens in yards adjacent to domestic dwellings. As a consequence, patterns in the distribution of plowzone derived materials can prove extremely useful in identifying the functions of nearby rooms and other spaces. For example, at King's Reach the servant's quarter and hall (kitchen) in the main house were found to have associated concentrations of coarse ceramics, bottle glass, and other utilitarian items, while the parlor had a higher proportion of table glass and fine ceramics dumped nearby. When added to the architectural data, this evidence provides important corroborating support for the identification of those areas. (*cf.* Pogue 1988a).

The maps of the distributions of tobacco pipes that follow were created with the aid of a computer, using a three-dimensional spline as the interpolation algorithm. The contour lines reflect percentiles of the frequency distribution of artifact counts (*cf.* Tukey 1977), with the three intervals shown conforming to the median and upper one-quarter and one-eighth quantiles.

Tobacco pipes have been demonstrated to be one of the most sensitive temporal indicators available. This is due to a systematic reduction in bore diameter over time, on average, as well as a general evolution in bowl shape, combined with the sometimes extremely precise evidence provided by maker's marks. The patterns in the spatial distributions of tobacco pipes plotted according to bore size have been most helpful in interpreting the homelot, and especially in tracing temporal shifts in refuse disposal patterns. In general, the patterns in pipe stem distributions support the overall results of the analysis of the distributions of the other artifact types (*cf.* Pogue 1988a).

The distribution of total measurable pipe stems serves to demonstrate the general patterns of artifact distribution at the site (Figure 3). Three major concentrations are indicated: to the rear of the main house (3a), centering on the house and extending to the south (3b), and between the house and quarter (3c). The rear concentration and that between the house and quarter are extensive sheet middens, originally deposited on ground surface. The concentration within the house stems from the existence of numerous large, trash-filled subsurface features located there. By plotting the distributions of measurable pipe stems by bore size, more sensitive indications of diachronic shifts in refuse disposal are possible. The pipe stems have been plotted in three groups: early (9-8-7/64th-inch), middle (6/64th-inch), and late (4-5/64th-inch). The three largest bore sizes were combined due to the relatively small number of stems involved (N=126); 4 and 5/64th-inch (N=1815) were combined due to the small number of 4/64th; 6/64th-inch totalled 765.

In comparing the three pipe stem distribution maps, a number of striking consistencies are apparent, as well as several important differences. First, all three maps again show major concentrations of pipes behind the main house and between the house and quarter. Major concentrations also occur within both the house and quarter on two of the three maps, with the third showing less dense concentrations there (Figures 4-6). These areas correspond with significant concentrations of virtually all other types of artifacts as well. These have been interpreted as representing extensive surface middens behind the house and between that structure and the quarter, which apparently served throughout the entire occupation of the site as the main areas of refuse dumping.

The concentrations within the two structures apparently derive from artifacts being plowed out of one large cellar in the quarter and from several cellars under the house. Therefore, these concentrations also represent the deposition of refuse, but inside subsurface features after they had ceased in their original storage functions. The artifacts within the subsurface dumps would seem more likely to represent restricted temporal ranges, as they would be completely filled at some point, unlike the surface middens that could continue to accrue debris over the entire span of the site's occupation. A number of smaller outlying concentrations also correspond with the suspected locations of numerous door openings, which are further supported by similar concentrations of other types of materials. These are best shown in the distribution of the early pipes (Figure 4a).

The three maps exhibit some striking differences as well. The most interesting of which is the change in the shape of the large concentration located between the house and quarter. In the distribution map of the early pipes, the concentration is extensive and focused between the house and a fence line that ran from the center of the south wall of the quarter and finally terminated at the southeast corner of the house (Figure 4b). This fence enclosed the area between the two structures and created a mutual foreyard. By the period of the second distribution map, that fence had been replaced by a second one that was located closer to the house and which created a smaller enclosure. The pipes still show a significant concentration within the fence, but a second and more intense concentration occurs just beyond it (Figure 5a). Finally, by the time of the third map, the major concentration in the area is just on the other side of the second fence line (Figure 6a). This sequence seems to document a slight change in disposal practice -- over the fence line instead of within it -- as well as supports the interpretation for when the fence was replaced. But the greater significance may be the evidence it provides for the type of subtle changes that plotting the pipe stem distributions may identify (*cf.* Pogue 1988a).

THE PIPES -- PLOWZONE

Several thousand pipe fragments were recovered from the plowzone, but no attempt will be made here to analyze all of that substantial collection. Instead, all maker's marks and any other decorations, and all pipe bowls complete enough to be identified as to type, have been selectively examined. Following this discussion, a more in-depth analysis of pipes recovered from a number of subsurface features will be conducted and the results of the two analyses will be compared.

Of the thousands of white clay tobacco pipe fragments recovered from plowzone, 2706 stems are measurable as to bore diameter. The great majority of the bores are 5/64th-inch (63.60%), with 28.2% measuring 6/64th, 4.0% at 7/64th and the remaining 4.2% comprised of 4/64th, 8/64th, and 9/64th-inch bores, combined. In comparison with the histograms for temporal ranges established by Harrington (1954), this distribution suggests a *circa* 1690 to 1730 range of occupation. The overwhelming preponderance of 5/64th-inch bores points to a relatively short span of habitation. In comparison, the pipe mean date computed using the Binford (1962) formula is 1727.24 (mean of 5.348). This date is at least 20 years later than expected based on the overall artifact analysis. Analyses of pipe bowl shapes and maker's marks (see below) also support an earlier date.

The sample size involved has been shown in other instances to be sufficient to yield a relatively accurate result. The Binford formula also has been demonstrated to be most effective for the period from *circa* 1680 to 1780. Therefore, the late mean date for the King's Reach plowzone pipes is puzzling. The reason for the later than expected date may lie in the site's apparent brief span of occupation, which may have resulted in the preponderance of pipes of 5/64th-inch bores.

Binford (1962) suggests that a more intensive occupation over a limited period within a site's overall span may skew the mean date accordingly.

A total of 18 different apparent maker's marks were recovered from plowzone. Of these, nine are legible and/or complete enough to be identified (Table 1). Of the nine, three may be associated with a high degree of confidence with known makers: Edward Reed and one of the three Robert Tippets, from Bristol, and one of the two William Manbys of London. Two others may well be the product of Isaac Evans and Thomas Owens, both of Bristol. The four remaining marks "IW", "IP", "WW", and "IM", have not been attributable to specific producers, with multiple pipe makers with those initials known to have been operating in Bristol and/or London during the years just before and after the turn of the 18th century. Each mark will be described below in some detail, along with the other characteristics of the pipes that seem pertinent to this analysis.

Edward Reed (ER)

A single bowl fragment was recovered that includes a portion of a cartouche containing the raised initials "ER" (Figure 7A). The fragment is from the apparent mid-section of the bowl and suggests placement on the side, probably the right. Typically, the bowls on which this mark are found are of the spur-less and heel-less "American Export" type. Edward Reed was a Bristol maker whose dates of production cover the period 1706-23 (Walker 1977(C):1478-9). Bowls with the "ER"

Table 1: King's Reach Site maker's marks: plowzone and features.

Mark	No.	Maker	Production	Bore	Provenience
ER	1	Edward Reed, Bristol	1706-1723	--	198PZ
R/TIPPETT	1	Robert Tippet, Bristol	1660-1720	--	238PZ
IE	8	Isaac Evans, Bristol	1698-1713	5/64	166PZ, 184PZ, 196E, G, H
WM	1	William Manby, London	1681-1696	5/64	228PZ
TO	3	Thomas Owen, Bristol	1698-1739	5-6/64	212PZ, 213P, S
IW	1	--	--	5/64	200PZ
IP	1	--	--	6/64	181PZ
WW	2	--	--	5/64	198PZ, 213PZ
IM	1	--	--	5/64	256PZ
RT	3	Robert Tippet, Bristol	1660-1720	--	196E, 182R, 228M
AS	1	Ann Smith, Bristol	?ca. 1672-1696	6/64	182SS
AI	1	--	--	6/64	213H

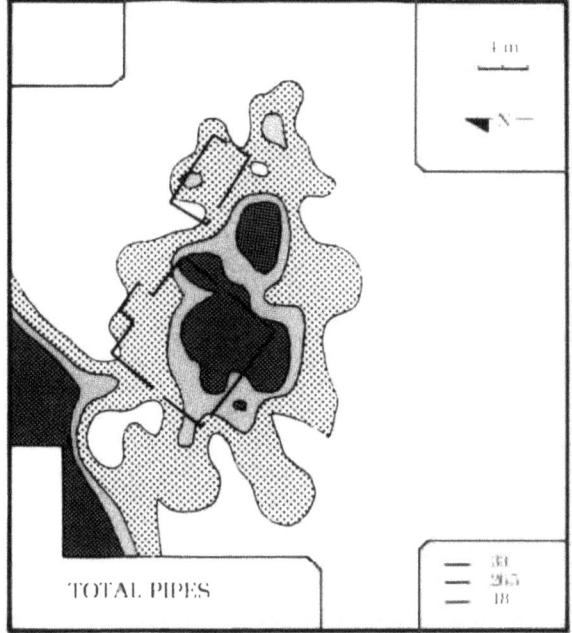

Figure 3: Distribution map of total pipe stem fragments, King's Reach.

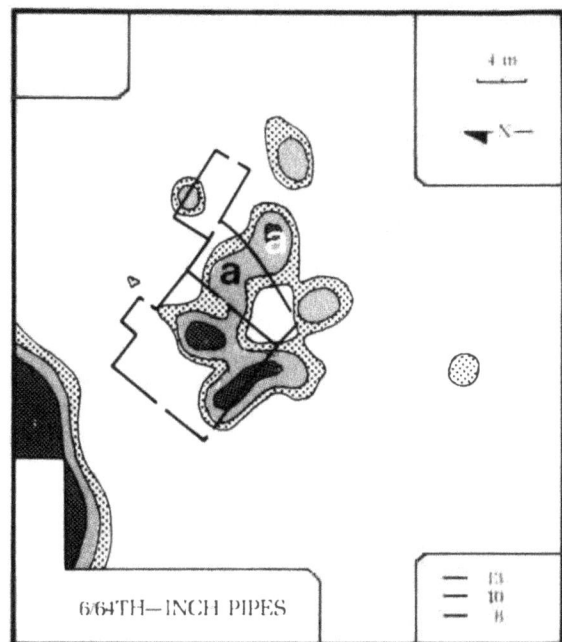

Figure 5: Distribution map of middle pipes (6/64th-inch), King's Reach.

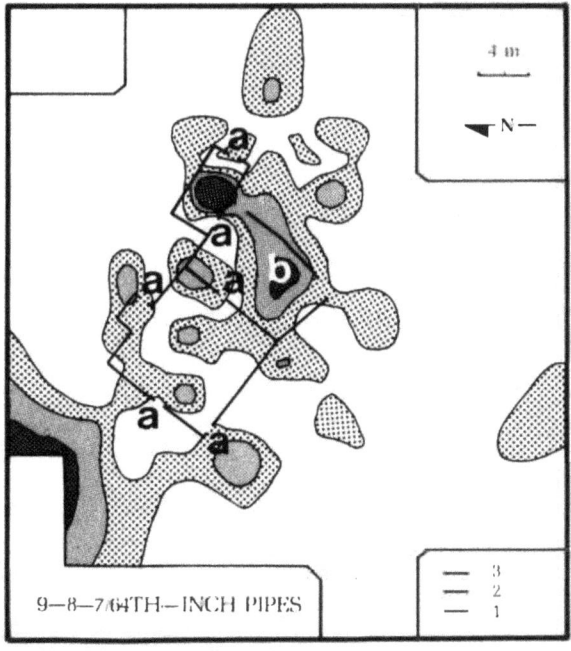

Figure 4: Distribution map of early pipes, (9-8-7/64th-inch), King's Reach.

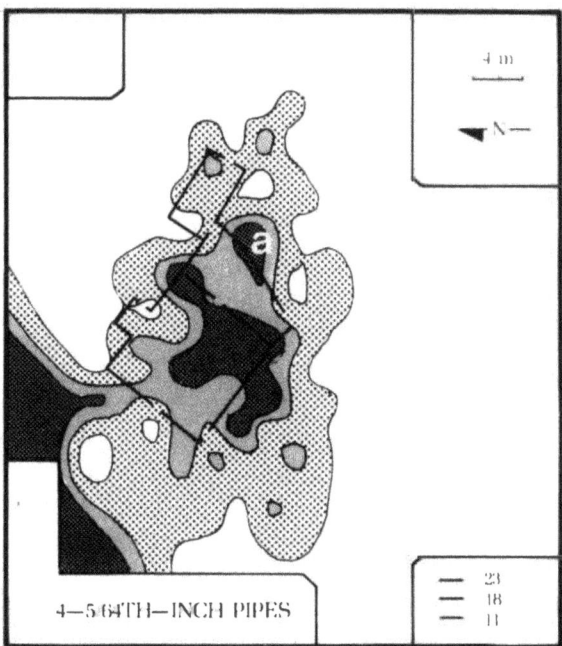

Figure 6: Distribution map of late pipes (4-5/64th-inch), King's Reach.

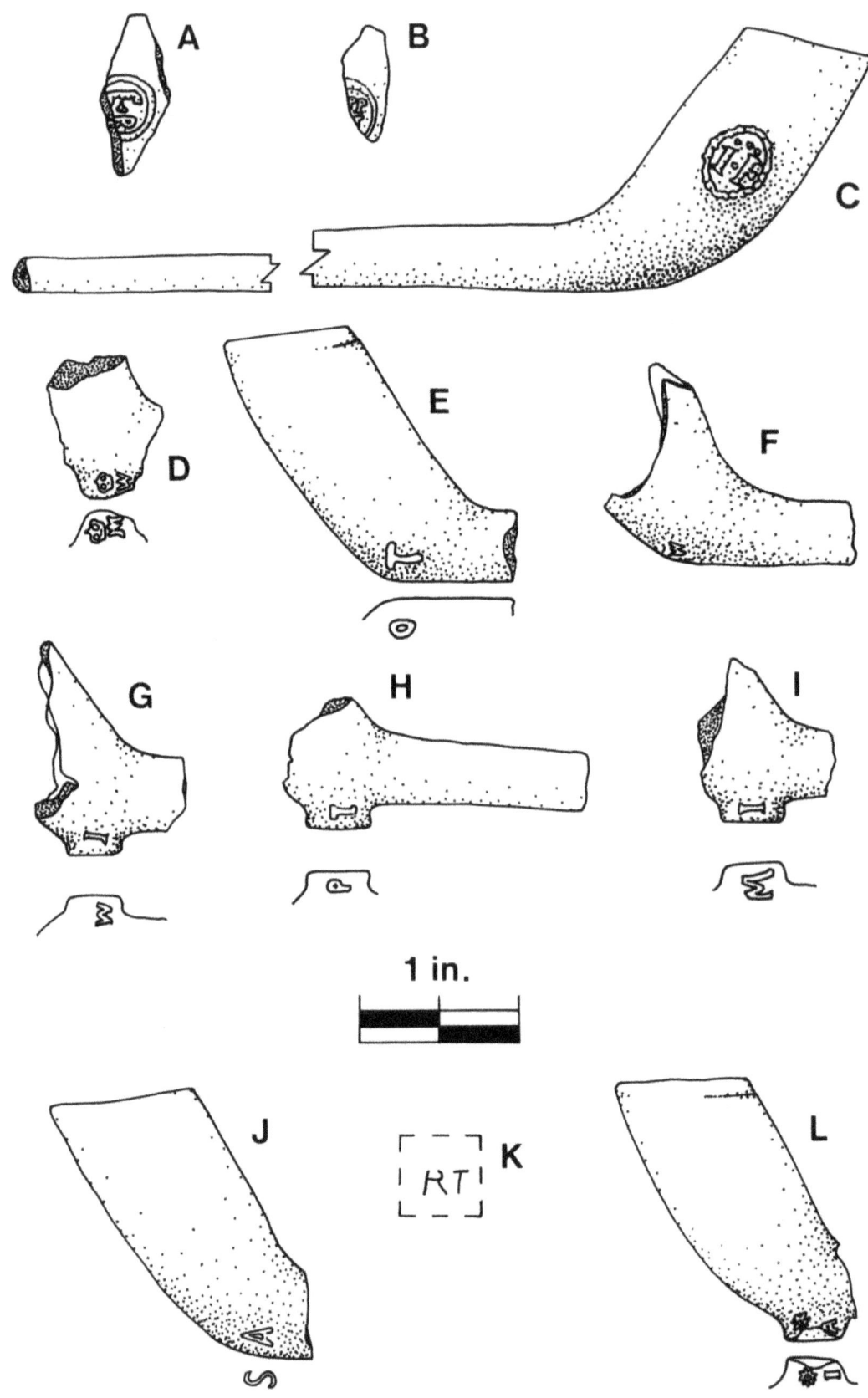

Figure 7: Maker's marks, King's Reach.

mark inside a cartouche are well known, with the King's Reach example similar in a number of ways to several Reed marks illustrated in Walker (1977(C):1479f). However, this example may be unusual as the initials appear to read from top to bottom instead of left to right.

Robert Tippet (R/Tipp/et)

A second bowl sherd also exhibits a fragment of a cartouche with a partial mark. That mark is undoubtedly "R/Tipp/et," although four of the letters do not survive (Figure 7B). This mark also is well known and matches any number of virtually identical examples (*cf.* Walker 1977(C):1495-1501). Again, the cartouche was located midway up the side of the bowl, probably on the right, which most likely was of the American Export type. Unfortunately, at least three Bristol pipe makers named Robert Tippet are known to have made tobacco pipes over the period *circa* 1660-1720, and it is virtually impossible to distinguish between their wares.

Isaac Evans (IE)

A third Bristol pipe maker was Isaac Evans, of the pipe making Evans family, who made pipes beginning in 1698 and likely continued at least until 1713 (Walker 1977(C):1130-31). Several bowls and bowl fragments with an oval cartouche and a raised "IE" inside were recovered, and have been tentatively identified as most likely the product of Isaac Evans. Again, the cartouche is located midway up the right side of the bowl, which is the American Export type (Figure 7C). The bowl shape is similar to those of several others that have been identified as Isaac Evans products (*cf.* Walker 1977(C):1427e), and along with the style of cartouche points to Bristol as the place of manufacture. However, this style of mark is not identical to any of the other Isaac Evans marks that appear in the literature, although he seems to have employed several different styles of mark and cartouche.

William Manby (WM)

Unlike the previous three marks, all of which are initials inside a cartouche and are most likely located on the side of the American Export type bowl, this mark is located on either side of the heel. The initial "W" is on the left and the "M" on the right, with a crown over each (Figure 7D). This mark also is well known and is almost surely that of one of the William Manbys of London. William Manby, Sr. was producing pipes from 1681-1696 (Oswald 1975:142) and pipes with the WM mark, with and without crowns, on either side of the heel have been reported from London excavations in contexts from *circa* 1690 throughout the first half of the 18th century (Walker 1966:99).

Thomas Owen (TO)

The fifth mark may be that of one of three Bristol piype makers named Thomas Owen, whose combined production spanned the period 1698-1739 (Walker 1977(C):1232-33). The raised letters "T" and "O" are located on either side of the base of an American Export type bowl (Figure 7E). No mark that has been attributed to the manufacture of any of the Owen's has been found; therefore, this attribution is somewhat conjectural. However, the time span for the Owens's pipe production, especially Thomas Owen I (1698-1725), and the apparent preponderance of Bristol-made pipes at the site, provides some support for that identification.

Figure 7 (opposite): Maker's marks, King Reach Site.

A. Bowl fragment with partial mark; cartouche with raised "ER", mark of Edward Reed of Bristol;
B. Bowl fragment with partial mark; cartouche with raised "-- PP/T-", mark of Robert Tippet of Bristol;
C. Nearly complete pipe, American Export type, with mark on right side of bowl; oval cartouche with raised "IE", possibly mark of Isaac Evans of Bristol (5/64th-inch);
D. Bowl fragment with raised initials on either side of heel; "W" on left and "M" on right, with crown above each initial, probably mark of William Manby of London;
E. American Export type bowl with rouletting around rim, with raised initials on either side of bottom of bowl; "T" on left and "O" on right, possibly the mark of Thomas Owen of Bristol (6/64th-inch);
F. Bowl fragment, with initials on either side of bottom of bowl; "W" on left and "W" on right (5/64th-inch);
G. Bowl fragment, with initials on either side of heel; "I" on left and "W" on right;
H. Bowl/stem fragment, with initials on either side of heel; "I" on left and "P" on right (5/64th-inch);
I. Bowl fragment, with initials on either side of heel; "I" on left and "M" on right (5/64th-inch);
J. Bowl fragment, with initials on either side of bottom of bowl; "A" on left and "S" on right (6/64th-inch);
K. Stamped "RT" mark, on bowl fragment, mark of Robert Tippet of Bristol;
L. Bowl fragment, with initials on either side of heel, with rouletting around rim; "A" on left and "I" on right, with starburst above each initial (6/64th -inch).

Even less is known about the remaining four marks recovered from plowzone: WW, IW, IP, and IM. Like the TO-marked pipes, the raised letter "W" is located on either side of the base of an American Export type bowl (Figure 7F). In Bristol, one maker with those initials, William Williams, was producing pipes during the period of the site's occupation, *circa* 1707 (Oswald 1975:160). The three remaining marks all are raised letters located on either side of heeled bowls (Figures 7g-i). Several makers with the initials IW were working in London and Bristol from the 17th to mid-18th centuries. In Bristol alone, two makers with those initials were operating between 1707 and 1722: John Wilson (1707-1722) and Joel Williams (1713-1722), and Wilson is known to have exported pipes to America (Oswald 1975:159). Similarly, one Bristol maker, John Massie, was producing pipes, and is known to have been exporting his product to America, from 1700-1726 (Oswald 1975:155). A number of makers with the initials IP were working in Bristol and London during that period (Oswald 1975:143 and 156).

Of the literally thousands of fragments of pipe bowls recovered from plowzone, very few are complete enough to be able to classify completely. Nevertheless, all bowls were examined and separated into types where possible. Four varieties of American Export bowls have been identified, along with nine varieties of heeled bowls; no bowls with spurs were recovered from plowzone. Examples of each of the varieties identified are illustrated in Figure 8. Many of these varieties also were recovered in more complete form from subsurface features and, therefore, will be discussed below in more detail. Based on shape and size, most of the bowls that are complete enough to allow analysis appear to date to the late 17th-early 18th centuries, although a very few exhibit characteristics generally ascribed to somewhat earlier types (see Figure 8g). Rouletting around the bowl mouth occurs on a large percentage of the fragments.

THE PIPES -- FEATURES

In addition to the pipes recovered from plowzone, large numbers of fragments were recovered from the numerous subsurface features excavated. Most of these were located within the structures and have been interpreted as cellars that were used as handy trash receptacles once they ceased being used in their original storage functions. The one exception is an irregularly shaped hole that appears to be a clay borrow pit. Pipes from six features will be analyzed in detail, both separately and together, and then compared with the plowzone pipes. The features were selected for analysis because they yielded a sufficient quantity of pipe fragments, including measurable bores, to allow reasonable assurance of reliability. Table 2 lists the six contexts and total numbers of pipes, measurable stems, marks, the calculated pipe stem means and standard deviations from the mean, and Binford mean pipe date. A seventh collection (228) also is included, although the small number of measurable bores (11) makes it untrustworthy in terms of temporal analysis.

Of the seven features, two (228 and 184) appear to have been filled relatively early in the life of the site, with a substantial gap in time between those two and the third (213), and with the remaining four dating much later and being relatively closely clustered (Table 2). Unfortunately, only 11 measurable stems were recovered from provenience 228, making its dating questionable. However, with more than 100 measurable bores recovered from 184, that collection is one of the most trustworthy of the seven. As for the Binford mean dates that have been calculated, all but the first two seem much too late when compared with all other evidence. However, with one exception, their relative chronology (probably better represented by the means) generally conforms with the seriation derived by examination of complementary archaeological data.

Figure 8 (opposite): Representative pipe bowls recovered from plowzone, King's Reach.

A. American Export type bowl fragment (5/64th-inch);
B. American Export type bowl fragment, with rouletting around the mouth (5/64th-inch);
C. American Export type bowl fragment, with rouletting around the mouth (6/64th-inch);
D. American Export type bowl fragment (5/64th-inch);
E. Bowl fragment with vestigial heel (7/64th-inch);
F. Heeled bowl fragment (6/64th-inch);
G. Heeled bowl fragment, with rouletting around rim (7/64th-inch);
H. Heeled bowl fragment (5/64th-inch);
I. Heeled bowl fragment;
J. Heeled bowl fragment (6/64th-inch);
K. Heeled bowl fragment (6/64th-inch);
L. Heeled bowl fragment (5/64th-inch);
M. Heeled bowl fragment (6/64th-inch).

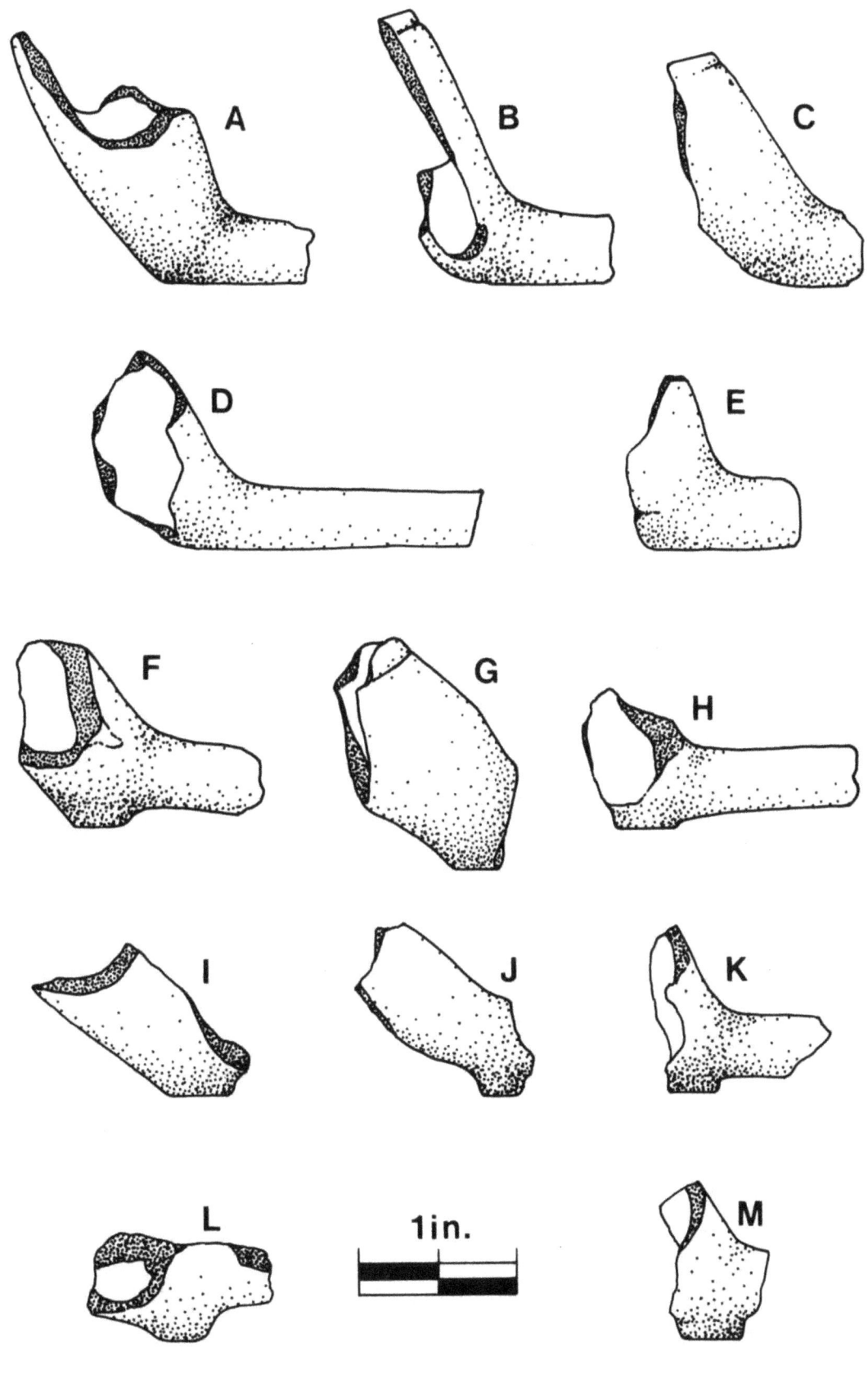

Figure 8: Representative pipe bowls recovered from plowzone, King's Reach.

Table 2: King's Reach Site, total pipes from seven subsurface features.

Prov.	Total Pipes	Bores	Marks	Mean	SD	Binford
228	35	11	RT	6.09	0.84	1698.85
184	149	109	--	6.07	0.40	1699.5
213	319	135	AI/TO	5.53	0.63	1720.47
182	190	71	RT/AS/IE	5.18	0.64	1733.55
196	89	39	RT/IE	5.10	0.72	1736.6
200	106	43	--	5.05	0.69	1738.82
197	149	47	--	5.00	0.39	1743.0

The single exception is the 196 cellar, which seems more likely to be the last of the seven to have been filled. This interpretation is based on the presence of large quantities of structural debris recovered from a single thick stratum, which seems likely to represent destruction fill capping a cellar that had been only partially filled at the time of the demolition of the dwelling. That feature is the only one exhibiting such a stratum. The difference between the pipe date from that feature and the other two with later mean dates (200 and 197) is not great, however (2.22 and 6.4 years), and the discrepancy may be a function of sample bias (Table 2).

A second form of analysis also supports this interpretation of the relative chronology for the six features. In addition to the mean bore diameter, the standard deviation from the mean also has been calculated for each collection (Table 2). The standard deviation (SD) indicates the variation in bore sizes within a given collection, with a smaller SD indicating smaller variance. The overall trend indicated by plotting all the standard deviations is an increase over time (Table 2). However, a notable exception to this apparent trend is the SD for feature 197, which is relatively small, given its chronological placement based on the mean.

In order to address possible explanations for this inconsistency, it is necessary to consider what the SD may represent in archaeological terms. The SD indicates the variance from the mean for each collection of measurable bores, and it has been demonstrated that in general the average size of pipe bores decreased over time. As early as 1962, Binford (1962) suggested that the SD could give "a rough estimate of the length of time over which the sample was accumulating." A second possibility also exists, that the SD reflects the duration of the site's occupation; or it could result from a combination of the two. If a pit is purposely filled over a short period, or with debris generated over a limited period, then it is likely that the pipe stems deposited would reflect that process, resulting in a small variance from the mean. Conversely, if a site has been occupied for a number of years, the normal processes of refuse disposal, that include both primary deposition and secondary redeposition of residual materials, make it likely that the pipes deposited will derive from a broader span of time, with a resulting greater SD (Neiman 1988 and personal communication). This second scenario seems to be more likely at sites occupied for any appreciable length of time.

If the variance from the mean is linked with the relative span of time over which a given feature is filled, then plotting the SD for individual assemblages over time would not seem likely to form a pattern of steadily increasing variance. Instead it would seem more likely that the variances would be completely divorced from the features' relative chronology and would produce a

---

Figure 9 (opposite): Representative pipe bowls from features, King's Reach.

A. American Export type pipe, with rouletting around mouth (6/64th-inch);
B. Heeled bowl, with rouletting around rim (6/64th-inch);
C. Heeled bowl (6/64th-inch);
D. Spurred bowl fragment, with rouletting around rim (6/64th- inch);
E. American Export type bowl fragment (5/64th-inch);
F. Heeled bowl fragment, with rouletting around rim;
G. Heeled bowl fragment, with rouletting around rim (6/64th-inch);
H. Apparent heeled bowl, with rouletting around rim; heel appears to have been removed (5/64th-inch);
I. American Export type bowl (5/64th-inch).

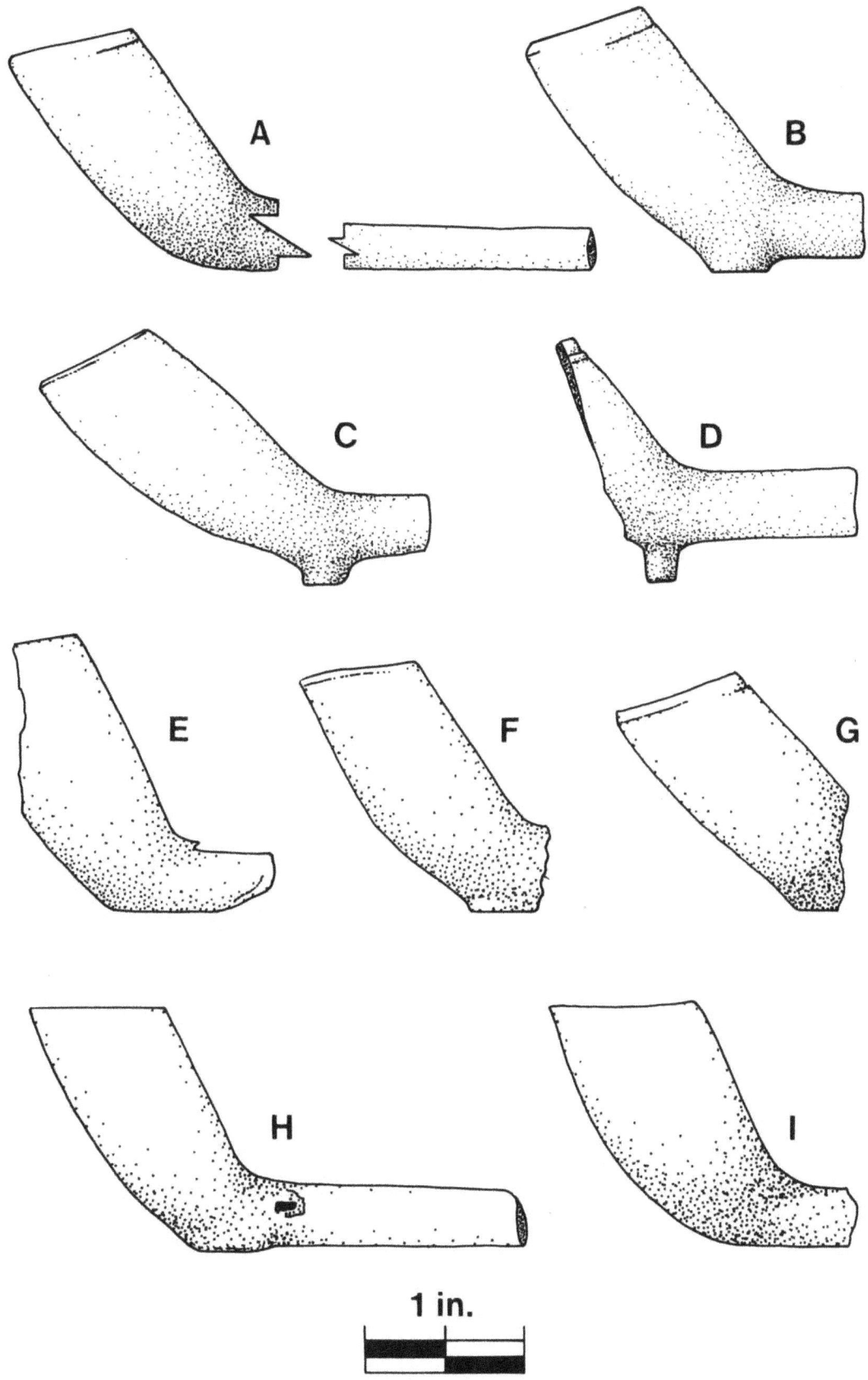

Figure 9: Representative pipe bowls from features, King's Reach.

seemingly random pattern linked to the individual depositional histories of the features involved. Therefore, the general trend toward increased variance over time exhibited by the King's Reach features suggests that the variances there are a result of the point withinthe site history when the features were filled, rather than how quickly that occurred. Therefore, features such as 182, 197, 200, and 196, all of which apparently were filled late in the history of the site, would be expected to exhibit increased variance. Similarly, a feature such as 184, which seems to have been filled early on, would be expected to have a small variance. As this is in fact the pattern revealed, then in this case the means and the standard deviations from them both are interpreted as indicative of depositional chronology.

That feature 197 does not fit the general chronological pattern indicated by the standard deviations (i.e. has a small SD in relation to its mean) is inferred to indicate that the feature's depositional history includes some unknown variable that has affected those results. The feature's chronological placement based solely on the mean also appears slightly off (too late), but could be explainable as a function of sample size. The smaller than expected SD may be the result of a high percentage of the pipe collection having been deposited together purposely in a single depositional episode. Therefore, the bore mean could be a relatively accurate temporal indicator even while the SD may be abnormally small.

A third type of analysis provides an additional means of addressing the question of intrasite chronology. It has been subjectively observed by a number of authors that rouletting around the mouth of pipe bowls seems to have decreased in frequency beginning in the first years of the 18th century. Therefore, since the King's Reach Site was occupied for approximately 25 years spanning that period, it was hypothesized that the proportion of rouletted bowls at the site would decrease over time.

In order to test this hypothesis, the percentage of bowl fragments with rouletting was calculated for the pipes recovered from the six features listed above. Again, a strong pattern emerges, with the percentage of rouletted bowls decreasing steadily from 52.17% for 184 to 3.84% for 200 and 0% for 197 (Table 3). When it is considered that pipe bowls are most often only rouletted on a portion of the rim, it is obvious that the percentage of archaeologically recovered rouletted pipe fragments never will approach 100% unless the collection is small and/or composed almost entirely of complete bowls. Therefore, the 52.17% of rouletted bowls from 184 probably represents a high percentage. This is corroborated by the fact that all nine of the largely complete bowls recovered exhibit rouletting. When the two earliest collections (184 and 213) are combined and compared with the four later collections, the contrast is similarly marked -- 36.2% to only 4.28%. These data then support the observed diachronic reduction in rouletted bowls over this period.

Bowls with five different maker's marks were recovered from the excavated features (Table 2). Two of these, "IE" and "TO," also were recovered from plowzone and have been tentatively attributed to Isaac Evans and Thomas Owen, both of Bristol. The three additional marks are "RT," "AS," and "AI." The RT mark is well known as another of the marks used by the Robert Tippets of Bristol, whose combined production spanned the *circa* 1660-1720 period (Walker 1977(C):1316-18). Unlike the other Tippet mark recovered (Figure 7b), however, the three examples of this mark are stamped into the rear of the bowls, and are without a cartouche of any other type of ornamentation (Figure 7j). Numerous virtually identical examples are illustrated in Walker (1977(C):1497).

The AS mark consists of the raised initials on either side of the bottom of an American Export type bowl (Figure 7k). The maker has not been positively identified, but one Bristol maker with those initials was Ann Smith, making pipes during the last quarter of the 17th century (Oswald 1975:158 and Walker 1977(C):1298). The AI mark also consists of raised letters, but they are located on either side of a heeled bowl, and include a starburst above each initial (Figure 7l). Such treatment has been identified as particularly characteristic of London makers (Atkinson and Oswald 1969:18), although no maker from that city with those initials so far has been identified. A Bristol maker with those initials, Abraham Johnson, was operating *circa* 1706 (Oswald 1975:154).

Figure 10 (opposite): Representative pipe bowls from features, King's Reach.

A. American Export type bowl (5/64th-inch);
B. American Export type bowl (5/64th-inch);
C. American Export type bowl (5/64th-inch);
D. American Export type bowl (5/64th-inch);
E. Bowl fragment with "mulberry tree" decoration;
F. Stem fragment with three finger impressions;
G. Stem fragment with carved tapering points at both ends;
H. Rouletted decoration from red clay pipe recovered at 18 Cv 232 (Figure 13j).

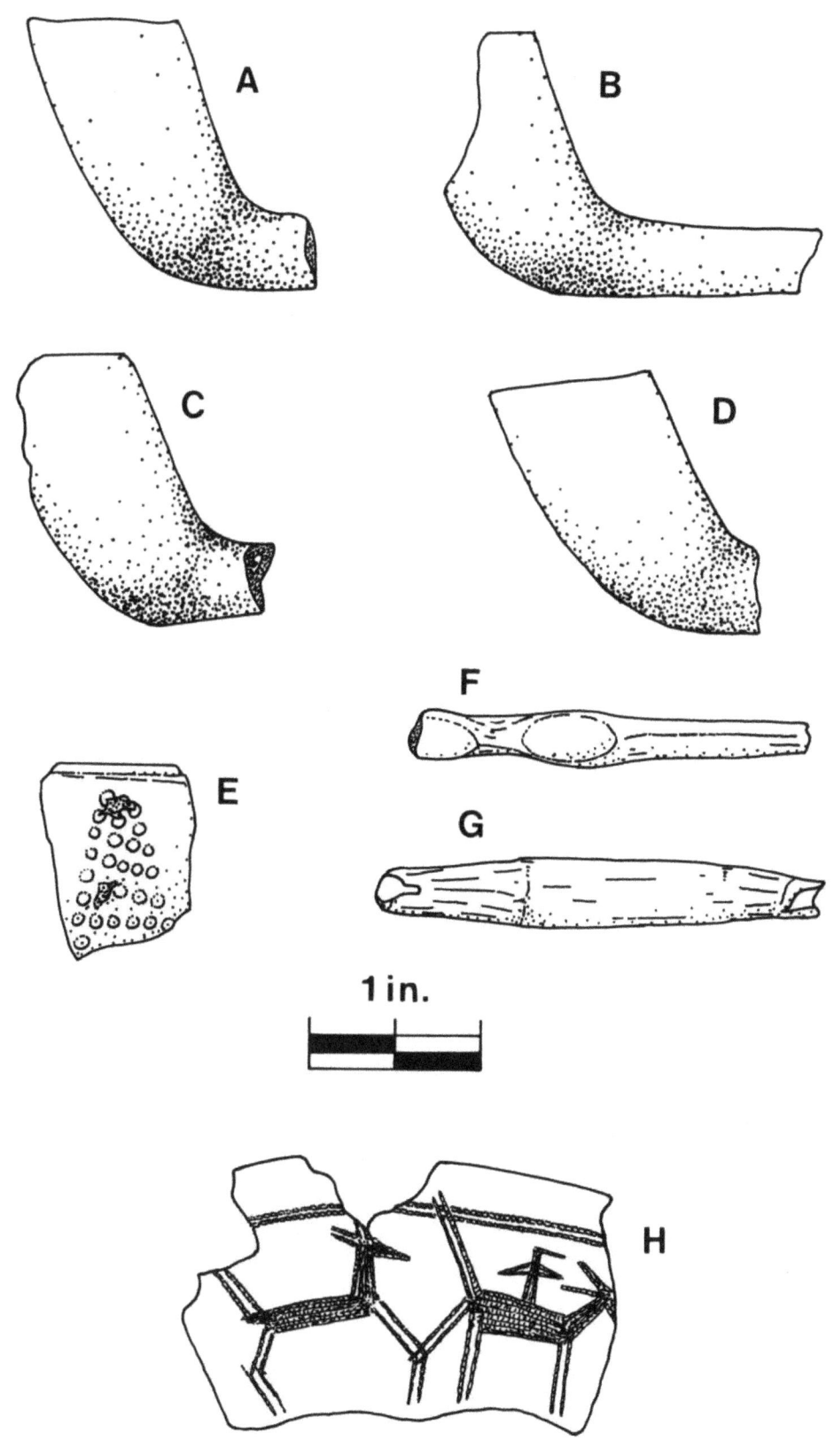

Figure 10: Representative pipe bowls from features, King's Reach, rouletted decoration from 18 Cv 232.

Table 3: Percentages of rouletted bowls and American Export type bowls for six features, King's Reach.

Prov.	% Rouletted	No. Rim Frags.	% Am. Export	No. Bowls
184	52.17	23	63.60	11
213	26.71	35	66.66	18
182	5.45	52	81.80	11
196	10.00	20	00.00	7
200	3.84	26	83.33	6
197	0.00	40	100.00	9

The small number of marked pipes recovered from features, and especially those for whom dating evidence is available, limits their utility as temporal indicators. In addition, the years of production for some of the makers -- particularly Robert Tippet I- III and Thomas Owen I-III, -- span almost the entire period of the site's occupation. Six bowl fragments with the IE mark were recovered from feature 196, which is interpreted as most likely having been filled very late in the occupation of the site. In contrast to this relatively large number of examples from one feature, only two identically marked fragments were recovered from plowzone and only one example was excavated from another feature (182). That feature also appears to have been finally filled at a relatively late date. This suggests that the IE-marked pipes may have been introduced to the King's Reach Site toward the end of the site's occupation, which provides some additional support for the end of that occupation as *circa* 1715.

Unlike the larger collection of bowl fragments recovered from plowzone, the overwhelming majority of bowls from the six features consist of the heel-less and spur-less American Export type. Also of interest, based on the evidence of the pipes from subsurface contexts, the percentage of American Export type bowls increased in general over time (Table 3).

In feature 184, 11 largely complete bowls were recovered, of which seven (63.6%) are American Export, two are heeled, and two have spurs. All of the American Export bowls are virtually identical (Figure 9a), as are the two heeled examples (9b); the two spurred bowls are quite different (9c and d). All of these bowls fit Oswald's (1961) Type 8 and 9 categories, however, and therefore fall within the *circa* 1680-1730 time period.

Of the 18 bowl fragments recovered from feature 213, 12 are of the American Export type, with six heeled. The 12 American Export bowls consist of only two varieties, however, with three varieties of heeled bowls. Two of the five total varieties are marked (TO and AI) and are illustrated in Figures 7e and 7l. Two of the three remaining varieties represent only slightly different versions of pipes already discussed. The remaining American Export variety (9e) is similar to a bowl fragment recovered from plowzone (8a); the example from 213 includes the rear of the rim, which is not rouletted. The second heeled variety (9f) is similar to the AI- marked example, but with a slightly larger heel and without rouletting as well as without the mark. The third heeled specimen (9g) has a more forward thrusting bowl and less pronounced heel; it also includes rouletting around the rear of the rim. Again, all these varieties fit Oswald's (1961) Types 8 and 9 (*circa* 1680-1730).

Although 190 pipe fragments were recovered from the 182 cellar, only 13 bowl fragments are complete enough to identify as to type -- with 10 American Export and two heeled. The remaining bowl appears to have been heeled originally, but the heel has been removed through cutting and scraping (9h). Both of the heeled bowl fragments are quite small and incomplete and do not allow further analysis. Two varieties of American Export bowls have been identified, one of which has the AS mark and is illustrated in Figure 7K. The second is only slightly different from numerous others recovered at the site (9i).

The remaining three features (197, 200, and 196), all of which seem to have been filled late in the history of the site, yielded almost exclusively American Export type bowls (Table 3). Only a limited number of varieties of that type of bowl are present as well, with one each from 196 and 200 and three from 197. All three from 197 are similar in size and shape, and are without rouletting or any other ornamentation (Figure 10a-c). The mouths of the bowls are nearly parallel with the line of the stem, which is an uncommon feature in the collection as a whole. The example from feature 200 (10d) is similar to these three, but the bowl is slightly forward thrusting. Finally, numerous fragments of one variety of American Export bowl were recovered from feature 196. These all exhibit the IE mark and the most complete example is illustrated in Figure 7C. Once again, all these bowls fit the Oswald (1961) Type 9c, generally dating to the period 1680-1730.

Five additional white clay pipe fragments were recovered that are of some interest. The first, and most diagnostic, is a bowl fragment that exhibits a number of closely spaced raised dots forming what appears to be a triangular shape, with the tip pointed toward the bowl's mouth (Figure 10e). While fragmentary, this appears certain to be what has been termed a "mulberry tree" decoration. Pipes with such decorations have been attributed to both Dutch and English production, and are well known on English sites beginning *circa* 1650 (*cf.* Oswald 1975:96-97 and Faulkner and Faulkner 1987:171). Pipes with similar decorations have been recovered at St. Mary's City (Miller: personal communication) and elsewhere in contexts dating to the second half of the 17th century (*cf.* McCashion 1979:118). Two stem fragments with a series of pinched, finger impressions also were recovered (10f); similar examples have been recovered from a number of sites (*cf.* Noel Hume 1979:24). A third stem fragment, with both ends carved to tapering points, may have been adapted as a bead (10g). Finally, a small bowl fragment with what appears to be molded hair, or possibly a mane, was recovered from plowzone. Unfortunately, its fragmentary condition makes any more complete interpretation difficult.

RED CLAY PIPES

While the white clay pipe fragments recovered number in the thousands, only eight fragments of red clay pipes were found. In addition, all eight were recovered from plowzone, so their usefulness in this analysis is even more limited. Of the eight, three are undecorated stem fragments, two are undecorated bowl fragments, and three are bowl fragments with the remnants of rouletted designs. The rouletting on these last fragments is similar to that found on pipes attributed to Indian manufacture, and which are commonly found on sites in the region before *circa* 1670 (Miller 1983:83; *cf.* Henry 1979). It is impossible to tell whether the remaining five fragments also are Indian-made or made instead by Colonists using imported molds. Such pipes also are often found on sites in the region, but seem first to occur with general frequency beginning *circa* 1670 (Miller 1983:83).

DISCUSSION

The King's Reach tobacco pipe assemblage, as a whole, supports the interpretation of the site's temporal range of occupation as spanning the period of the last decade of the 17th century and the first 10 to 20 years of the 18th century. The overwhelming majority of pipe bowls recovered fit this period, with only a few that seem to date slightly earlier. The five marks that have been attributable as to maker all fall within that period. The virtual absence of identifiable Dutch pipes and the extremely small number of Indian-made pipes both support a post-*circa* 1670 date of occupation. The prevalence of pipes of Bristol manufacture, and especially the preponderance of American Export bowls, provides additional support for a late 17th-early 18th-century occupation. Since pipes with the mark of the Bristol maker, Llewellin Evans, are some of the most commonly found on sites dating before *circa* 1690, the absence of any pipes with that mark at King's Reach also supports a post-1690 date. Finally, analysis of the pipes recovered from features points to a reduction over time in the percentage of rouletted bowls.

The use of pipe stem bore measurements in spatial analyses proved extremely helpful in interpreting the King's Reach homelot. In addition, computation of the bore diameter means for pipes from the six features studied also proved useful, and provides additional support for the validity of the hypothesized general reduction in bore diameters over time. However, computation of mean dates for both the site as a whole, based on more than 2700 measurable pipe stems from plowzone, and for pipes from five subsurface features seems to have yielded uniformly later dates than all other avenues of analysis would suggest. The mean date computed based on the plowzone pipes is 1727.24, almost 20 years later than expected. One feature interpreted as having been filled relatively early in the occupation of the site did yield a mean date of 1699.5 (109 stems), which is consistent with other evidence. However, the remainder of the six collections yielded dates as late as 1736.6 (39 stems), 1738.82 (43 stems), and 1743 (47 stems). All these dates seem much too late.

One explanation for the seemingly "faulty" dates may be the small numbers of measurable stems upon which the calculations are based. However, the fact that the means for the six collections correlate remarkably well with the chronological seriation of those features seems to indicate that the means are valid at least in relative terms. Another possible explanation could be that the occupation of the site may have been more intensive, i.e. had a larger population, during the latter years, which could have produced a disproportionately large percentage of the pipes deposited. As Binford (1962) has warned, such an increased rate of accumulation for the later period could "skew the total sample from the site in favor of a later date." The fact that the refuse from four of the seven subsurface features examined above appear to have been deposited late in the site's history may support this hypothesis.

A similar discrepancy between the mean dates for several features based on measurement of pipe bore diameters and other dating evidence seems to be the case at another late 17th-century Maryland site, Harmony Hall (Potter: personal communication). As at King's Reach, all other evidence points to an earlier range of occupation, from *circa* 1690-1720, but the mean date for the site based on 1033 stems is 1727.55. In addition, the mean dates for three features all are later than expected, yet their relative dates conform to the complementary archaeological data (Potter: personal communication). This similar result suggests the possibility that during this period pipes may have exhibited a greater proportion of 5/6th-inch bore diameters than expected.

MATTAPANY-SEWALL (18 St 390)

Mattapany-Sewall was the residence of Charles Calvert, Governor of the Maryland Colony from 1663 to 1678, who then inherited the title of third Lord Baltimore and the position of second Lord Proprietor of Maryland. In addition to serving as the Governor's residence, the manor also often was used as a meeting place for the Governor's Council. It was at Mattapany-Sewall that the Calverts' Proprietary government surrendered to the Protestant insurrectionists during the Revolution of 1689. The site was discovered in 1981 at the 6500-acre Patuxent River Naval Air Station during a federally-mandated cultural resources survey of the facility (Figure 1) (*cf.* Pogue 1987).

Through excavation of more than 300 shovel tests, the site was discovered and its limits demarcated. A total of 23 five x five foot test units were excavated within the area of highest artifact density, revealing a complex of subsurface features that included a single post hole/mold and four large pits filled with both structural and domestic debris. Portions of those features were excavated in hopes of retrieving an artifact sample sufficient to assign a temporal range for the site's occupation. Analysis of the resulting artifact assemblage points to a period of occupation spanning the second half of the 17th century. The abundant surviving documentary evidence pertaining to Mattapany-Sewall points to a similar time span of *circa* 1663-1700 (*cf.* Pogue 1987).

THE PIPES

A total of 540 tobacco pipe fragments were recovered, of which 526 are white clay and 14 are red. Of the 526 white pipes, 328 have measurable stem bores. The bore diameter totals in 64ths of an inch are given in Table 4. With 61.5% measuring 7/64th-inch, 26.5% 8/64th, and only 5.7% 6/64th, the bore diameter data support a *circa* 1660-1690 period of occupation (Harrington 1954). The preponderance of 7/64th-inch bores and precipitous drop-off to 6/64th points to a virtual abandonment of the site in the late 17th century, which corresponds with other archaeological and documentary evidence. It is well known that results of the Binford (1962) pipe bore formula are suspect when the total sample is less than approximately 1000 fragments, and even more questionable when the site studied dates before *circa* 1680. The Mattapany-Sewall pipe evidence further demonstrates these limitations, as a date of 1655.52 was produced. The other pipe data, i.e. maker's marks and bowl shapes, also support the Harrington derived period of *circa* 1660-1690 over the Binford mean date, which appears to be much too early.

Of the 37 white clay pipe bowl fragments complete enough to allow identification, 20 have heels, two are spurred, and 15 are the spur-less, heel-less, American Export type. A total of eight varieties have been identified: five heeled (Figure 11a-e), one spurred (11f), and two American Export (11g-h). The great majority of the bowls recovered, and all five identifiable varieties with intact rims, are rouletted around the mouth, a decorative treatment quite common on pipes dating to the 17th century. All the identifiable bowls are forward-thrusting and appear to fall within the *circa* 1650-1700 period (*cf.* Oswald 1961).

Only three bowl "marks" are present: a stamped "I" or "H" on a heel bottom (11c), a fragment of a stamped floral design, also on a heel bottom (11i), and a stamped "LE" on a bowl back (11g). The "LE" mark is the only one identified so far, and is well known as that of Llewellin Evans, a Bristol craftsman making pipes from 1661-1689 (Walker 1977(C):432), who was active in the export trade and whose wares are some of the most commonly represented on Chesapeake sites from the period. In addition, two stem decorations are present, two vaguely floral stamps on top of a heeled specimen (11e), and three with bands of continuous impressed diamonds with raised dots, bounded by

---

Figure 11 (opposite): Tobacco pipes from Mattapany-Sewall (18 St 390).

A. Heeled bowl, with rouletting around mouth (7/64th-inch);
B. Heeled bowl fragment, with rouletting around mouth (6/64th- inch);
C. Heeled bowl fragment, with "I" or "H" mark stamped on bottom of heel (9/64th-inch);
D. Heeled bowl fragment;
E. American Export type bowl fragment, with stamped "LE" mark on back of bowl, and rouletting around mouth (7/64th-inch).
F. American Export type bowl fragment, with rouletting around mouth (7/64th-inch);
G Heeled bowl/stem fragment, with stamped decoration on top of stem (8/64th-inch);
H. Spurred bowl/stem (6/64th-inch);
I. Heel fragment, with incised floral decoration;
J. Red clay pipe bowl fragment, with punctate and rouletted decorations;
K. Red clay heeled bowl, with rouletting around mouth, mold-made (6/64th-inch).

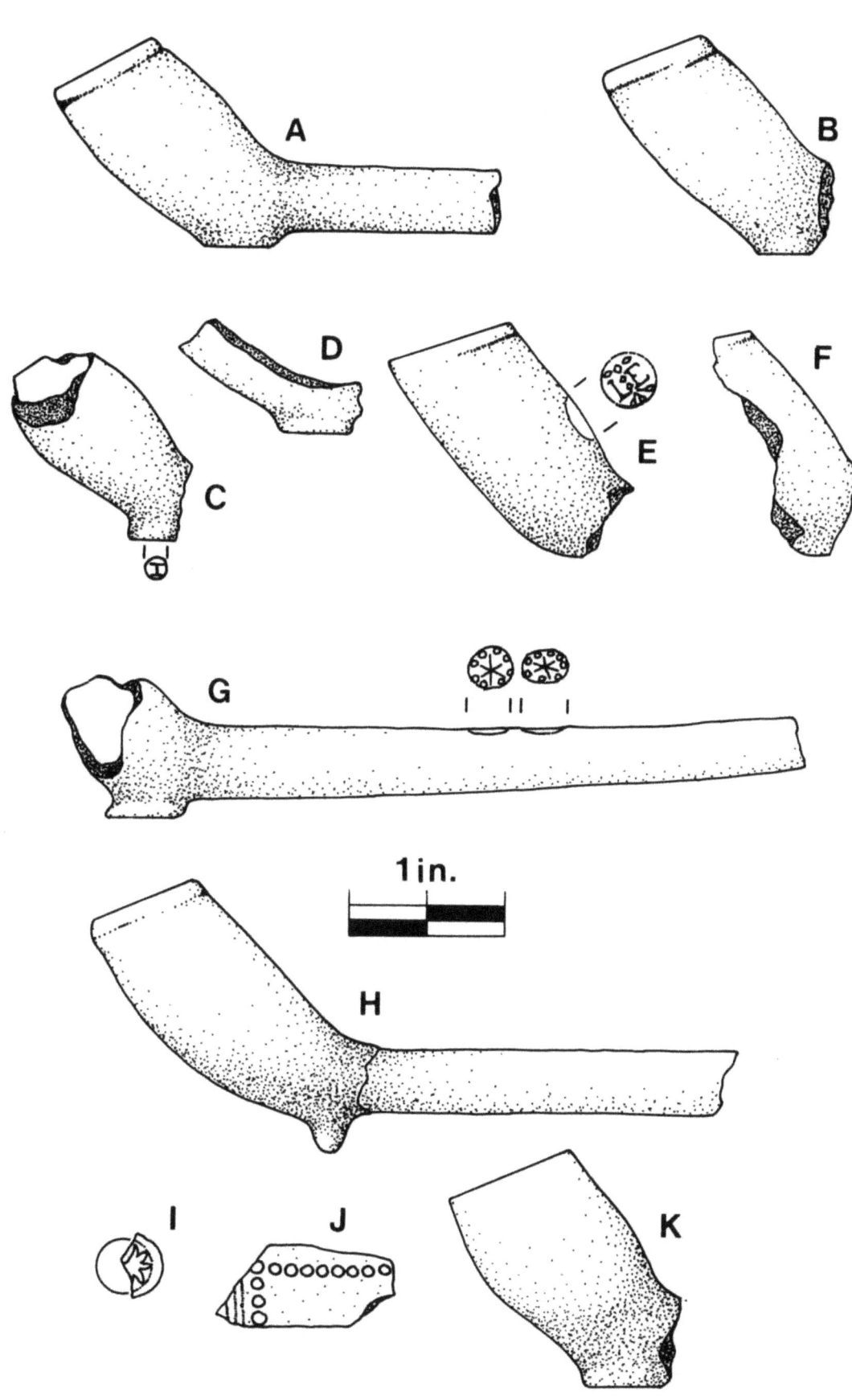

Figure 11: Pipes from Mattapany-Sewall (18 St 390).

dashed lines, encircling the stem. Stem decorations of the latter type are characteristic of Bristol manufacture during the second half of the 17th century (Walker 1977 (B):607). All the bowls appear to be English in origin and, since the marked bowl and stems have been attributed to Bristol manufacture, that city may well have been the source for most of the white clay pipes recovered. The absence of any identified Dutch pipes also supports a post-1660 date, as Dutch pipes seem to be relatively scarce on Chesapeake sites dating after that year (Miller 1983:83).

Of the 14 red clay pipe fragments, 13 are undecorated and appear to be of Colonial manufacture, using imported molds; the other is arouletted and punctate-decorated bowl fragment of Indian make (Figure 11j). Two complete, and a third fragmentary, heeled bowls were recovered. All three are well finished and obviously made using imported molds. The two complete specimens have rouletting around the rim; their shapes fit the general 1680-1700 period (11k). Pipes made by Indians are commonly found on Maryland sites in contexts dating before *circa* 1670; in contrast, Colonial- made pipes appear to date between *circa* 1670 and the end of the century (Miller 1983:83). The presence of locally made pipes on a site with as prestigious a resident as Charles Calvert may be attributable to at least two possible causes -- use by the plantation's servants and/or slaves, or by the countless visitors known to have congregated there.

Table 4: Mattapany-Sewell site pipe bore diameters.

Diameter	Number	Percent
5/64 inch	9	2.7
6/64	19	5.7
7/64	202	61.5
8/64	87	26.5
9/64	10	3.0
10/64	1	0.3

18 Cv 169

Limited archaeological investigations were carried out intermittently over a four-month period in 1987 at 18 Cv 169 to assess the negative impact on the site due to long-term, and continuing, agricultural cultivation. Investigations included systematically collecting artifacts from the plowed field surface and excavating seven two-by-two-meter test units within the area of highest artifact density. A complex of subsurface features was revealed below plowzone, which have been interpreted as a portion of a structure and associated refuse-filled pits. As the goal of the field work was limited to discerning the level of negative impact on site integrity, the subsurface features were recorded but not excavated. Since the site was found to contain extensive and significant subsurface remains, and they are believed to be in great danger of destruction if continued plowing is permitted, the site core as identified by this investigation was removed from active cultivation (*cf.* Pogue 1988b).

THE PIPES

A total of 421 white clay tobacco pipe fragments were recovered as a result of surface collection and plowzone excavation. Of that total, 239 are stems with measurable bores; Table 5 records the bore diameters in 64ths of an inch. With 41.42% measuring 6/64th- inch, 38.91% 7/64th, and only 12.55% at 8/64th, the distribution of bore diameters suggests a *circa* 1665-1695 period of occupation, in comparison to the histograms for temporal ranges established by Harrington (1954) and using interpolated periods prepared by Stone (1977). No red clay pipes were recovered.

Computation of the Binford (1962) pipe bore formula has yielded a date of 1679.91. The total number of measurable bores is only 239, and considerable research over the years has demonstrated that to be too few for a dependable mean date to be produced. However, that date fits extremely well with the approximate range of

---

Figure 12 (opposite): Tobacco pipes from 18 Cv 169.

A. American Export type bowl/stem, with rouletting around mouth (6/64th-inch);
B. American Export type bowl, with rouletting around mouth (7/64th-inch);
C. American Export type bowl, with rouletting around mouth (6/64th-inch);
D. American Export type bowl/stem, with rouletting around mouth (7/64th-inch);
E. American Export type bowl fragment, with rouletting around mouth (7/64th-inch).
F. American Export type bowl/stem fragment, with stem mark consisting of incised bands and repeating diamond (7/64th-inch) (see Figure 13e);
G. American Export type bowl fragment, with rouletting around mouth and with stamped "LE" mark on back of bowl;
H. Heeled bowl fragment (7/64th-inch);
I. Spurred bowl fragment (7/64th-inch);

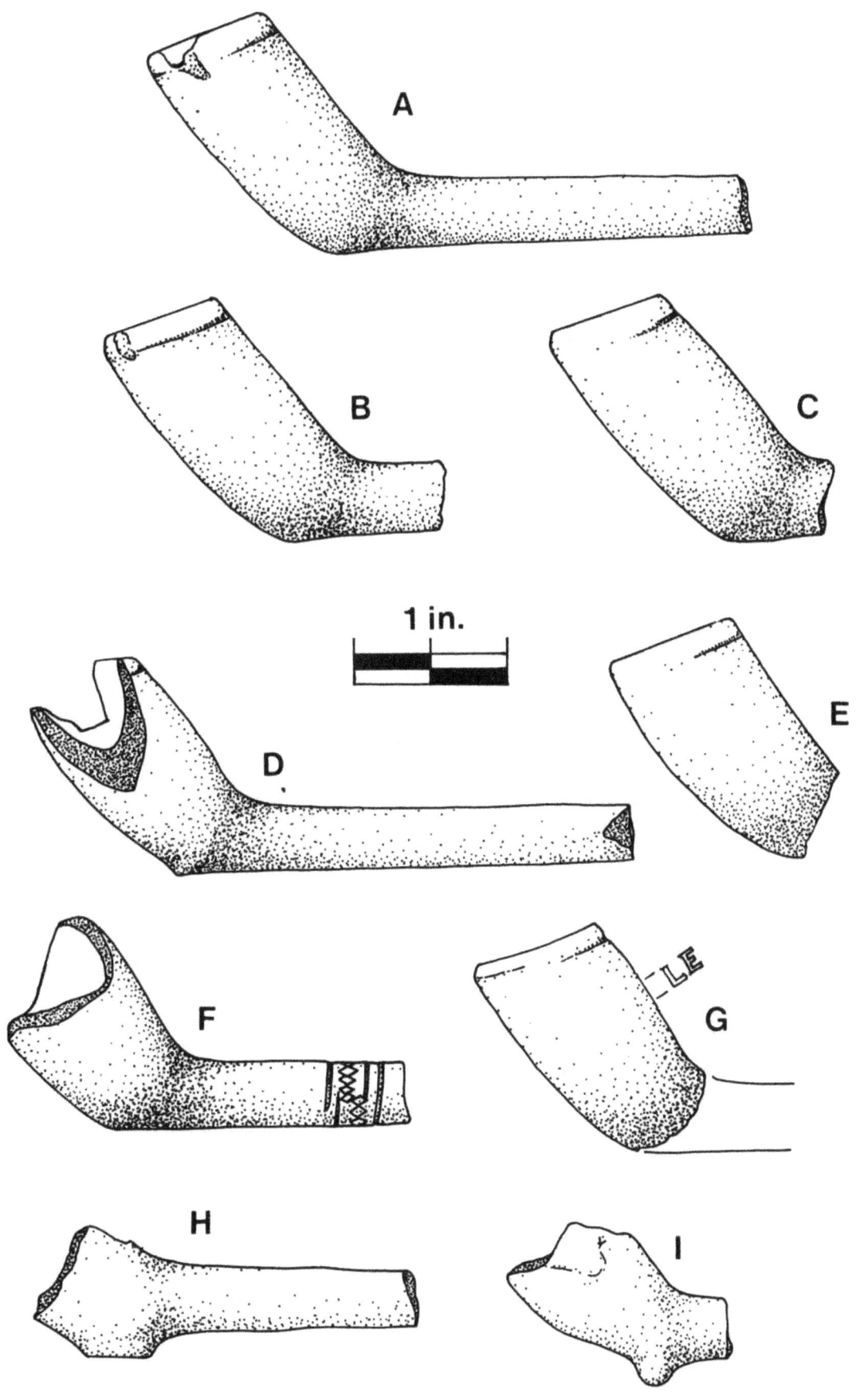

Figure 12: Pipes from 18 Cv 169.

occupation suggested by the Harrington (1954) pipe distribution, and by analysis of the entire artifact assemblage.

In addition to the measurable stems, a number of other pipe fragments were recovered that provide dating information. Two bowl fragments and six stem fragments with maker's marks were recovered, along with several decorated stems. Two of the marks are incomplete, but the remainder are identifiable as "LE" and "WE." These marks are well known as belonging to members of the pipemaking Evans family of Bristol, England. Llewellin Evans was making pipes from *circa* 1661-1689 (Walker 1977(C):1131-32), and appears to have specialized in the overseas export market. His LE-marked wares have been recovered in large numbers from archaeological sites all along the eastern seaboard in America, as well as abroad. The pipes of William Evans are almost as widespread, but two William Evans' successively manufactured pipes, and it is difficult to discriminate between them. Therefore, the general date range for WE-marked pipes is broad (*circa* 1660-1697). A William Evans, very possibly the son of Llewellin, began making pipes on his own in 1660, followed by his son, William, in 1667. At least one William Evans still was making pipes in 1697 (Walker 1977(C):1132-36).

Table 5: 18 CV 169 Site pipe bore diameters.

Diameter	Number	Percent
5/64 inch	16	6.69
6/64	99	41.42
7/64	93	38.91
8/64	30	12.55
9/64	1	0.41
TOTALS	239	99.9

The LE-marked pipe is of the American Export type (Figure 12a), with a forward-thrusting bowl and with rouletting around the rim. The mark consists only of the very plain and simple stamped letters, which occur on the back, facing the smoker. Unfortunately, the pipe is broken at the elbow and, as a result, the stem bore diameter is impossible to measure.

Of the 39 bowl fragments complete enough to identify with confidence, 23 are of the American Export type, corresponding with number 9c of Oswald's (1961) typology and dating to *circa* 1680-1730. At least six slightly variant forms of this type have been identified in this collection. Of the six relatively complete bowls of this type, all six have at least partial rouletting around the mouth; of the six with measurable bores, four are 7/64th and two are 6/64th-inch (Figure 12b-e). Of the remaining 16 bowl fragments, 15 have heels and one is spurred. The two heeled bowls with measurable bores have one 7/64th and one 6/64th-inch (12h); the spurred pipe has a 7/64th-inch bore (12i). Finally, of the 67 total pipe bowl rim fragments, 43 (64.17%) are rouletted and 24 (35.82%) do not show evidence of rouletting.

All three of the stems with LE marks have 7/64th-inch bores, and include a band of impressed diamonds encircling the stem as well as encircling rouletted bands enclosing the mark (Figure 13a and b). The WE-marked stem is similar in appearance to the LE type, but with an 8/64th-inch bore diameter (13c). In addition to these marked stems, three other varieties of decorated stems were recovered. One is similar to those described above, but without any initials, with a bore of 8/64th-inch (13d). The second is quite different, consisting of a series of repeating "X" marks within two incised bands, with a bore diameter of 6/64th-inch. The third is quite a different type altogether, consisting of two encircling, crudely incised bands, without any marks, with a bore of 5/64th-inch (13f).

Figure 13 (opposite): Decorated stems from 18 Cv 169, and tobacco pipes from 18 Cv 232.

A. Stem fragment with incised "LE" mark within encircling rouletted bands, and repeating impressed diamonds (7/64th inch);
B. Stem fragment with incised "LE" mark within encircling rouletted bands, and repeating impressed diamonds with dots in their centers (7/64th-inch);
C. Stem fragment with incised "WE" mark within encircling rouletted bands, and repeating impressed diamonds with dots in their centers (8/64th-inch);
D. Stem fragment with repeating impressed diamonds with dots in their centers (8/64th-inch);
E. Bowl/stem fragment with mark consisting of incised bands and repeating diamonds (see Figure 12f);
F. Stem fragment with two encircling crudely incised bands (5/64th-inch);
G. Heeled bowl with stamped "Tudor rose" decoration on bottom of heel (10/64th-inch);
H. Heeled bowl fragment, with rouletting around mouth and incomplete stamped mark on bottom of heel;
I. Heeled bowl fragment (7/64th-inch);
J. Red clay, hand-made bowl fragment, with rouletted "running deer" decoration (Figure 10h).

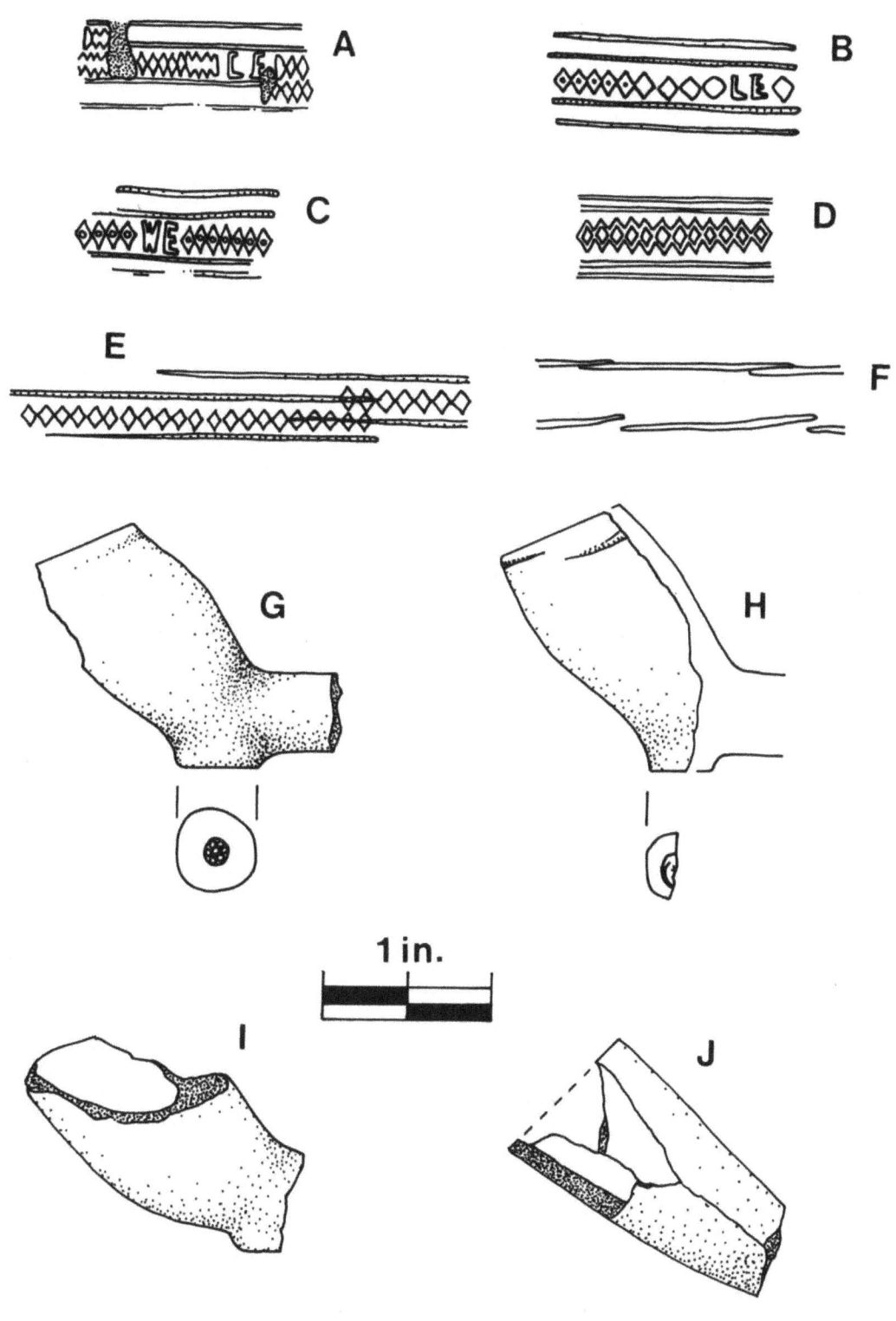

Figure 13: Decorated pipe stems from 18 Cv 169 and pipes from 18 Cv 232.

18 Cv 232

The fourth collection is both the smallest and the earliest, and derives from surface collecting an apparent domestic site located in an agricultural field overlooking nearby St. Leonard Creek (Figure 1). The surface collection was carried out in 1984 when the site was discovered, and yielded structural debris such as brick and mortar rubble and nails, as well as domestic materials such as ceramics, bottle glass, flint, and tobacco pipes. Evidence for two small, approximately four by five feet in dimension, roughly circular subsurface pits was observed, and the pipe fragments were found in their vicinity. The parcel of land on which the site is located was patented in 1651 by Peter Johnson and was called Brewhouse (Archives 51:68). Circumstantial evidence suggests that this may be the site of Johnson's residence.

THE PIPES

Of the 11 pipe fragments, eight are white clay and three are reddish brown. Seven of the white clay pipe bores are measurable, yielding two 10/64th-inch, one 9/64th, three 7/64th, and one 6/64th. Obviously, this number is far too small to yield any reliable dating evidence. Four white clay bowls were complete enough to allow identification as to type, with three heeled and one American Export. The American Export type has a 7/64th-inch bore; it is not complete enough for any additional analysis.

Two of the three heeled examples exhibit circular marks on their heel bottoms. Only one of the marks is complete, however, and it is a "Tudor Rose" design, a mark apparently used by both English and Dutch pipe makers (Miller 1983:78), and which by itself is not diagnostic (Figure 13g). The bowl with the "Tudor Rose" design does not have rouletting around the mouth; the second bowl, with only a fragmentary heel mark, is rouletted (13h). The third heeled bowl also is fragmentary and cannot be analyzed further (13i).

The shapes of the two more complete heeled bowls, large and barrel-shaped, with their broad heels, and forward thrusting posture, all suggest mid-century dates of production. They generally conform to Oswald's (1961) type 6b, which he dates to *circa* 1650-1680.

The three red clay pipe fragments mend and are part of a hand-formed, funnel-shaped bowl, with a rouletted design in the form of an animal (Figures 10h and 13j). This design has been termed the "running deer" motif (Henry 1979: 24 and 27 and Miller 1983:83). The method of manufacture, shape of the bowl, and the technique and type of decoration all point to its being made by American Indians. Virtually identical examples have been recovered from numerous sites throughout the Chesapeake in 17th-century contexts (Henry 1979); in Maryland, this type of pipe is most often found in contexts dating before *circa* 1670 (Miller 1983:83).

While the number of pipes from Cv 232 is admittedly quite small, this collection has been included here because of its apparent early date -- probably the earliest of the four studied. The pipes reflect this, including one bowl of native manufacture and at least one marked white clay bowl that may be of Dutch origin. In addition, while only seven measurable stems were recovered, their mean diameter is 8.00, by far the largest of the four collections examined.

COMPARATIVE DATA

Recent excavations at two additional 17th-century domestic sites in the Patuxent River valley provide valuable comparative data. The Compton Site (18Cv279) dates to the period *circa* 1651-1684 (Outlaw *et al.* 1989); the Patuxent Point Site (18Cv271) has been tentatively dated to the 1660s-1690s (Gibb: Personal communication). Both sites have been intensively excavated and have yielded significant quantities, thousands of fragments, of tobacco pipes. Unfortunately, the Patuxent Point excavation and analysis are not yet completed, but a report on the Compton Site is available for comparison.

In addition to a majority of English pipes, both sites yielded large numbers of pipes with Dutch maker's marks and decorations, as well as numerous locally-made red clay pipes. These include both molded and hand-formed types, interpreted as the product of Colonists and American Indians, respectively (Outlaw *et al.* 1989:104-116). Given that both sites were occupied beginning well before the year 1670, the presence of Dutch and locally-made pipes is expected.

Unfortunately the Compton Site report (Outlaw *et al.* 1989) does not list a complete break-down of the pipes by bore diameters, by nation of origin, by bowl shape, or by maker's mark. However, the discussion of the pipe data includes a more complete elucidation of the pipes excavated from a single large feature. A total of 1,448 pipe fragments were recovered, of which 1,162 are measurable stems and 78 are "datable" bowls. One Dutch maker's mark, "EB" for Edward Bird (1630-1665), is found on 37 of the bowls. Twelve bowls exhibit the molded "pilgrim/Minerva" design, and two stems are marked with *fleur-de-lis*, all believed to be Dutch (Outlaw *et al.* 1989:115).

Two other maker's marks were recovered at the site, "PE", probably Philip Edwards, and "Flower Hunt". Both Edwards and Hunt probably were Bristol pipe makers. Philip Edwards I made pipes from *circa* 1649-1669; his son, Philip Edwards II, also made pipes, from *circa* 1680-1696 (Walker 1977:1125-1126). Flower Hunt was making pipes from *circa* 1651-1672 (Walker 1977:1177).

The pipe mean dates derived from calculation of the

Binford regression formula for various assemblages all are significantly earlier than indicated by other artifact analyses. The date for the single large feature, based on a total of 1,162 measurable stems, is 1628.81. The mean date for all measurable pipes (1,234 stems) recovered from subsurface features was only slightly later - 1630.17 (Outlaw *et al.* 1989:111). Since diagnostically Dutch pipes were recovered in quantity, and it is well established that the bore diameters of Dutch pipes tend to be larger when compared with English pipes of the same period, this early date seems most likely attributable to that factor.

THE "PATUXENT PATTERN"

Together, the four sites span the relatively broad period from *circa* 1660-1715. The results of the preceding analyses provide additional evidence for changes in the types of tobacco pipes used along the Patuxent over the more than a half-century period involved. As the four collections span such a broad period, a comparison of the results of the analyses provides an opportunity to track these changes. In addition, significant trends seem to be reflected within the King's Reach Site collection alone.

Dutch pipes appear to make up an extremely small percentage of the total pipes recovered from the sites. Not a single maker's mark or decoration has been attributable to Dutch manufacture, although at least one possible Dutch mark is included in each of the King's Reach and Cv 232 collections. Evidence from elsewhere in the Chesapeake, including nearby St. Mary's City, suggests that the Dutch pipe industry had lost out to the British by between 1660 and 1670. Since the collections examined generally date after the former year, it is not surprising that Dutch wares are virtually unrepresented. The presence of Dutch pipes of the Compton and Patuxant Point Sites, both of which were occupied prior to 1670, gives additional support to this interpretation.

On the other hand, all but one of the attributable maker's marks recovered are believed to be of Bristol origin, with the lone exception from London. This evidence provides strong support for the contention that Bristol makers had virtually cornered the American tobacco pipe market during the second half of the 17th century. As for the distribution of marks, those of Llewellin Evans again have been shown to be plentiful on sites spanning his approximately 28 years of production.

The proportion of bowl shapes that are of the "American Export" type is high at all three of the sites from whom sizable collections were recovered. At the King's Reach Site, that type appears to have become more popular over time; at the other two, earlier sites, the proportion seems lower, but still significant (40.54% at Mattapany- Sewall and 58.97% at Cv 169). The question of whether that type of bowl actually increased in use needs to be addressed via examination of additional collections spanning the period.

Calculating the proportion of rouletted and nonrouletted bowls at the King's Reach Site has yielded interesting results. The number of rouletted bowls shows a marked decrease over the period of the site's occupation, suggesting that for the Bristol pipe industry, at least, rouletting went out of fashion during the period that King's Reach was occupied. The percentages of rouletted bowls at the Mattapany-Sewall and Cv 169 Sites are high, and again seem to reflect earlier dates of occupation.

Red clay pipes also make up a small percentage of the total, but were recovered in small numbers at three of the four sites. In Maryland, red clay pipes made by Indians are commonly found on sites dating before *circa* 1670; mold-made pipes made by Colonists first appear at about that time. Once again, the presence of locally-made pipes in apparently larger numbers at both Compton and Patuxent Point Sites, therefore, fits this pattern. Henry (1979) has compiled substantial evidence to suggest that the occurrence of such pipes may be an indication of the economic status of the occupants, and directly linked to fluctuations in the price of tobacco.

Clearly, additional collections of pipes from the area need to be examined before the apparent patterns outlined above may be taken as reliably indicative of trends in pipe use for the Patuxent River valley. The lack of collections from the earliest period of settlement (*circa* 1637-1660) is a particularly glaring gap in knowledge. Given the results from this study, however, and with reference to research carried out elsewhere in the region, it seems likely that both Dutch and locally-made pipes would comprise a much larger proportion of total pipes for that period.

REFERENCES CITED

Alexander, L.T.(1979). Clay pipes from the Buck Site in Maryland. *The archaeology of the clay tobacco pipe, II: The United States of America.* Edited by P.J. Davey, British Archaeological Reports International Series 60:37-61.

Atkinson, D. and Oswald, A. (1969). *London clay tobacco pipes.* Museum of London, London, England.

Binford, L.R. (1962). A new method of calculating dates from kaolin pipe stem samples. *Southeastern Archaeological Conference Newsletter* 9(1):19-21.

Carson, C., Barka, N.F., Kelso, W.M., Stone, G.W. and

Upton, D. (1981). Impermanent architecture in the Southern American colonies. *Winterthur Portfolio* 16(2/3):135-196.

Faulkner, A. and Faulkner, G. (1987). *The French at Pentagoet*. The Maine Historic Preservation Commission, Augusta, Maine.

Gibb, J.G. (1990) Personal communication.

Harrington, J.C. (1954). Datingstem fragments of seventeenth and eighteenth century clay tobacco pipes. *Quarterly Bulletin of the Archeological Society of Virginia* 9(1):9-13.

Henry, S.L. (1979). Terra-cotta tobacco pipes in 17th century Maryland and Virginia: a preliminary study. *Historical Archaeology* 13:14-37.

Keeler, R.W. (1978). *The homelot on the seventeenth century Chesapeake tidewater frontier*. Unpublished Ph.D. dissertation, Department of Anthropology, University of Oregon.

Kelso, W.M. (1984). *Kingsmill plantations, 1619-1800: archaeology of country life in Colonial Virginia*. Academic Press, New York.

King, J.A. (1988). A comparativemidden analysis of a household and inn in St. Mary's City, Maryland. *Historical Archaeology*, 22(2):17-39.

King, J.A. and Miller, H.M. (1987). The view from the midden: an analysis of midden distribution and variability at the van Sweringen Site, St. Mary's City, Maryland. *Historical Archaeology*, 21(2):37-59.

Lewarch, D.E. and O'Brien, M.J. (1981). Effect of short term tillage on aggregate provenience surface pattern. *Plowzone archaeology: contributions to theory and technique*, Edited by M.J.O'Brien and D.E. Lewarch, Vanderbilt University Publications in Anthropology No. 27:7-50.

Main, G. (1982). *Tobacco colony: life in early Maryland, 1650-1720*. Princeton University Press, Princeton, New Jersey.

McCashion, J.H. (1979). A preliminary chronology and discussion of seventeenth and early eighteenth century clay tobacco pipes from New York State sites. *The archaeology of the clay tobacco pipe, II: The United States of America*. Edited by P.J. Davey, British Archaeological Reports International Series 60:63-150.

Miller, H.M. (1983). A search for the "Citty of Saint Maries": report on the 1981 excavations in St. Mary's City, Maryland. *St. Maries City Archaeology Series No.1*.

Miller, H.M. (1983) Personal communication.

Neiman, F.D. (1988). Do formation processes distort or document what we want to know. Paper presented at the Jamestown Conference on Archaeology.

Neiman, F.D. (1988). Personal communication.

Neiman, F.D. (1980). Field archaeology of the Clifts Plantation Site, Westmoreland County, Virginia. Ms. on file, Jefferson Patterson Park and Museum, St. Leonard, Maryland.

Noel Hume, A. (1979). Clay tobacco pipes excavated at Martin's Hundred, Virginia, 1976-1978. *The archaeology of the clay tobacco pipe, II: The United States of America*. Edited by P.J. Davey, British Archaeological Reports International Series 60:3-36.

Oswald, A. (1975). *Clay pipes for the archaeologist*. British Archaeological Reports 14. Oxford, England.

Oswald, A. (1960). *The archaeology and economic history of English clay tobacco pipes*. The Museum of London, London, England.

Outlaw, A.C., and others (1989). *The Compton Site, circa 1651-1684*. Louis Berger and Associates, East Orange, New Jersey.

Pogue, D.J. (1988a). Spatial analysis of the King's Reach plantation homelot, Ca. 1690-1715. *Historical Archaeology* 22(2):40-56.

Pogue, D.J. (1988b). Archaeological investigations at 18 Cv 169, Jefferson Patterson Park and Museum, St. Leonard, Maryland. *Jefferson Patterson Park and Museum File Report*.

Pogue, D.J. (1987). Seventeenth-century Proprietary rule and rebellion: archeology at Charles Calvert's Mattapany-Sewall. *Maryland Archeology*, 23(1):1-37.

Stone, G.W. (1977). Dating seventeenth-century white clay tobacco pipe stem groups: a proposal to the seventeenth-century study group. Ms. on file, Historic St. Mary's City.

Tukey, J. (1977). *Exploratory data analysis*. Addison-Wesley, Reading, Massachusetts. *History and Archeology Series 11*

Walker, I.C. (1966). TD pipes -- a preliminary study. *Quarterly Bulletin of the Archaeological Society of Virginia*, 20(4):86-102.

Walker, I.C. (1977). *Clay tobacco pipes, with particular reference to the Bristol industry* (4 vols.). Parks Canada, Ottawa.

An Analysis of Clay Tobacco Pipes from Harmony Hall, Maryland

Stephen R. Potter and Robert C. Sonderman

INTRODUCTION

National Park Service archaeological excavations in 1985-87 resulted in the discovery of a late 17th century earthfast house site located on the grounds of Harmony Hall (18PR305), an 18th-century Georgian manor in Prince Georges County, Maryland (Figure 1). The property is owned by the National Park Service and was leased in October 1985 to a private firm under the provisions of the Historic Leasing Program. The discovery was made during an archaeological survey of the property to ensure that plans by the lessees for new construction and utilities would not destroy any significant historic resources.

The remains of the earthfast house consisted of a burned soil horizon found below a thin construction layer associated with the extant brick, Georgian manor known as Harmony Hall (Figure 2). Three sides and two corners of the post-in-the-ground structure were exposed, indicating it was 18 feet wide and probably three bays or 30-feet long. An existing gravel driveway covers the northeast end of the house; however, the maximum length of the burned house midden which was uncovered is 22-feet, indicating a structure of at least three, 10-foot bays. Based on the assemblage of artifacts, stratigraphy, and historical research, the earthfast house was occupied for a relatively short time, circa 1690-1720.

From an examination of the archaeological evidence, it appears that soon after the post-supported frame dwelling burned, the brick manor house, Harmony Hall, was erected. The traditional date for Harmony Hall's construction is 1723. However, historical research indicates the brick manor was most likely built either before 1721 or after 1763 (Nickels 1987). An analysis of the features and clay tobacco pipes from the site provides an opportunity to tightly date some pipes and to aid in dating events associated with both the earlier earthfast house and the later brick manor.

A BRIEF HISTORY OF HARMONY HALL: THE 17TH AND 18TH CENTURIES

Originally patented as 500 acres of land called Battersea, the property was surveyed in 1662 and recorded in the name of Humphrey Haggett. By the time the patent was granted six years later, the owner was Richard Fowke, who had married Haggett's widow.

In 1688, Fowke divided the property in half, selling one portion to Philip Mason and the other to Richard Iles. The tract sold to Mason contained the land upon which Harmony Hall now stands (Nickels 1987).

Shortly after acquiring the property, Mason sold it to Thomas Lewis in 1692. Four years later, Thomas Lewis willed 100 acres to his son Richard, which included the house his mother was living in. Since this 100 acre tract also incorporated the future site of Harmony Hall, the archaeological remains of the earthfast house probably represent the dwelling of Thomas Lewis and his wife. Depositions taken in 1745, from some of the areas earliest farmers, indicate the Battersea property was occupied and farmed some time during the period 1685-95 (Nickels 1987).

In 1709, Richard Lewis sold the 100 acres of land containing his parents' home to a carpenter named William Tyler. With Tyler's death in 1721, his "dwelling plantation called Battersea" was willed to his wife Elizabeth, and upon her death to his son William. Five years later, Elizabeth remarried and moved elsewhere to live with her new husband, Henry Massey. Elizabeth's son, William, never inherited the Battersea property, since his mother outlived him by two years, dying in 1757 (Nickels 1987).

At this time, the property passes to Elizabeth's grandson, John Tyler, who resided in adjacent Charles County. John, in turn, ultimately sold it to James Marshall in 1763. Six years later, the tract was purchased by Enoch Magruder and for nearly a century it remained in the Magruder family. It is during their ownership that the 18th century brick manor house acquired its' present name. In 1792, Walter and John Addison rented the Battersea house from Dennis Magruder, while their own houses were being built. The brothers and their brides spent their first year of marriage at Battersea, which they declared was such a pleasant time together that the house should be renamed "Harmony Hall" (Nickels 1987).

Given this brief overview of Battersea's early history, it is most likely that the brick manor of Harmony Hall was built either before the elder William Tyler's death in 1721 or after his grandson, John Tyler, sold the property in 1763. The results of the previous architectural investigations have been equivocal, as well. Therefore, information derived from the archaeological research and clay tobacco pipe analysis may assist in addressing this problem.

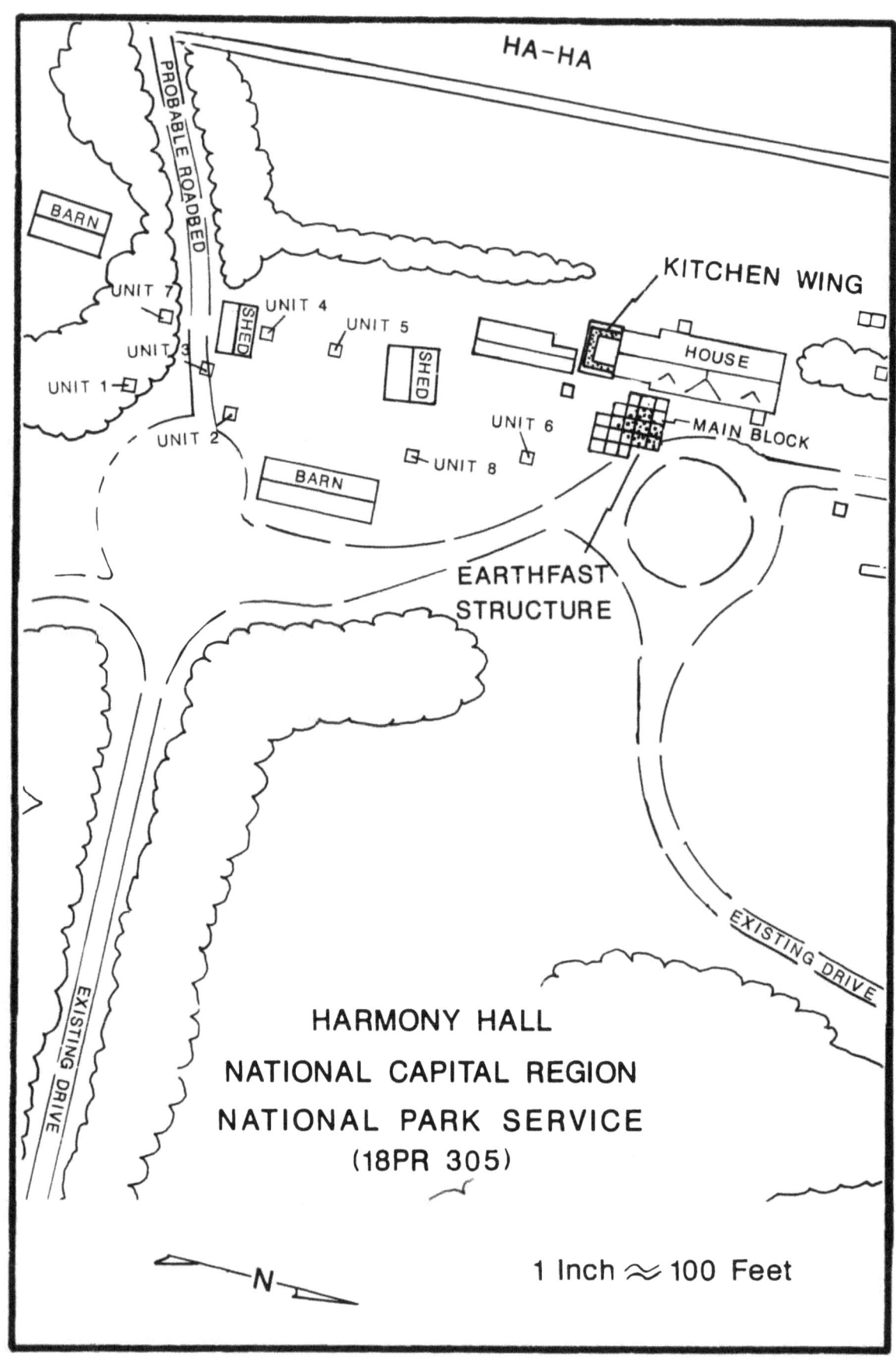

Figure 1: Area map of Harmony Hall (18PR305), Prince Georges County, Maryland

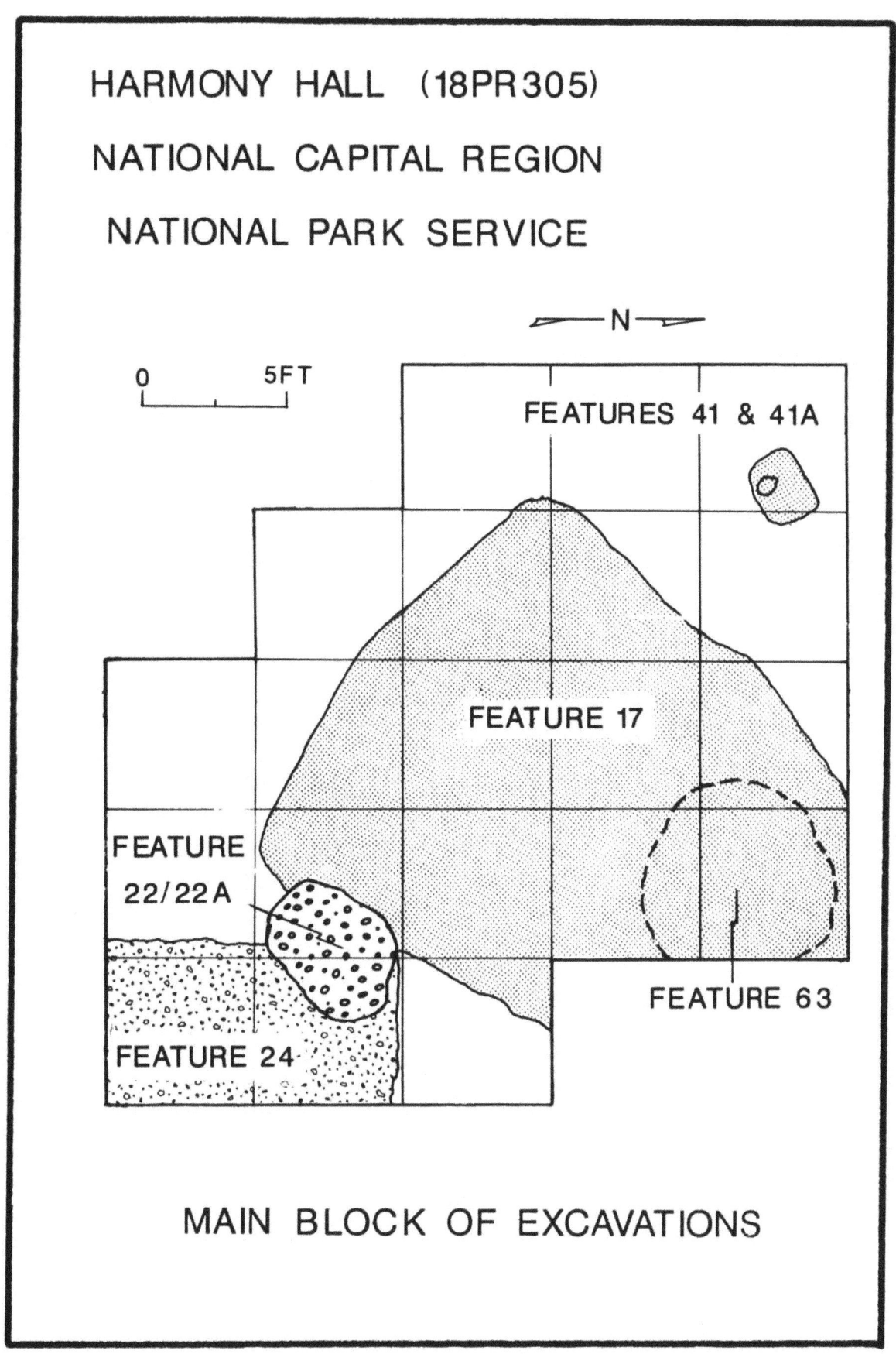

Figure 2: Plan view of the main block of excavations at the site of the earthfast house, Feature 17.

CLAY TOBACCO PIPE DESCRIPTION AND ANALYSIS

FEATURE 17, THE BURNED, EARTHFAST HOUSE MIDDEN (Figure 2):

The main block of archaeological excavations on the Harmony Hall property occurred at the site of the earthfast house. A total of 20 contiguous 5-by-5 foot units, were excavated in order to expose the post-supported frame dwelling and adjacent areas. Approximately 65% of the burned house midden was exposed, covering an area 18-by-22-feet and varying in thickness between 0.5 to 0.8 feet. Only 15% of the midden stain, describing three sides and two corners of the house, was excavated.

A Binford (1962) mean pipe date of 1715.3 was derived from a total of 247 pipe stems found in the house midden (Table 1). One of the stems, with a bore diameter of 6/64", shows signs of being a secondary mouthpiece. A detailed description of the pipe bowls from Feature 17 follows.

Figure 3a: A pipe bowl lacking a heel or spur, with a rounded base on the underside where the bowl and stem join. There is a slight swelling on the back of the bowl. On the smoker's right side of the bowl is a relief-molded cartouche bearing the initials "RC" over "PW."

This specimen is similar to one illustrated by McCashion (1979:146) except that it has no rouletting below the mouth of the bowl. According to McCashion, the pipe probably dates to circa 1690-1710 and, because of the bowl form and relief-molded cartouche, was most likely made in Bristol (I. Noel Hume 1970:305). Including this pipe, only three examples by the makers "RC/PW" have been reported for all of North America. Unfortunately, the pipemakers remain unidentified (McCashion 1988).

Stem hole diameter 5/64".

Figure 3b: A plain pipe bowl with a rounded base and no heel or spur. A slight swelling occurs on the back of the bowl.

Stem hole diameter 5/64".

Figure 3c: A plain pipe bowl fragment with slight swelling on the back. Although fragmentary, the bowl shape indicates this specimen was probably similar to the previous example (Figure 3b).

Stem hole diameter cannot be determined.

Figure 3d: A fragmentary bowl and stem, with a slight swelling on the back of the bowl, no rouletting and a rounded base.

Stem hole diameter 6/64".

Figure 3e: A fragmentary bowl and stem. The back is slightly swollen, there is no rouletting and the base is rounded. This specimen is similar to the previous pipe (Figure 3d).

Stem hole diameter 6/64".

Figure 3f: A fragmentary bowl and stem, with a slight swelling on the back of the bowl and a rounded base on the underside of the bowl-stem juncture. The lip of the bowl is flat and the wall is very thick (4 mm) at the back mold seam, but becomes much thinner (1.5 mm) away from the seam.

Stem hole diameter 6/64".

Table 1: Pipe-stem data.

Location	No. of stems by hole diameter					Total Stems	Binford Mean Date
	4/64"	5/64"	6/64"	7/64"	8/64"		
All excavations	85	575	323	41	9	1033	1727.55
Main block excavations	53	518	286	33	9	899	1726
Feature 17	4	106	113	18	6	247	1715.3
Feature 63	2	15	20	1	-	38	1720.43
Feature 22	1	18	10	-	-	29	1728.68
Feature 14	7	6	2	-	-	15	-

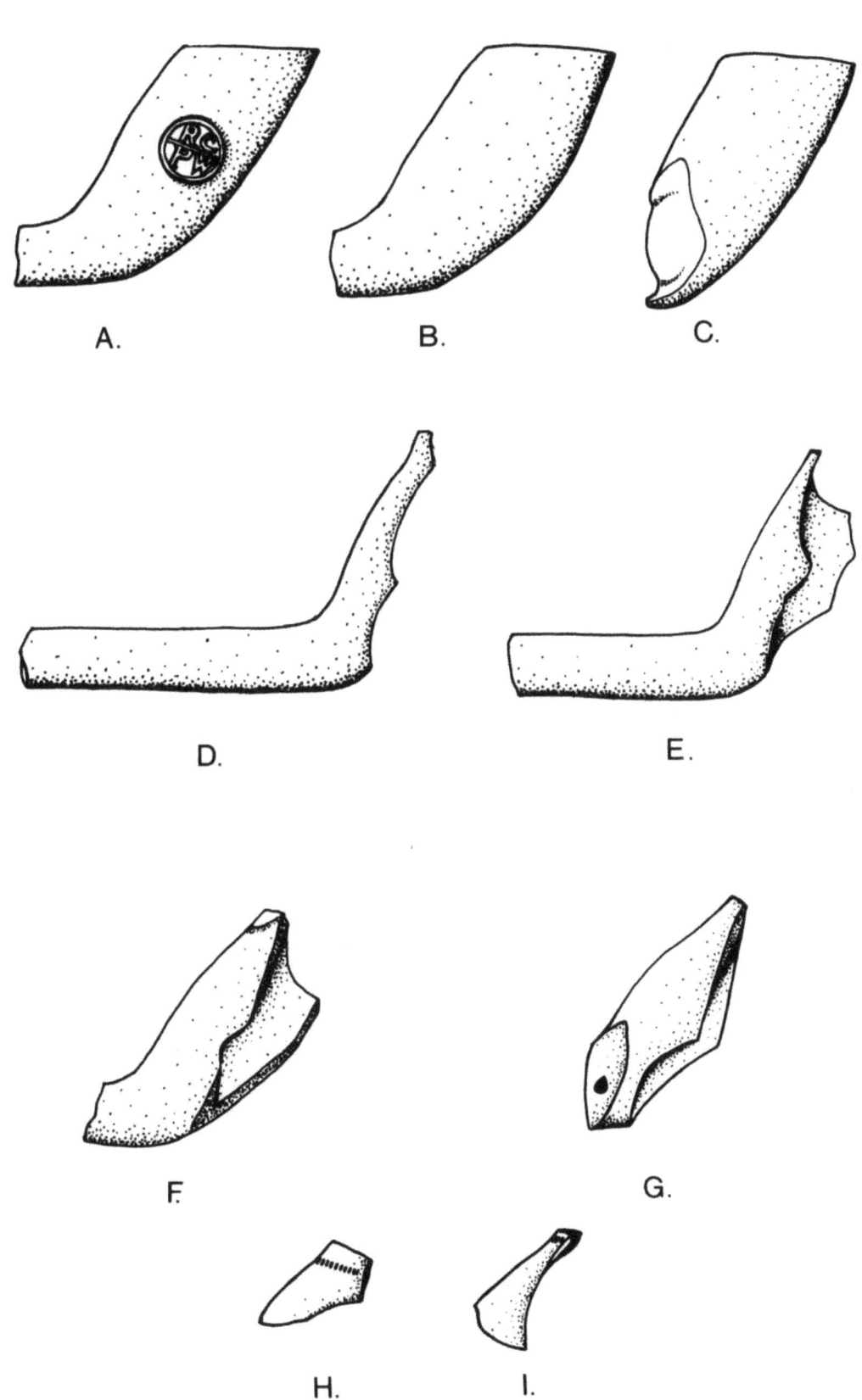

Figure 3: Clay tobacco pipes from Feature 17, the burned, earthfast house midden. Scale 1:1.

Figure 3g: A fragmentary bowl with a slightly swollen back and no rouletting. Like the previous example (Figure 3f), it has a flat lip and the wall of the bowl is thickest at the back mold seam (4 mm), tapering to 1.5 mm thick away from the seam.

Figure 3h: A fragment of a bowl, with a line of rouletting below the mouth. Examination of the cross-section indicates the pipe bowl had bulbous walls.

Figure 3i: A bowl fragment with rouletting below the mouth. The shape indicates the pipe had a bulbous bowl. This specimen is from a different pipe that the previous example (Figure 3h).

FEATURE 63, A STORAGE PIT BENEATH FEATURE 17 (Figure 2):

Originally dug to serve as a storage pit accessed through a floor panel of the earthfast house, the pit was filled with trash shortly before the house burned. The maximum dimensions of the feature are 6.5-by-6.0-by-2.0 feet. A total of 38 pipe stems were recovered, which give a Binford mean pipe date of 1720.43. Unfortunately, no pipe bowls were found (Table 1).

Feature 22, a trash pit:

The trash pit, measuring 4.5 feet in diameter and one foot deep, is intrusive in a burned clay horizon created by an on-site brick kiln used during construction of Harmony Hall (Figure 2). The 29 pipe stems from the feature yield a Binford mean pipe date of 1728.68 (Table 1). A small bowl fragment with part of an unidentifiable relief-molded cartouche was also found, along with two other pipe bowls described below.

Figure 4a: A plain pipe bowl and stem with a rounded base on the underside where the bowl and stem join.

Stem hole diameter 5/64".

Figure 4b: A plain pipe bowl of basic 18th century form, but with a narrow profile "indicative of an early date within the period" (I. Noel Hume 1966:56-57). The heel is short and round.

Stem hole diameter 5/64".

STRATUM ABOVE THE BURNED, EARHFAST HOUSE MIDDEN, FEATURE 17:

Sandwiched between the burned midden of the earthfast house and a soil horizon representing the historic grade associated with the construction of Harmony Hall, was a stratum varying between 0.1 to 0.2 feet in thickness. From this thin layer came two pipe stems with 6/64" bore diameters and their ends fashioned as secondary mouthpieces. Other finds include a small, eroded bowl fragment with an unidentifiable relief-molded cartouche and another bowl fragment with rouletting. Descriptions of additional pipe bowls or fragments from this stratum are given below.

Figure 4c: A plain, elongated, slightly bulbous bowl with a protruding lip. There is no heel or spur. This bowl form is similar to the type illustrated by Ivor Noel Hume (1970:Figure 97, No. 17) dating to circa 1680-1710.

Stem hole diameter 5/64".

Figure 4d: A fragmentary bowl and stem from a plain bowl, with neither a heel nor spur.

Stem hole diameter 5/64".

Figure 4e: A tobacco pipe heel and stem fragment, with the initials "IS" molded on the smoker's left and right sides of the heel, respectively. The "I" is very thick. This specimen is similar to one found at Tutter's Neck, Virginia (I. Noel Hume 1966:57).

Stem hole diameter 5/64".

Figure 4f: A heel and stem fragment with the initials "SI" molded on the smoker's left and right sides of the heel, respectively. The initial "S" is twice the height of the "I".

Stem hole diameter 5/64".

FEATURE 14, A MID 18TH CENTURY TRASH PIT:

The trash pit is located on the river-side lawn of Harmony Hall (Figure 1). A portion of the feature extends into the west wall of the excavation units. The north-south axis of the feature is 7.5 feet and it is 2.2 feet deep. The bore diameters of 15 pipe stems from the pit are given in Table 1. In addition, a fragmentary bowl was found with incuse initials "IA" on the back of the bowl and a stem hole diameter of 5/64" (Figure 4g).

Ceramics from the feature include sherds of Buckley ware, Staffordshire slipware, both monochrome blue and plain white delftware, and a rimsherd from a cup of refined, white salt-glazed stoneware. The latter specimen, in particular, dates the trash pit to the mid-18th century, which is consistent with the bore diameters of the 15 pipe stems (Table 1).

LATE 18TH AND 19TH CENTURY PIPES FROM DISTURBED CONTEXTS:

In the main block of archaeological excavations, there is a mantel of landscaping material and fill varying in depth from 1.1 to 2.0 feet, which lies

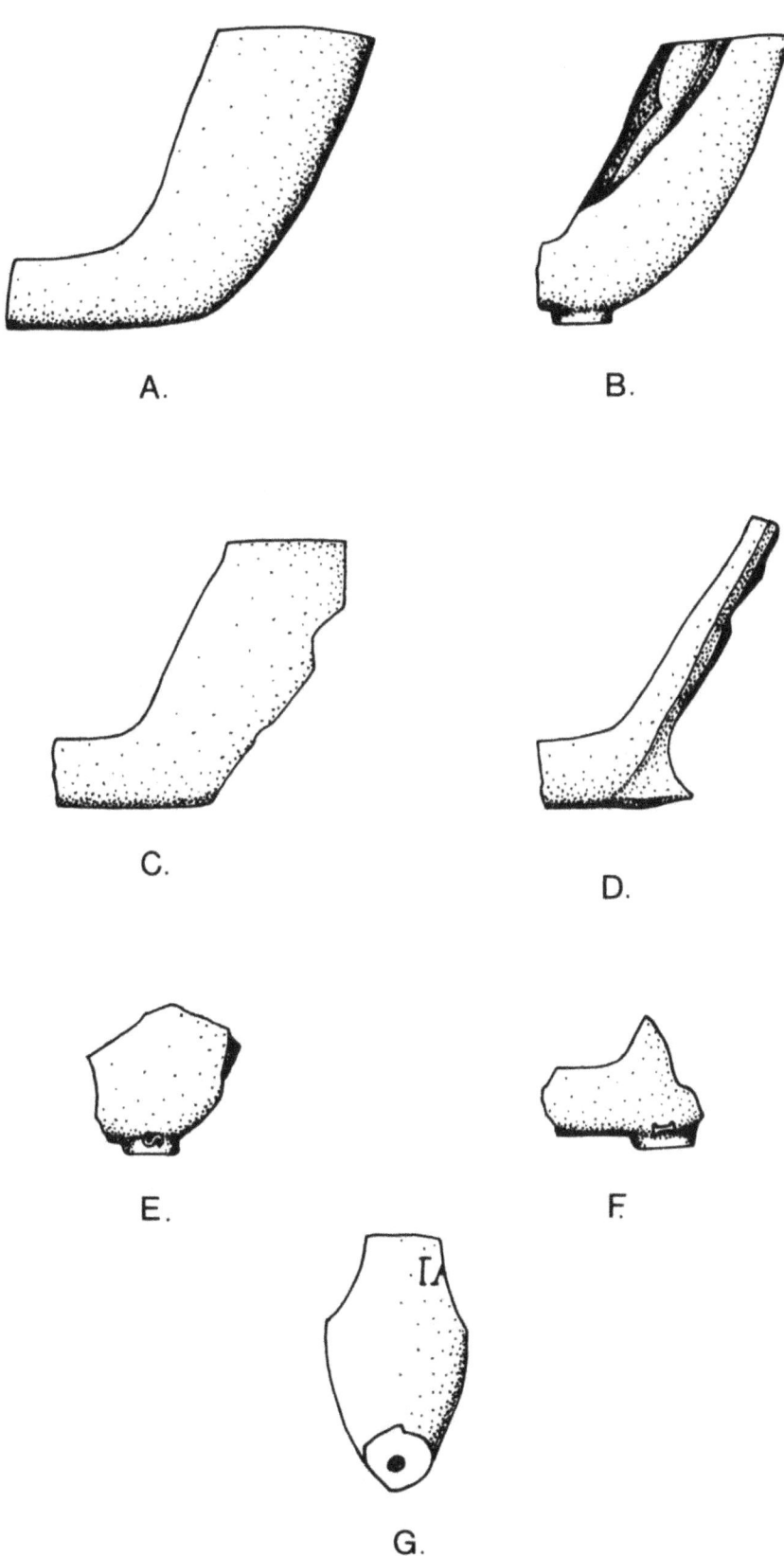

Figure 4: Clay tobacco pipes A and B from Feature 22, a trash pit. Pipes C-F from stratum above Feature 17. Pipe G from Feature 14, a trash pit. Scale 1:1.

above the historic grade associated with the building of Harmony Hall. With the exception of two rouletted pipe bowl fragments from the 17th or early 18th centuries, all the other diagnostic pipe fragments from these disturbed contexts date to the late 18th or 19th centuries. This collection includes two pillar-molded bowl fragments; two bowl fragments with the front mold seams decorated with a branch design or a frond of opposing leaves; two stem fragments with relief-molded ribbing; one bowl and stem fragment with fluting and relief-molded ribbing; one spur and stem fragment with a triangular pattern of two raised dots on the smoker's left of the spur; one bowl fragment with a line of small, relief-molded rosettes circumscribed by the bowl rim and an incuse line; one bowl fragment with an incuse "D"; one stem with "2," "K," and "DAVIDSON" impressed on the smoker's left and "GLASGOW" on the smoker's right; and, one bowl and stem fragment from a red clay, reed-stemmed pipe.

DISCUSSION

The clay tobacco pipes from the excavations at Harmony Hall not only provide an opportunity to further test the accuracy of the Binford pipe stem dating formula (Binford 1962), but they also provide another means of unraveling the historical events associated with the 17th-century Battersea plantation and the 18th-century brick manor of Harmony Hall. Although there are several caveats which must be kept in mind when using the Binford formula (A. Noel Hume 1963, 1979; I. Noel Hume 1982: 119-122; Alexander 1979:39-45), its application to the pipes from Harmony Hall is appropriate for several reasons. The occupation of the earthfast house and the possible pre-1721 construction date for Harmony Hall fit comfortably within the range (circa 1680-1760) of acceptable accuracy for the pipe stem dating formula (I. Noel Hume 1970:300). Although a minimum of 900-1000 fragments are necessary to "provide a consistently reliable date" (A. Noel Hume 1963:22), datable pipe bowls and ceramics from the features, and the stratigraphic relationship of the features, serve as independent checks on the mean pipe dates derived from the stems. And finally, the features represent short-term events, especially the filling of the storage and trash pits.

Feature 17, the burned midden of the earthfast house, is probably the archaeological remains of the home of Thomas Lewis, built in 1692. Ceramics from the midden include North Devon gravel-tempered earthenware, black-glazed earthenware, Staffordshire slipware, monochrome blue and polychrome delftware, and Rhenish blue and manganese incised stoneware. These wares were in common use during the period 1675-1720. However, a few sherds of slip-dipped white salt-glazed stoneware were found at the top of the burned midden, along with an English brown salt-glazed stoneware mug bearing a "GR" excise mark. The former dates circa 1715-1775 (South 1977:211) and the latter is post 1714 (Oswald et al. 1982:278). These ceramics likely were in use near the end of the occupation of the earthfast house.

Pipe stems from the midden provide a Binford mean date of 1715.3 (Table 1). Comparing this with the datable ceramics, 1715 seems closer to an end date than a median. This discrepancy is probably due to the limited sample size.

The storage pit beneath the earthfast house, Feature 63, was abruptly filled with trash shortly before the house burned. Among the discarded items were Staffordshire slipware, black-glazed earthenware, and a rim/handle sherd from a Rhenish blue-gray incised stoneware mug. Again, the ceramics fit well within the hypothesized life of the dwelling, from 1692 until circa 1715-1720.

The sample of 38 stem fragments provides a Binford mean date of 1720.43 (Table 1). Once again, this does not seem to be a mean date for the occupation of the house, but is either a terminal date or one that falls a few years after the house was destroyed. However, as a relative date it supports the interpretation that the storage pit was filled late in the structure's history, which is probably why the Binford date for the storage pit (1720) is slightly later than that (1715) for the burned house midden above, since the house midden includes pipe stems discarded throughout the entire life of the structure. Stone (1974:151) has also pointed out the usefulness of Binford pipe dates in providing a relative chronology for activities at a given site.

The trash pit, Feature 22, intrudes into a burned clay horizon created by brick making during Harmony Hall's construction. The top of the burned clay horizon corresponds with the construction horizon that overlies the nearby site of the earthfast house. Scattered over the construction horizon were little piles of cut bricks, including one cluster that contained a reverse"S"-scroll water table brick which matches exactly the water table bricks of Harmony hall. Thus, the construction horizon is the historic ground surface that the masons walked upon while erecting the brick manor. Since Feature 22 is intrusive, it must date after the construction of Harmony Hall.

Mixed in the trash pit were sherds of Rhenish blue and manganese decorated stoneware, monochrome blue and polychrome delftware, and English brown salt-glazed stoneware. The small sample of stems yields a Binford mean pipe date of 1728.68 (Table 1). One of the two pipe bowls from the pit is typical of forms in use early in the 18th century. Taken together, the stratigraphy and artifacts indicate the trash pit was filled sometime during the 1720s.

Based on the above information, the following historical interpretation is presented. In 1692, Thomas Lewis built a post-supported frame dwelling on a portion of the original Battersea patent. This structure and its lands were purchased by William Tyler, the elder, in 1709. The earthfast house continued to be occupied until its' destruction sometime after 1715 and before 1720. Shortly thereafter, William Tyler built the brick manor, Harmony Hall, prior to his death in 1721.

Such an interpretation accords well with the clay tobacco pipe analysis. First, the pipe bowls and bowl fragments are typical of Bristol manufacture during the period circa 1692-1720s. The mix of English-made pipes -- some with rouletting, most without; some with heels, most with rounded bases; and three with cartouches -- is exactly what one would expect of an assemblage that straddles in time the "mould-size agreement" of November 10, 1710 (Jackson and Price 1974:16-17). The agreement dealt with the size of pipes and was signed by some 40 Bristol tobacco pipe makers. Other makers signed the agreement over a period from 1710 until about 1725. During this time, rouletting around the rim disappears, as noted by McCashion (1988). Second, the quick succession of events -- destruction of the earthfast house, construction of the brick manor, and the digging and filling of the trash pit, Feature 22 -- all within six to ten years' time, means that there will be little variation in the pipe and ceramic assemblages. And third, the second point helps to explain the Binford mean date of 1726 for the main block of excavations, where an adequate sample of 899 stems does exist (Table 1). Since the total number of pipe stems from the main block reflect events associated with the history of the earthfast house, the construction of Harmony Hall, and daily activities around the brick manor after its erection, it follows that the pipe date should be closer to the end of the first quarter of the 18th century if Harmony Hall was constructed before the elder William Tyler's death in 1721.

And last, two other items are worth mentioning. The discovery of the Bristol-made RC/PW pipe bowl in an unequivocal context of 1692-1720 fits perfectly with the temporal contexts of the two previously reported examples by these makers (McCashion 1988). The specimen from Harmony Hall, however, does not have rouletting, unlike the other two pipes from New York state. It is also interesting to note that absolutely no terra-cotta pipe fragments, mold or hand-made, were found. This is intriguing since the occupancy of the earthfast house occurred during the lengthy tobacco depression of 1680-1713, when one might expect to see more locally-made pipes in use along the western frontier of late 17th and early 18th century Maryland (Henry 1979:33-35). Perhaps, the of terra-cotta pipes at Harmony Hall, especially hand-made ones, reflects the reduction and dispersal of one of the groups responsible for their production, the local Algonquian Indians, who left the area in 1697 to settle in Piedmont Virginia (Cissna 1986:176, 180-185).

ACKNOWLEDGEMENTS

The authors would like to thank the following individuals for their assistance with various phases of the research: Dr. Marilyn Nickels, John H. McCashion, Matthew Virta, Janice Bailey, Pamela Crane, Lynette Volz, and Peter Morrison.

REFERENCES CITED

Alexander, L.T. (1979) Clay pipes from the Buck Site in Maryland. *The archaeology of the clay tobacco pipe II: The United States of America.* Edited by Peter Davey. British Archaeological Reports, International Series, 60:37-61.

Binford, L.R. (1962) A new method for calculating dates from kaolin pipe stem samples. *Southeastern Archaeological Conference Newsletter* 9(1): 19:21.

Cissna, P.B. (1986) The Piscataway Indians of Southern Maryland: an ethnohistory from pre-European contact to the present. Ph.D. dissertation, The American University.

Henry, S.L. (1979) Terra-cotta tobacco pipes in 17th century Maryland and Virginia: A preliminary study. *Historical Archaeology* 13:14-37.

Jackson, R.G., and Price R.H. (1974) Bristol clay pipes: a study of makers and their marks. *Bristol City Museum: Research Monograph No. 1.* City of Bristol.

McCashion, J.H. (1979) A preliminary chronology and discussion of seventeenth and early eighteenth century clay tobacco pipes from New York State sites. *The Archaeology of the Clay Tobacco Pipe, II: The United States of America.* Edited by Peter Davey. British Archaeological Report International Series, 60:63-149.

McCashion, J.H. (1988). Personal communication.

Nickels, M. (1987). Harmony Hall history. Manuscript on file, National Park Service, National Capital Region. Washington, D.C.

Noel Hume, A. (1963). Clay tobacco pipe dating in the light of recent excavations. *Quarterly Bulletin.* Archaeological Society of Virginia, 18(2): 22-25.

Noel Hume, A. (1979). Clay tobacco pipes excavated at Martin's Hundred Virginia, 1976-1978. *The Archaeology of the clay tobacco pipe, II: The United States of America.* Edited by Peter Davey, British Archaeological Report, International Series, 60:3-36.

Noel Hume, I. (1966). Excavations at Tutter's Neck. Contributions from the Museum of History and Technology, Papers 52-54 On Archaeology. *Bulletin,* 249:31-72.

Noel Hume, I. (1970) *A guide to artifacts of Colonial America*. Alfred A. Knopf, New York.

Noel Hume, I. (1982). *Martin's Hundred*. Alfred A. Knopf, New York.

Oswald, A., Hildyard, R.J.C. and Hughes, R.G. (1982). *English brown stoneware 1670-1900*. Faber and Faber, London.

South, S. (1977). *Method and theory in historical archaeology*. Academic Press, New York.

Stone, L.M. (1974). Fort Michilimackinac 1715-1781: an archaeological perspective on the revolutionary frontier. Publications of the Museum, Michigan State University, *Anthropological Series*, Vol. 2.

A Descriptive Analysis of the White Clay Tobacco Pipes from the St. John's Site in St. Mary's City, Maryland.

Silas D. Hurry and Robert W. Keeler

INTRODUCTION

Excavations at St. John's, a major 17th-century archaeological site in Maryland's first settlement, produced an impressive collection of white clay tobacco pipes spanning the period 1638 to circa 1720. The site began as a tobacco plantation established by John Lewger, Maryland's first Secretary of State. Through its long life, the site served a variety of functions, being at various times the residence of the colony's Governor, an official meeting place, a public inn, and a government records office (Stone 1974:146-168).

Excavations were conducted at the site by the museum staff of Historic St. Mary's City from 1972 through 1975, and again in 1982. This work produced a major assemblage of tobacco pipes from both feature and plow disturbed contexts. The focus of this study is the morphology of the tobacco pipe bowls, the identification of the makers' marks, and the description of the decorations. Based on this important artifact class, suggestions as to marketing patterns and depositional activities are forwarded.

HISTORICAL AND EXCAVATION BACKGROUND

The St. John's Site (18 St 1-23) in St. Mary's city, Maryland, was excavated in the 1970s by the archaeologists of Historic St. Mary's City under the direction of Garry Wheeler Stone and Alexander H. Morrison II. The house at St. John's was built in 1638 by John Lewger, first Secretary of State for the Colony of Maryland. St. John's was one of the earliest substantial structures built in the new Maryland colony. Lewger held the property until 1654-5 when Simon Overzee, a Dutch merchant, made St. John's his home. In 1661 Charles Calvert, governor of the colony and son of Cecil Calvert, the second Lord Baltimore, occupied St. John's. Charles Calvert, who later inherited his father's title, resided at St. John's until approximately 1666 or 1667, when he married a wealthy widow and moved to her plantation. Following Charles Calvert's removal from St. John's, the historical record of the occupants becomes somewhat murky. For the remainder of the 17th century the Calverts appear to have leased St. John's as an ordinary or public inn and to have occasionally used it as a government records storage office. A 1678 lease between Calvert and Henry Exon details improvements and repairs to the house and indicates its use, at that time, as an ordinary. The last documentary reference to St. John's is in 1693 when the building was used to house the colony's probate office. In 1695 the capital of the colony was moved to Annapolis and in 1708 the county seat for St. Mary's County was moved to Leonardtown. Archaeological data suggest the building was used up to the end of the first decade of the 18th century, when it and the rest of St. Mary's City began to pass into the archaeological record (Stone 1974:146-168).

The excavations at the St. John's Site uncovered evidence of a hall and parlor, center chimneyed principal dwelling with a partial cellar, a detached quarter later converted to a kitchen, a later servant's quarter, and a myriad of yard features and trash deposits. Despite having been plowed after abandonment, considerable subsurface deposits remained intact. A large proportion of the artifacts, however, were recovered from the plow disturbed soils which were systematically screened. Given the 17th-century habit of disposing of refuse in surface middens around dwellings and service buildings, this artifact sample, though homogenized by the action of the plow, provides the lion's share of the recovered tobacco pipes (see Keeler 1978 and King 1988). From a contextual perspective, they can only be dated to the bracket dates of the occupation of the site (1638- circa 1720). Utilizing ceramic chronology, the subsurface features, however, have been divided into three phases of occupation: Phase 1 (1638-circa 1660), Phase II (circa 1660-circa 1685), and Phase III (ca. 1685- ca.1720).

THE SAMPLE

The sample for this analysis is comprised of the white clay tobacco pipe fragments which fall into the following categories: bowls complete enough to be typed (112), specimens with makers' marks (168), and decorated specimens (238). Other undecorated and unmarked specimens have been excluded from this analysis. Also excluded are non-white clay tobacco pipes recovered. Both non-white clay tobacco pipes and generalized bore analyses of both decorated and undecorated pipe stem fragments have been addressed elsewhere (Henry 1979 and Stone 1977).

ORGANIZATION

This report is organized into a number of discrete discussions addressing different aspects of the St. John's pipe assemblage. First, bowl forms are described and referenced to the standard typologies. Second, marked specimens are described and identified. This section is further divided into subsections based on where the mark appears on the specimen: heel marks, stem marks, base marks, and bowl marks. Following the discussion of marked specimens, we turn to the specimens which are decorated but lack makers' marks. These examples are subdivided similarly to the marked examples: decoration on stems and decoration on bowls. In the following analysis, the context of the specimens being described will be referenced to the previously described scheme of site chronology: Phase I, Phase II, Phase III, or nondiagnostic (for specimens from plow disturbed soils and undated subsurface features). Bore diameters are given for all specimens in 64ths of an inch. Specimens without measurable bores are described as N.B. (no bore). Indecipherable initials in makers' marks are indicated by a question mark (?). All bowl illustrations are at actual size (scale of 1:1) and all mark and decoration illustrations are at twice natural size (scale of 2:1).

BOWL FORM DESCRIPTION

Each bowl is described in reference to the standard typologies formulated by Oswald (1975), Atkinson and Oswald (1969), and Noel Hume (1963 and 1970). These typologies are supplemented by Lawrence (1979) for York pipes, Watkins (1979) for Hull pipes, and Davey and Rutter (1980) for Chester pipes, and examples illustrated by Duco (1981) and McCashion (1979) for Dutch pipe forms.

Type A, Variety 1

ILLUSTRATION: Figure 1 a-c.

DESCRIPTION: Short fat bulbous bowl with a large pedestal heel and rouletted rim.
NUMBER OF SPECIMENS: three
BORE DIAMETER: 8/64 (3)
COMPARISONS: Similar to Oswald's general Type 5 (1975: 39), and the Hull varieties of Yorkshire bulbous IIc (Watkins 1979: 87).
MAKER'S MARK: none
CONTEXT: nondiagnostic (3)
DATE: circa 1640-1660 (Oswald 1975: 39,41), 1650-1675 (Watkins 1979: 87).

Type A, Variety 2

ILLUSTRATION: Figure 1 d-f

DESCRIPTION: Similar to Type A, Variety 1, but with a taller, more slender bowl, and a more slender, underdeveloped, pedestal heel.
NUMBER OF SPECIMENS: three
BORE DIAMETER: 7/64 (1), 6/64 (1), 9/64 (1)
COMPARISONS: Similar to Oswald's general Type 5 (1975: 39), and Yorkshire bulbous Type 7 (Lawrence 1979: 61), these specimens also show similarities to McCashion's (1979) early Dutch belly bowls.
MAKER'S MARK: none
CONTEXT: Phase 1 (1), Phase 11 (1), nondiagnostic (1)

DATE: circa 1640-1660 (Oswald 1975: 39,41), 1650-1675 (Lawrence 1979: 61), 17th century (McCashion 1979).

Type A, Variety 3

ILLUSTRATION: Figure 1 g-o (three specimens not illustrated)

DESCRIPTION: Similar to other Type A pipes but with a slightly taller, more slender bowl, and a slender more developed pedestal heel.
NUMBER OF SPECIMENS: 12
BORE DIAMETER: 9/64 (2), 8/64 (10)
COMPARISONS: Similar to Oswald's general Type 5 (1975: 39), and Yorkshire bulbous Type 7 (Lawrence 1979: 61). Greatest similarity is with the Chester pipes (Rutter and Davey 1980: 58,59).
MAKER'S MARKS: none
CONTEXT: Phase I (3), Phase II (1), Phase III (1), and nondiagnostic (7)
DATE: circa 1640-1660 (Oswald 1975: 39,41), 1650-1675 (Lawrence 1979: 61),1610-1650 (Rutter and Davey 1980: 58,59).

Type A, Variety 4

ILLUSTRATION: Figure 2 a-f

DESCRIPTION: Similar to Type A, Varieties 2 and 3, but with an even taller, more slender bowl and an even smaller pedestal base.
NUMBER OF SPECIMENS: six
BORE DIAMETER: 8/64 (6)
COMPARISONS: Similar to Oswald's general Type 5 (1975: 39) and Noel Hume's Type 8 (1970: 303).
MAKER'S MARKS: none
CONTEXT: Phase I (1), Phase II (1), nondiagnostic (4)
DATE: circa 1640-1660 (Oswald 1975: 39, 41), 1645-1665 (Noel Hume 1970: 303).

Type A, Variety 5

ILLUSTRATION: Figure 2 g

DESCRIPTION: Similar to other Type A bowls, but very bulbous, and with a very small heel which is almost a spur.
NUMBER OF SPECIMENS: one
BORE DIAMETER: 8/64 (1)
COMPARISONS: Similar to Oswald's general Type 5 (1975: 39).
MAKER'S MARKS: none
CONTEXT: nondiagnostic (1)
DATE: circa 1640-1660 (Oswald 1975: 39, 41)

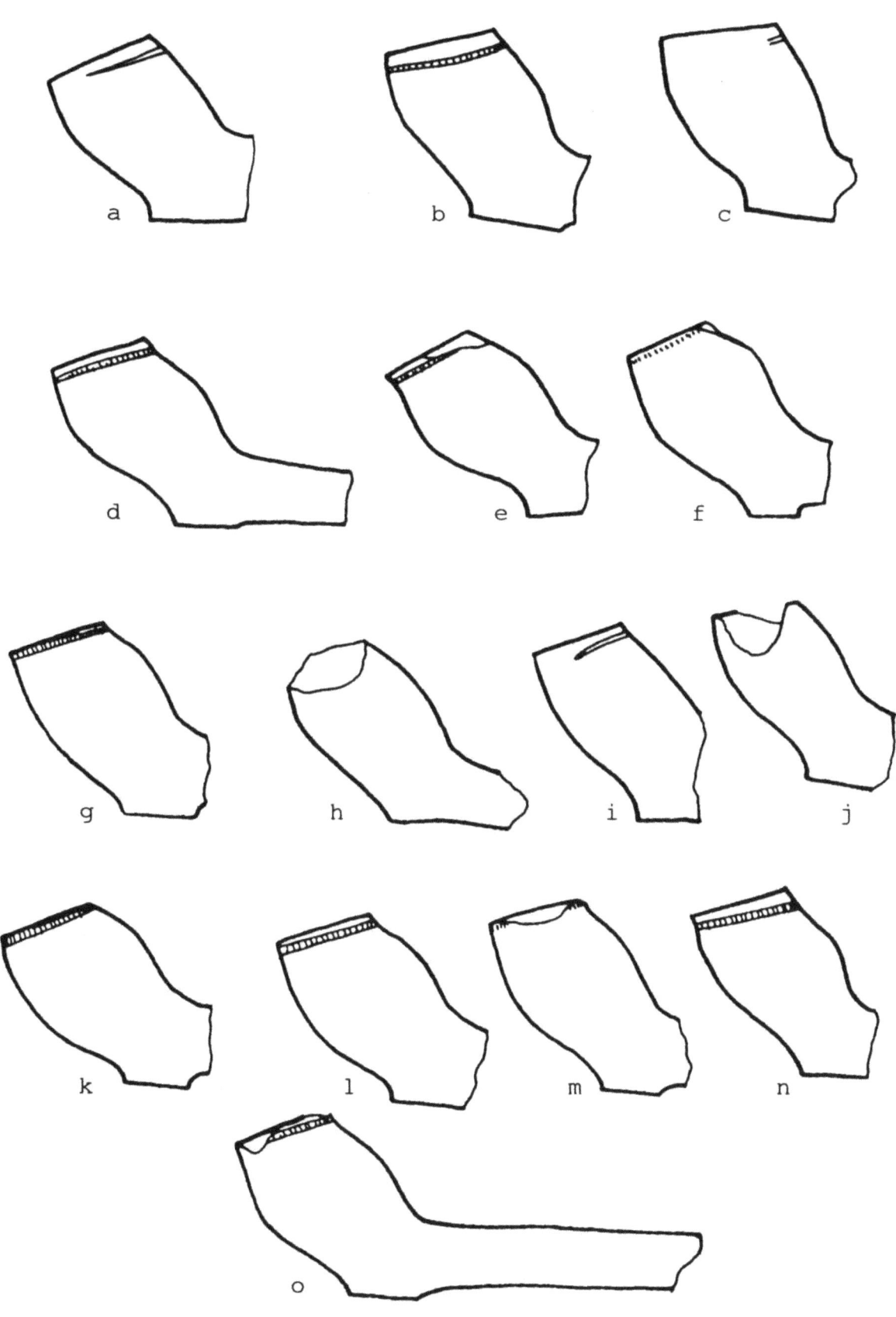

Figure 1: Type A bowls: Variety 1 a-c; Variety 2 d-f; Variety 3 g-o

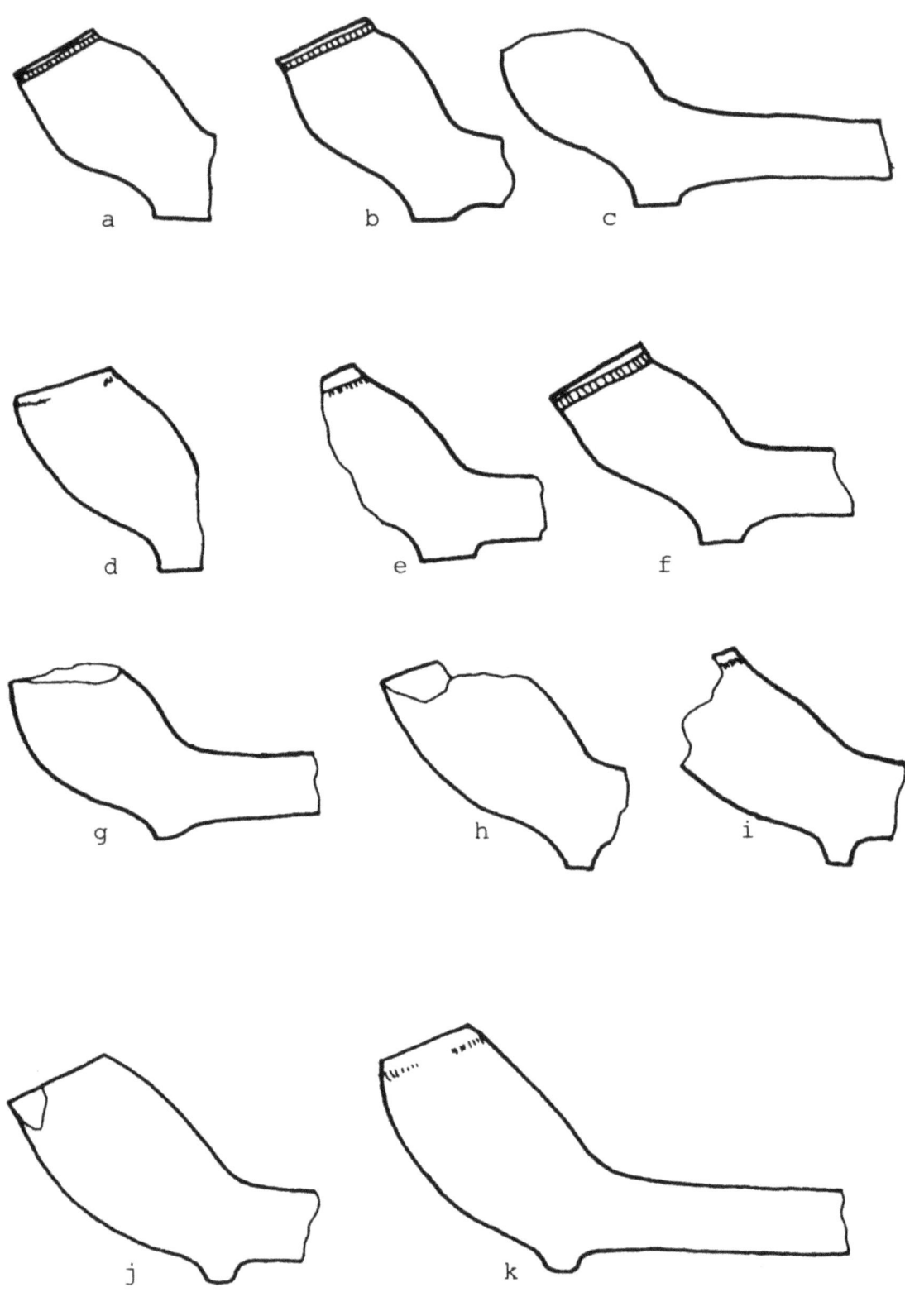

Figure 2: Type A bowls: Variety 4 a-f. Type B bowls: Variety 1 h-i; Variety 2 j-k

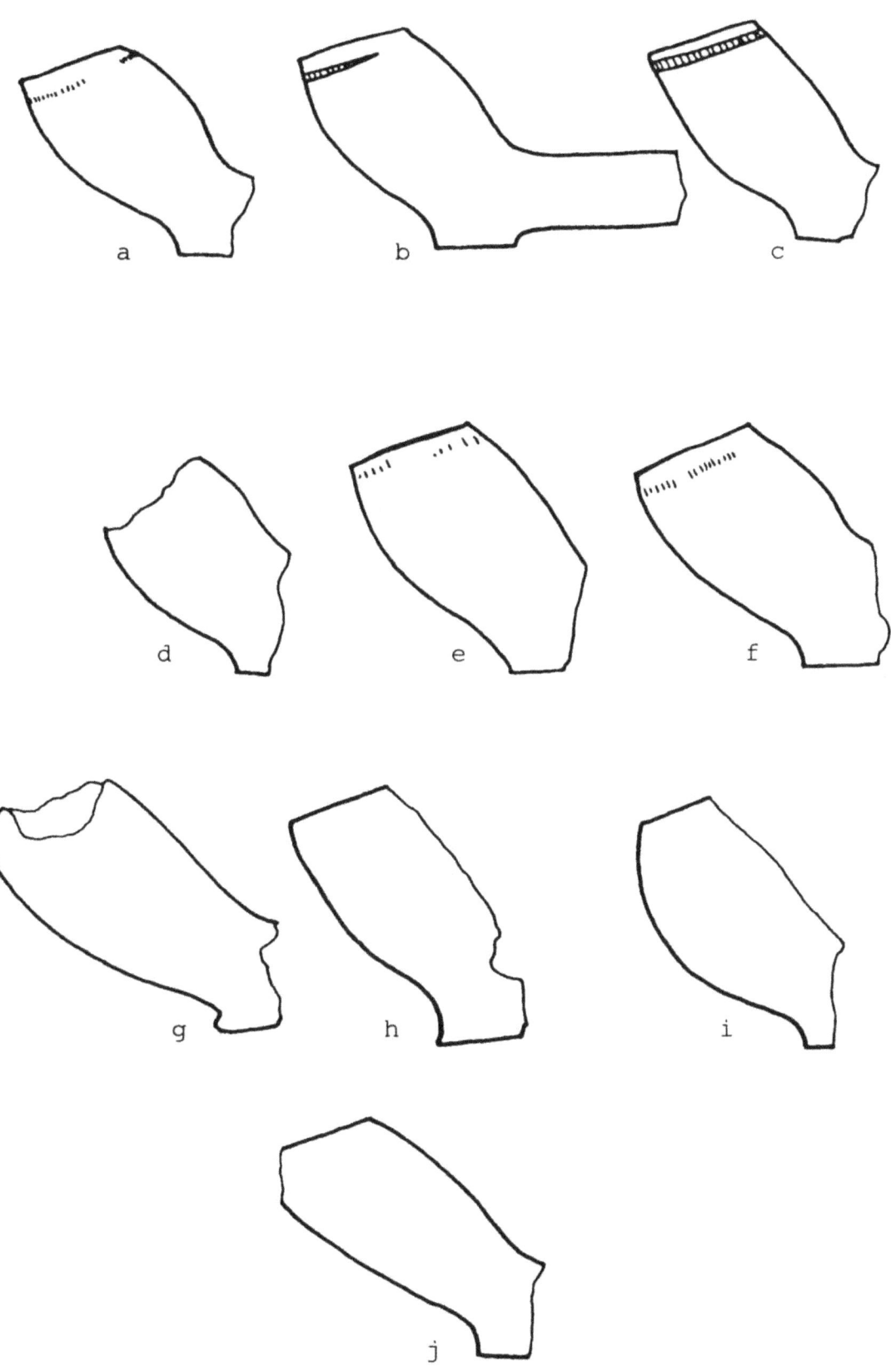

Figure 3: Type C bowls: Variety 1 a-c; Variety 2 d-f. Type D bowls: g-h. Type E bowls i-j

Type B, Variety 1

ILLUSTRATION: Figure 2 h-i

DESCRIPTION: Bulbous bowl with rudimentary spur/pedestal heel, and rouletted rim.
NUMBER OF SPECIMENS: two
BORE DIAMETER: 8/64 (2)
COMPARISONS: Similar to Oswald's general Type 9 (1975: 39), but the bowl is less bulbous, Noel Hume's Type 11 (1970: 303) is very similar but with a more fully developed spur; these specimens may represent transitional forms.
MAKER'S MARKS: One with relief molded decoration in the Mulberry tree motif (see decorated bowls below).
CONTEXT: nondiagnostic (2)
DATE: 1680-1710 (Oswald 1975: 39,41), 1650-1680 (Noel Hume 1970: 303).

Type B, Variety 2

ILLUSTRATION: Figure 2 j, k

DESCRIPTION: Similar to Type B, Variety 1, but proportionately larger.
NUMBER OF SPECIMENS: two
COMPARISONS: Oswald's general Type 9 (1975:39) is similar, but the bowl is less bulbous; Noel Hume's Type 11 (1970: 303) is very similar but with a more fully developed spur; these specimens may represent transitional forms.
MAKER'S MARKS: none
CONTEXT: nondiagnostic (3)
DATE: 1680-1710 (Oswald 1975: 39,41), 1650-1680 (Noel Hume 1970: 303).

Type C, Variety 1

ILLUSTRATION: Figure 3 a-c

DESCRIPTION: Elongated bulbous bowl, with flat pedestal heel and rouletted rim.
NUMBER OF SPECIMENS: three
BORE DIAMETER: 7/64 (1), 8/64 (1), and 9/64 (1)
COMPARISONS: Similar to Oswald's general Type 6 (1975: 39), Yorkshire Bulbous Type 11f (Watkins 1979: 87), Atkinson and Oswald's London Type 12 (1969), Noel Hume's Type 8 (Noel Hume 1970: 303), and McCashion's (1979) Dutch belly bowl.
MAKER'S MARKS: One specimen with the "EB" heel mark of Edward Bird (see below).
CONTEXT: Phase II (1), nondiagnostic (2)
DATE: 1660-1680 (Oswald 1975: 39, 41), 1660-1700 (Watkins 1979: 87), 1640-1670 (Atkinson and Oswald 1969),1645-1665 (Noel Hume 1970: 303), and 17th century (McCashion 1979).

Type C, Variety 2

ILLUSTRATION: Figure 3 d-f

DESCRIPTION: Similar to Type C, Variety 1, but bowl is more bulbous and larger.
NUMBER OF SPECIMENS: three
BORE DIAMETER: 8/64 (3)
COMPARISONS: Similar to Oswald's general Type 6 (1975: 39), Yorkshire bulbous Type 14 (Lawrence1979: 61),Hull Type 11b (Watkins 1979: 87), and McCashion's Dutch belly bowl (1979).
MAKER'S MARK: none
CONTEXT: Phase III (1), nondiagnostic (2)
DATE: 1660-1680 (Oswald 1975: 39,41), 1670-1700, (Lawrence 1979: 61), 1660-1700 (Watkins 1979: 87), and 17th century (McCashion 1979).

Type D

ILLUSTRATION: Figure 3 g, h

DESCRIPTION: Narrow, elongated bulbous bowl with flat, splayed heel and rouletted rim.
NUMBER OF SPECIMENS: two
BORE DIAMETER: 6/64 (1), N.B.(1)
COMPARISONS: Similar to Oswald and James' Brosely Type 2b (in Oswald 1975).
MAKER'S MARKS: none
CONTEXT: nondiagnostic (1)
DATE: 1660-1680 (Atkinson's dating, Oswald 1975)

Type E

ILLUSTRATION: Figure 3 i, j

DESCRIPTION: Forward-leaning, elongated, bulbous bowl with small, flat spur-like heel, and rouletted rim.
NUMBER OF SPECIMENS: two
BORE DIAMETER: 6/64 (1), 7/64 (1)
COMPARISONS: Transitional between Oswald's general Type 8 and Type 9 (Oswald 1975: 39, 41).
MAKER'S MARKS: none
CONTEXT: nondiagnostic (2)
DATE: 1680-1710 (Oswald 1975: 39, 41)

Type F

ILLUSTRATION: Figure 4 a, b

DESCRIPTION: Forward-leaning, elongated, slightly bulbous bowl with a very small, flat, spur-like heel and rouletted rim.
NUMBER OF SPECIMENS: two

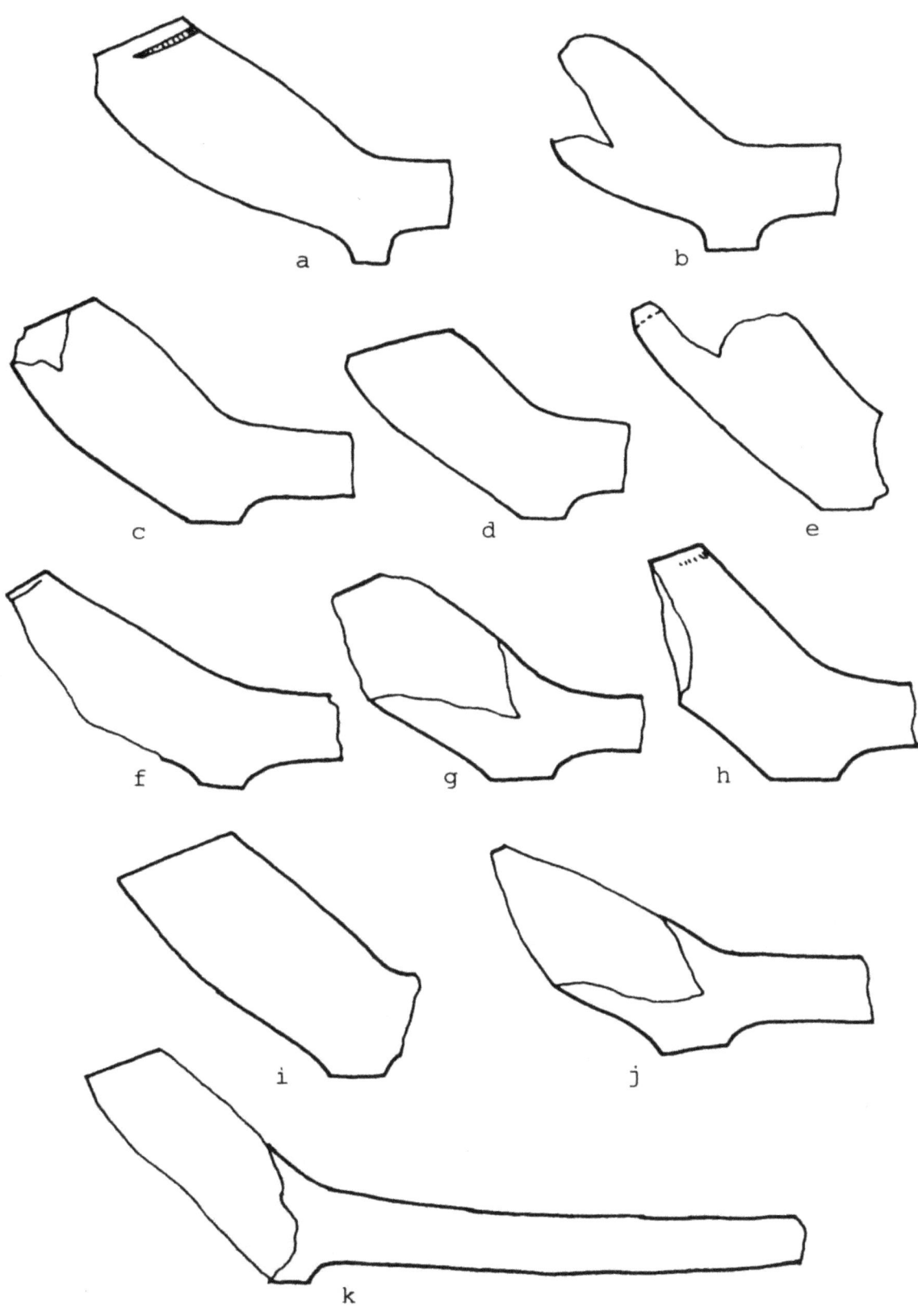

Figure 4: Type F bowls: a-b. Type G bowls: c-k

BORE DIAMETER: 6/64(1), 7/64(1)
COMPARISONS: Similar to Oswald's general Type 8 (1975: 39), and Noel Hume's Type 13 (1970: 303).
MAKER'S MARKS: none
CONTEXT: Phase III(1), nondiagnostic (1)
DATE: 1680-1710 (Oswald 1975: 39, 41, Noel Hume 1970: 303)

Type G

ILLUSTRATION: Figure 4 c-k

DESCRIPTION: Forward-leaning, very slightly bulbous bowl, with a flat heel and a rouletted rim.
NUMBER OF SPECIMENS: nine
BORE DIAMETER: 6/64(7), 7/64(1), 8/64(1)
COMPARISONS: Similar to Oswald's general Type 8 (1975: 39) and Noel Hume's Type 12 (1970: 303).
MAKER'S MARKS: One specimen with initials "IP" molded on side of heel, one decorated with the Mulberry Tree motif relief molding (see makers' marks and decorated bowls below).
CONTEXT: Phase III (1), nondiagnostic (8)
DATE: 1680-1710 (Oswald 1975: 39,41), 1650-1680 (Noel Hume 1970: 303).

Type H

ILLUSTRATION: Figure 5a

DESCRIPTION: Slightly curving bowl with pronounced, pointed spur.
NUMBER OF SPECIMENS: one
BORE DIAMETER: 7/64 (1)
COMPARISONS: Similar to Oswald's general Type 19 (1975: 41), Noel Hume's Type 19 (1970: 303).
MAKER'S MARKS: none
CONTEXT: nondiagnostic (1)
DATE: 1690-1710 (Oswald 1975: 39, 41), 1690-1750 (Noel Hume 1970: 303).

Type 1

ILLUSTRATION: Figure 5 b

DESCRIPTION: Bowl is slightly flared with rudimentary spur, rim is rouletted and nearly parallel with stem.
NUMBER OF SPECIMENS: one
BORE DIAMETER: 7/64 (1)
COMPARISONS: Similar to Oswald's general Type 20 (1975:41).
MAKER'S MARKS: none
CONTEXT: nondiagnostic (1)
DATE: 1690-1730 (Oswald 1975: 41)

Type J

ILLUSTRATION: Figure 5 c

DESCRIPTION: Slightly curving sides with the bowl in a nearly "upright" position, no heel, rouletted rim, bowl is polished.
NUMBER OF SPECIMENS: one
BORE DIAMETER: 8/64 (1)
COMPARISONS: Similar to McCashion's Dutch export funnel elbow type (1979).
MAKER'S MARKS: none
CONTEXT: Phase III (1), nondiagnostic (2)
DATE: 17th century (McCashion 1979)

Type K

ILLUSTRATION: Figure 5 d-g

DESCRIPTION: Bowl has parallel curving sides and small, flat heel.
NUMBER OF SPECIMENS: four
BORE DIAMETER: 6/64 (2), 7/64 (1), N.B.(1)
COMPARISONS: Similar to Oswald's general Type 11 (1975: 39), and transitional between Noel Hume's Types 15 and 16 (1970: 303).
MAKER'S MARKS: none
CONTEXT: Phase III (1), nondiagnostic (3)
DATE: 1730-1760 (Oswald 1975: 39), 1700-1770, 1730-1790 (Noel Hume 1970: 303).

Type L

ILLUSTRATION: Figure 5 h,i

DESCRIPTION: Curving bowl with a flattened area at the base, but not a true heel.
NUMBER OF SPECIMENS: two
BORE DIAMETER: 7/64 (2)
COMPARISONS: Similar to Oswald's general Type 10 (1975: 39).
MAKER'S MARKS: none
CONTEXT: nondiagnostic (1)
DATE: 1700-1740 (Oswald 1975: 39)

Type M, Variety 1

ILLUSTRATION: Figure 6 a-n

DESCRIPTION: Spurless, heel-less bowl, with bowl curving sharply from stem, rim of bowl is rouletted, but not parallel with stem.
NUMBER OF SPECIMENS: fourteen
BORE DIAMETER: 6/64(4), 7/64 (7), 8/64 (2), N.B. (1)
COMPARISONS: Similar to Atkinson and Oswald's London Type 24 (1969), Noel Hume's 1690-1720 type (1963: 262).

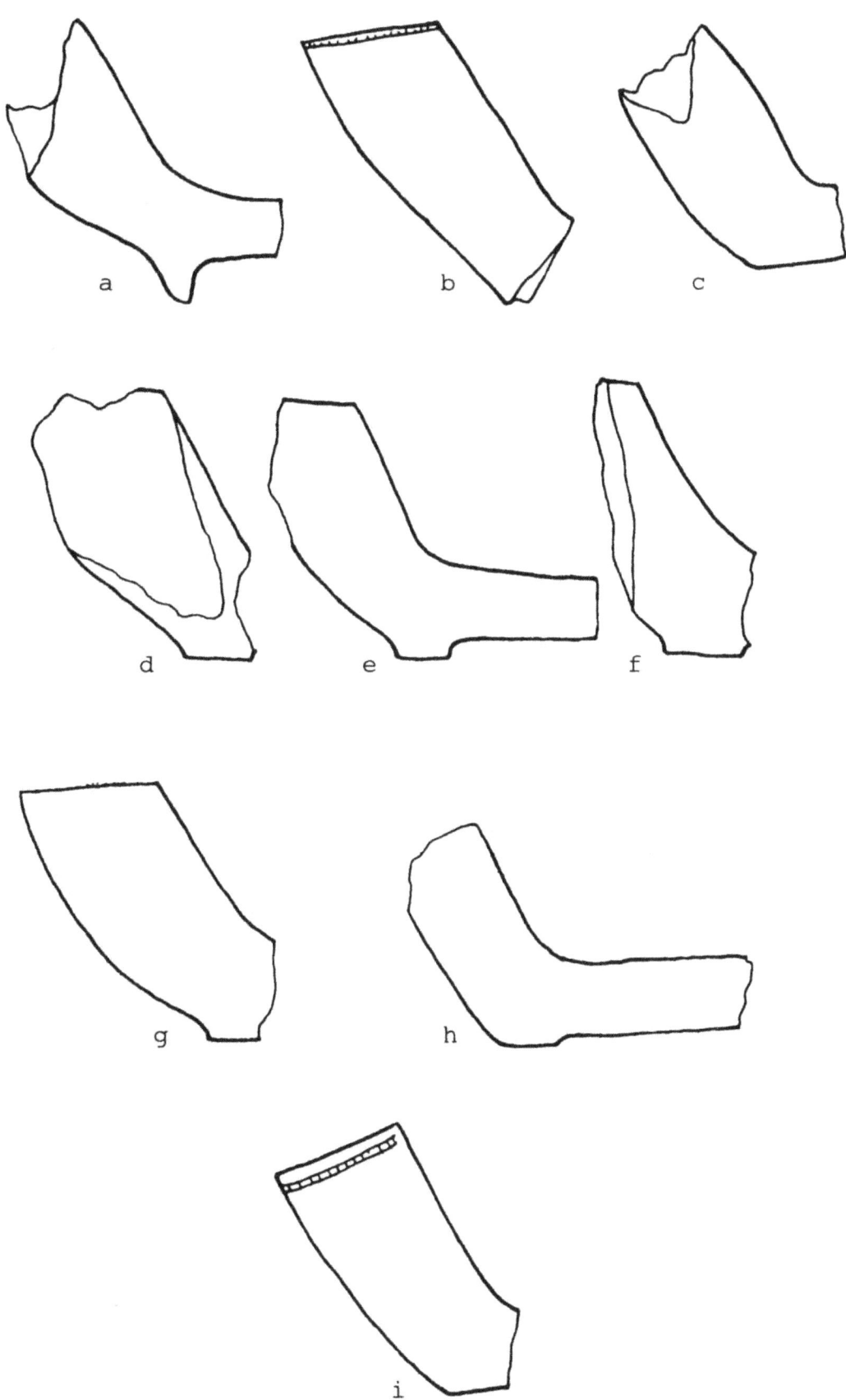

Figure 5: Bowls: Type H a; Type I b; Type J c; Type K d-g; Type L h-i

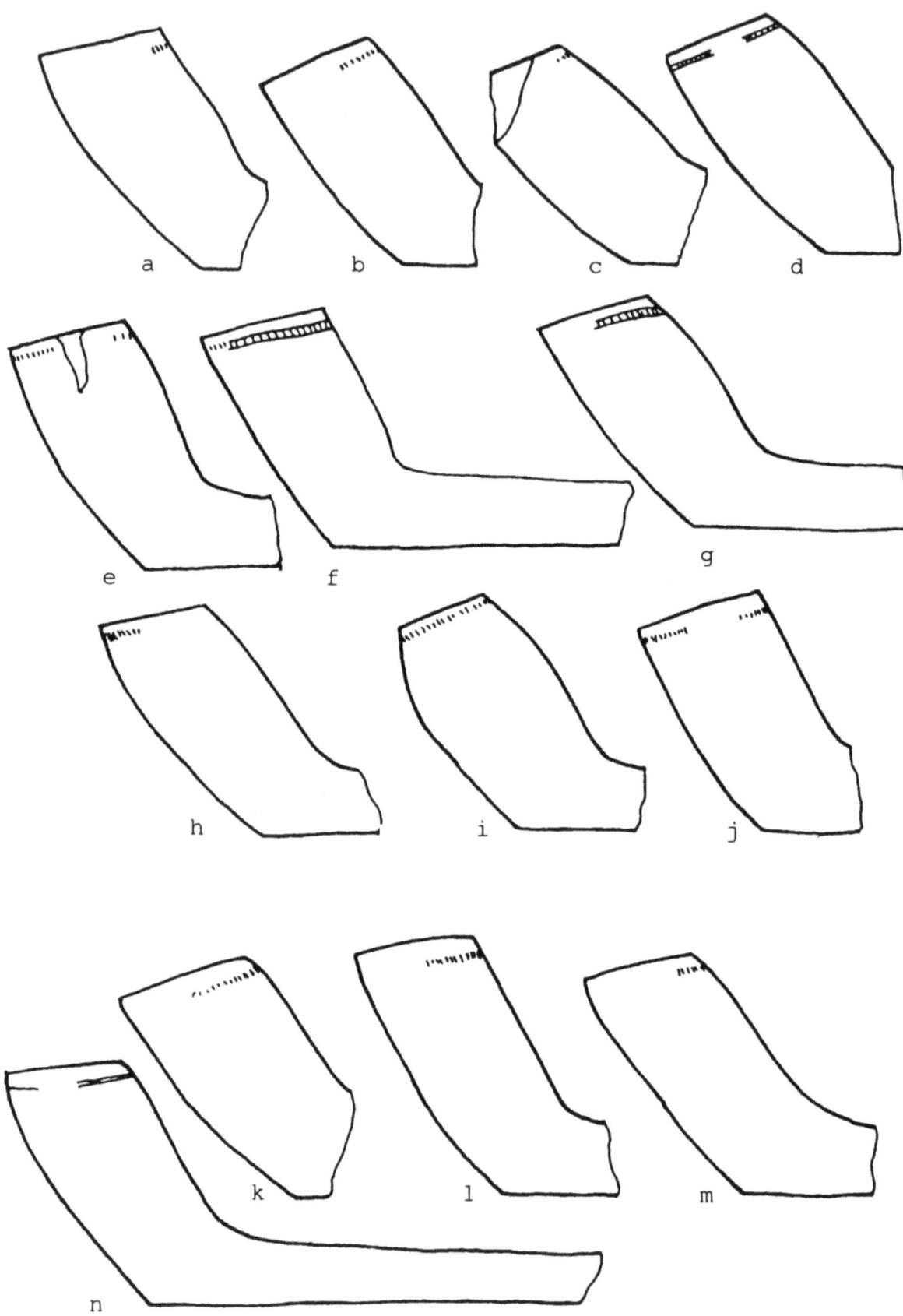

Figure 6: Type M bowls: Variety 1 a-n

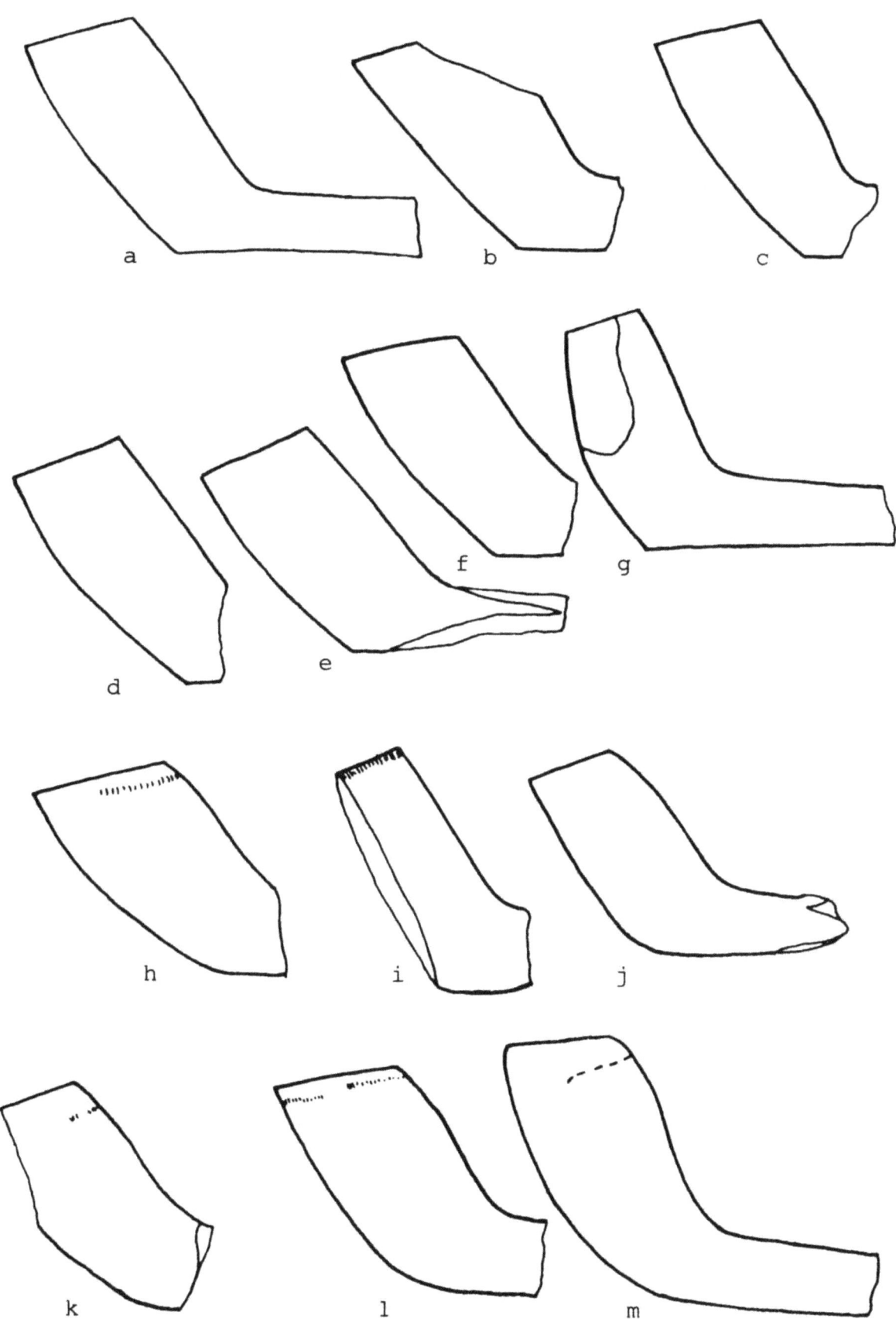

Figure 7: Type M bowls: Variety 2 a-g; Variety 3 h-m

Figure 8: Type M bowls: Variety 4 a-n

MAKER'S MARKS: One specimen with the mark of William Evans (I or II) of Bristol. An additional William Evans (I or II) mark appears on a M Type bowl for which the variety is not identifiable (see makers' marks below).
CONTEXT: Phase III (2), nondiagnostic (12)
DATE: 1700-1740 (Atkinson and Oswald 1969), 1690-1720 (Noel Hume 1963: 262).

Type M, Variety 2

ILLUSTRATION: Figure 7 a-g

DESCRIPTION: Spurless, heel-less bowl, with bowl curving sharply from stem, rim of bowl is not parallel with stem or rouletted.
NUMBER OF SPECIMENS: seven
BORE DIAMETER: 5/64 (1), 6/64 (2), 7/64 (3), 8/64 (1)
COMPARISONS: Similar to Atkinson and Oswald's London Type 24 (1969), Noel Hume 1690-1720 type (1963: 262).
MAKER'S MARKS: One specimen is marked with a Llewellin Evans mark, additionally, a William Evans (I or II) mark appears on a type M bowl for which the variety is not identifiable (see makers' marks below).
CONTEXT: Phase III (2), nondiagnostic (5)
DATE: 1700-1740 (Atkinson and Oswald 1969), 1690-1720 (Noel Hume 1963: 262).

Type M, Variety 3

ILLUSTRATION: Figure 7 h-m

DESCRIPTION: Spurless, heel-less bowl, with bowl curving gently from stem, rim of bowl is rouletted and not parallel with stem.
NUMBER OF SPECIMENS: six
BORE DIAMETER: 6/64 (2), 7/64 (3), 8/64 (1)
COMPARISONS: Similar to Noel Hume's 1680-1740 type (1963: 262).
MAKER'S MARKS: None definitely, but a William Evans (I or II) mark appears on a Type M bowl for which the variety is not identifiable (see below).
CONTEXT: nondiagnostic (5)
DATE: 1680-1740 (Noel Hume 1963: 262)

Type M, Variety 4

ILLUSTRATION: Figure 8 a-n and Figure 9 a-d

DESCRIPTION: Spurless, heel-less bowl, with bowl curving gently from stem, rim of bowl is not rouletted or parallel with stem.
NUMBER OF SPECIMENS: 18
BORE DIAMETER: 5/64 (2), 6/64 (11), 7/64 (4), N.B. (1)
COMPARISONS: Similar to Noel Hume's 1680-1740 type (1963: 262).
MAKER'S MARKS: None definitely, but a William Evans (I or II) mark appears on a Type M bowl for which the variety is not identifiable (see makers' marks below).
CONTEXT: Phase III (4), nondiagnostic (14)
DATE: 1680-1740 (Noel Hume 1963: 262)

Type M, Variety 5

ILLUSTRATION: Figure 9 e, f

DESCRIPTION: Spurless, heel-less bowl, with bowl curving sharply from stem, rim of bowl is parallel with stem and rouletted.
NUMBER OF SPECIMENS: two
BORE DIAMETER: 6/64 (1), 8/64 (1)
COMPARISONS: Similar to Oswald's general Type 26 (1975: 39), Noel Hume's Type 18 (1970: 303).
MAKER'S MARKS: None definitely, but a William Evans (I or II) mark appears on a Type M bowl for which the variety is not identifiable (see below).
CONTEXT: nondiagnostic (1)
DATE: 1680-1710 (Oswald 1975: 39,41, Noel Hume 1970: 303).

Type M, Variety 6

ILLUSTRATION: Figure 9 g

DESCRIPTION: Spurless, heel-less bowl, with bowl curving sharply from stem, rim of bowl is parallel with stem and not rouletted.
NUMBER OF SPECIMENS: one
BORE DIAMETER: 8/64 (1)
COMPARISONS: Similar to Oswald's general Type 26 (1975: 39), Noel Hume's Type 18 (1970: 303).
MAKER'S MARKS: None definitely, but a William Evans (I or II) mark appears on a Type M bowl for which the variety is not identifiable (see makers' marks below).
CONTEXT: nondiagnostic (1)
DATE: 1680-1710 (Oswald 1975: 39, 41, Noel Hume 1970: 303)

Type M, Variety 7

ILLUSTRATION: Figure 10 a-c

DESCRIPTION: Spurless, heel-less bowl, with bowl curving gently from stem, rim of bowl is parallel with stem and rouletted.
NUMBER OF SPECIMENS: three
BORE DIAMETER: 6/64 (3)
COMPARISONS: Similar to Oswald's general Type 26 (1975: 39), Noel Hume's Type 17 (1970: 303).
MAKER'S MARKS: None definitely, but a William Evans (I or II) mark appears on a Type M bowl for which the variety is not identifiable (see makers' marks below).

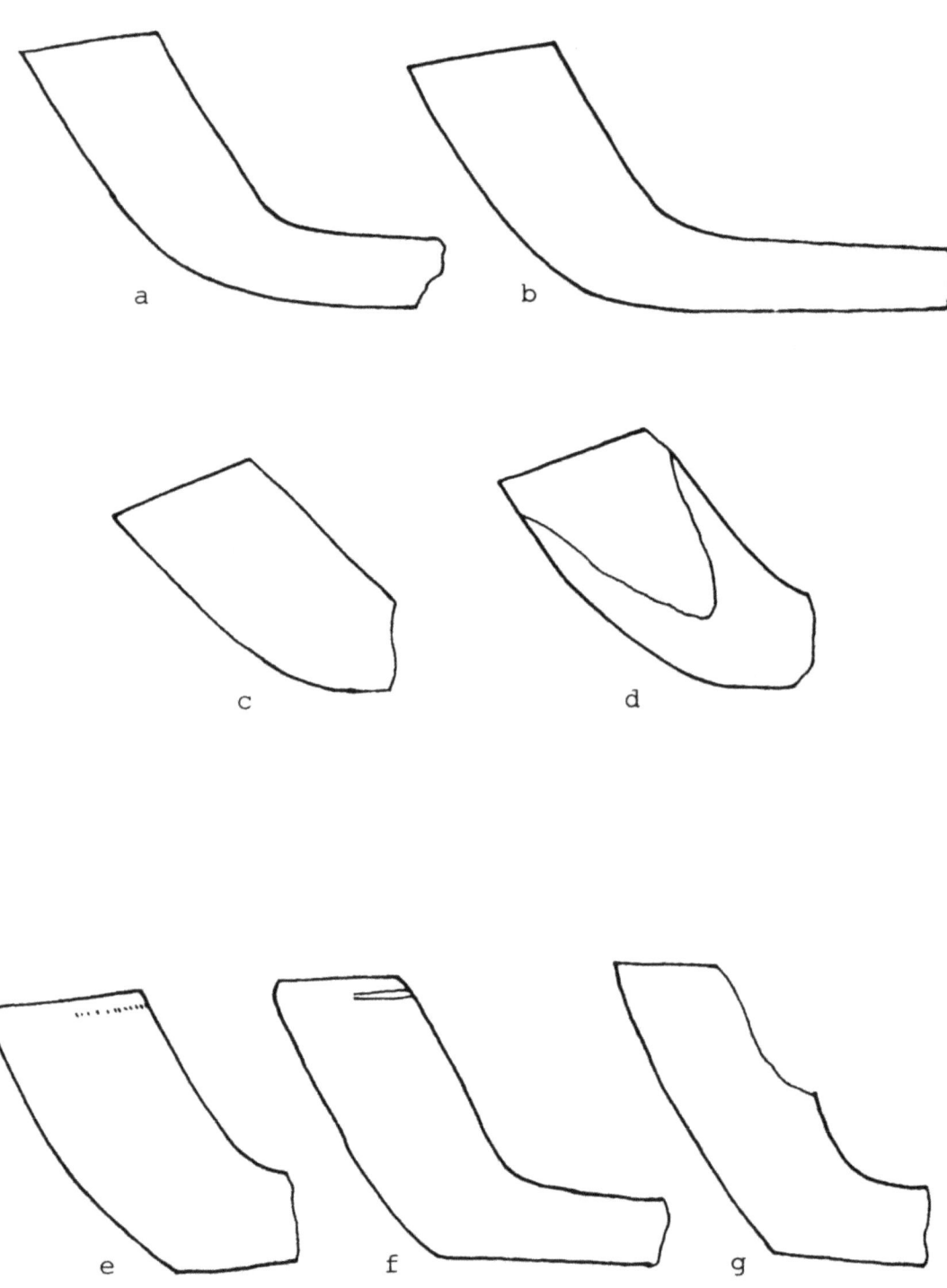

Figure 9: Type M bowls: Variety 4 a-d; Variety 4 e-f; Variety 6 g

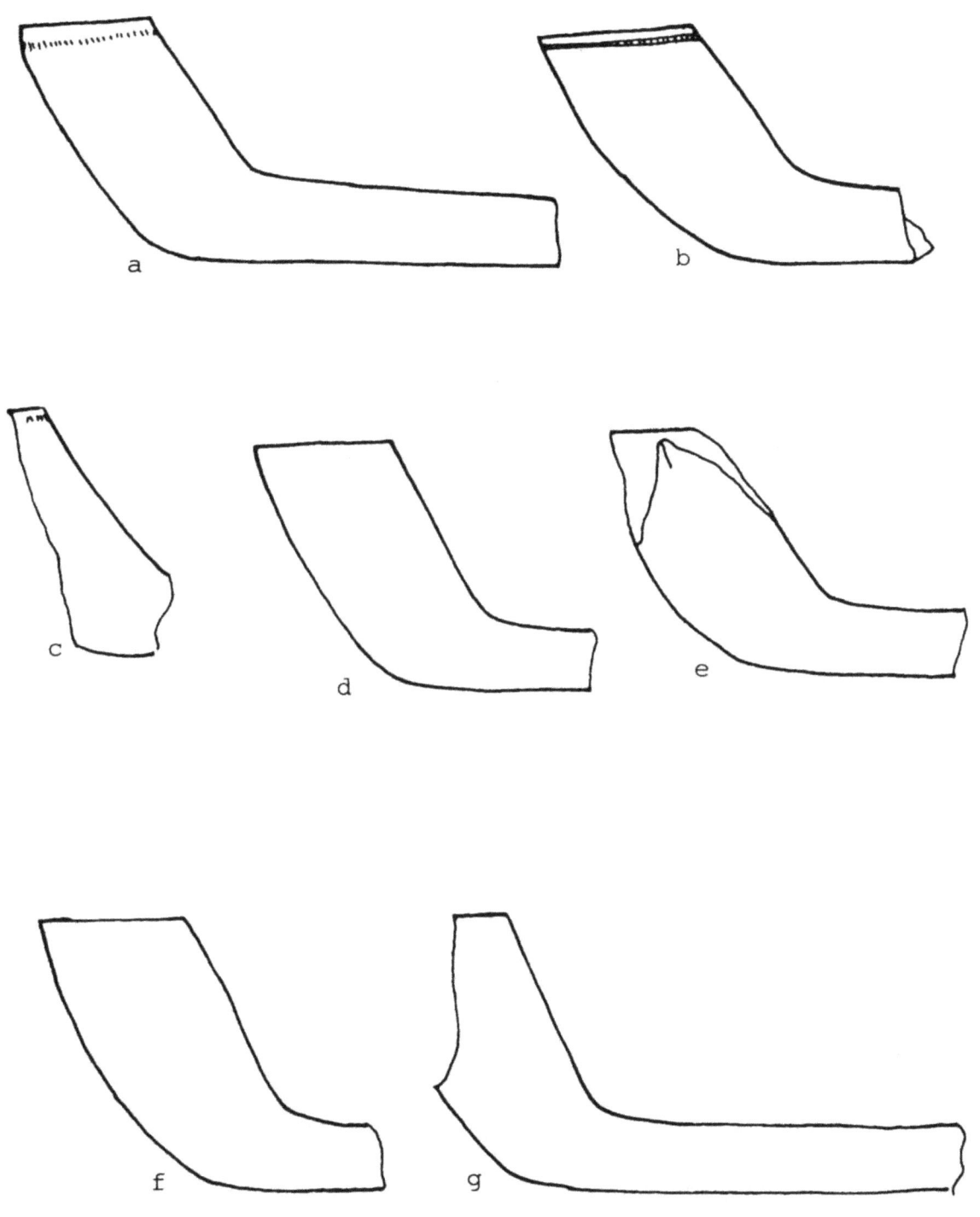

Figure 10: Type M bowls: Variety 7 a-c; Variety 8 d-g

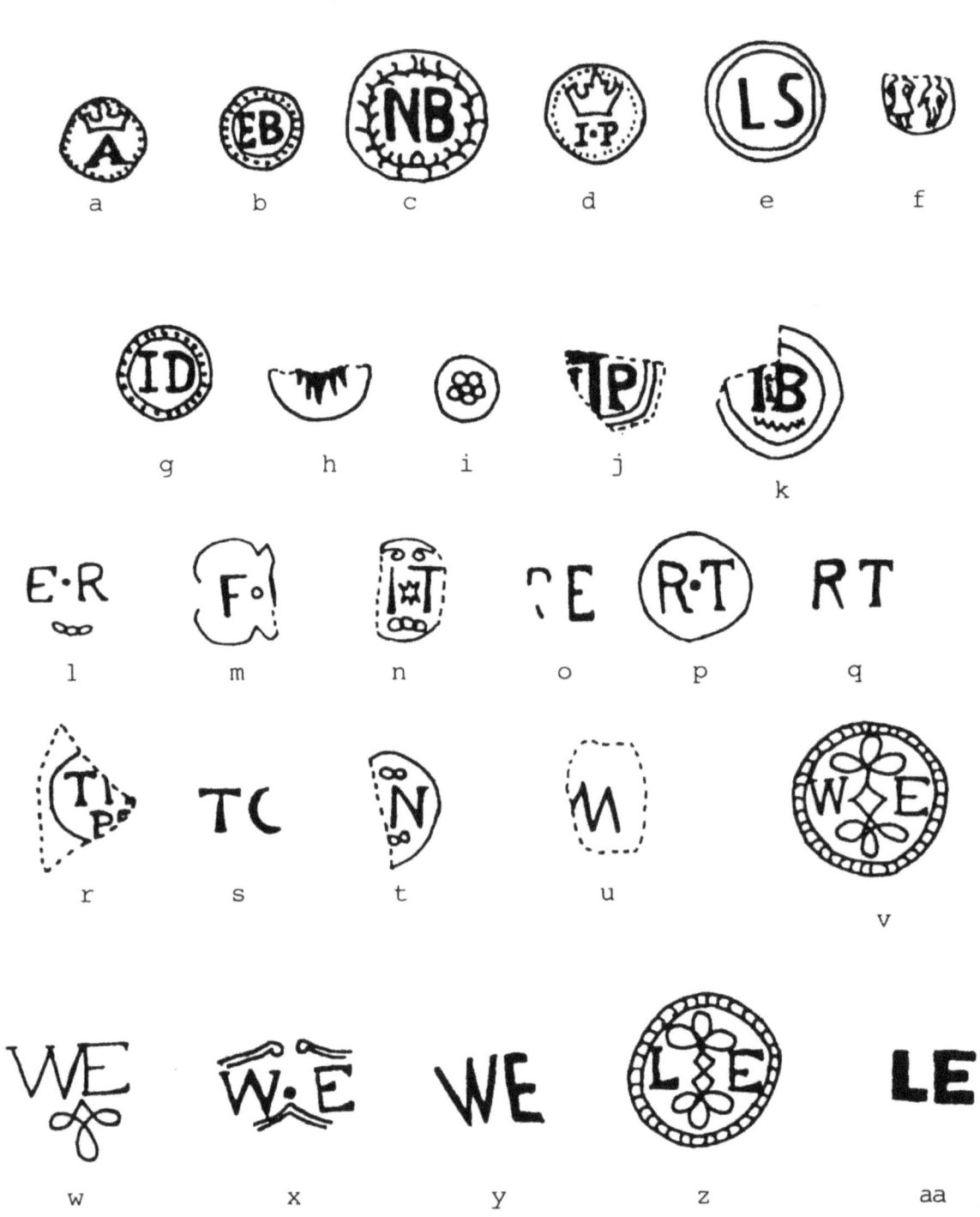

Figure 11: Makers' marks: heels a-k; bowl marks l-aa

CONTEXT: nondiagnostic (4)
DATE: 1680-1710 (Oswald 1975: 39, 41, Noel Hume 1970: 303)

Type M, Variety 8

ILLUSTRATION: Figure 10 d-g

DESCRIPTION: Spurless, heel-less bowl, with bowl curving gently from stem, rim of bowl is parallel with stem.
NUMBER OF SPECIMENS: four
BORE DIAMETER: 6/64 (3), 7/64 (1)
COMPARISONS: Similar to Oswald's general Type 25 (1975: 39), Noel Hume's Type 17 (1970: 303).
MAKER'S MARKS: None definitely, but a William Evans (I or II) mark appears on a Type M bowl for which the variety is not identifiable (see makers' marks below).
CONTEXT: Phase III (1), nondiagnostic (3)
DATE: 1680-1710 (Oswald 1975: 39, 41, Noel Hume 1970: 303)

MAKERS' MARKS: HEELS

ILLUSTRATION: Figure 11 a

DESCRIPTION: Upper case "A" surmounted by a crown.
NUMBER OF SPECIMENS: one
BORE DIAMETER: 6/64 (1)
TYPE OF BOWL: unknown, heeled bowl
COMPARISONS: Duco (1981) and McCashion (1979) illustrate similar crowned marks with different initials and attribute them to Dutch manufacture. Miller (1983) illustrates an identical mark from the Village Center of St. Mary's City.
CONTEXT: nondiagnostic (1)
MAKER: unknown, probably Dutch
DATE: unknown

ILLUSTRATION: Figure 11 b

DESCRIPTION: Upper case "E B" surrounded by concentric circles.
NUMBER OF SPECIMENS: two
BORE DIAMETER: 6/64 (1), 9/64 (1)
TYPE OF BOWL: One Type C, 1 bowl, one on a very fragmentary Type J funnel-shaped elbow pipe.
COMPARISONS: McCashion (1979) and Duco (1981) identify the maker as Edward Bird of Holland. See also Miller (1983), Mitchell (1983), Faulkner and Faulkner (1987), and Gibson (1980) for identical marks.
CONTEXT: nondiagnostic (2)
MAKER: Edward Bird of Holland
DATE: 1635-1665 (McCashion 1979: 92)

ILLUSTRATION: Figure 11 c

DESCRIPTION: Upper case "N B" surrounded by a wreath-like circle.
NUMBER OF SPECIMENS: two
BORE DIAMETER: 9/64 (2)
TYPE OF BOWL: unknown, heeled bowl
COMPARISONS: Duco (1981) illustrates similar marks, but with different initials. Miller (1983: 70) illustrates a very similar mark from the Village Center at St. Mary's City.
CONTEXT: nondiagnostic (2)
MAKER: unknown, probably Dutch
DATE: unknown

ILLUSTRATION: Figure 11 d

DESCRIPTION: Upper case "I P" separated by a dot and surmounted by a crown.
NUMBER OF SPECIMENS: one
BORE DIAMETER: N.B.
TYPE OF BOWL: unknown heeled bowl
COMPARISONS: Duco (1981) illustrates similar marks. Miller (1983: 70) illustrates a similar crowned, two-initial mark from the Village Center at St. Mary's City. See also "I P" stem and base marks, below.
CONTEXT: nondiagnostic (1)
MAKER: unknown, probably Dutch
DATE: unknown

ILLUSTRATION: Figure 11 e

DESCRIPTION: Upper case "L S" in circle on heel.
NUMBER OF SPECIMENS: one
BORE DIAMETER: 7/64 (1)
TYPE OF BOWL: Unknown heeled bowl with a splayed heel similar to Brosely pipes.
COMPARISONS: Rutter and Davey (1980: 121) illustrate a similar but not identical mark which they tentatively attribute to Lawrence Starkey.
CONTEXT: nondiagnostic (1)
MAKER: Lawrence Starkey of Chester
DATE: Circa 1670 (Rutter and Davey 1980: 121)

ILLUSTRATION: Figure 11 f

DESCRIPTION: Two human (?) figures in a circle.
NUMBER OF SPECIMENS: one
BORE DIAMETER: 6/64 (1)
TYPE OF BOWL: unknown heeled bowl
COMPARISONS: McCashion (1979) illustrates similar, but not identical specimens.
CONTEXT: Phase III
MAKER: unknown, possibly Dutch
DATE: unknown

ILLUSTRATION: Figure 11 g

DESCRIPTION: Upper case "I D" surrounded by a circle.
NUMBER OF SPECIMENS: one
BORE DIAMETER: 7/64 (1)
TYPE OF BOWL: Extremely fragmentary Type J funnel-shaped elbow pipe.
COMPARISONS: Duco (1981) illustrates an identical mark and variations on the mark, and attributes it to John Draper.
CONTEXT: nondiagnostic (1)
MAKER: John Draper of Holland
DATE: 1630-1645 (Duco 1981)

ILLUSTRATION: Figure 11 h

DESCRIPTION: Indiscernible mark on elongated heel, possibly an inverted tulip.
NUMBER OF SPECIMENS: one
BORE DIAMETER: 8/64 (1)
TYPE OF BOWL: unknown, heeled bowl
COMPARISONS: McCashion (1979) and Duco (1981) illustrate tulip marks.
CONTEXT: nondiagnostic (1)
MAKER: unknown, possibly Dutch
DATE: unknown

ILLUSTRATION: Figure 11 i

DESCRIPTION: Impressed five-petaled, stylized Rose mark enclosed in a circle.
NUMBER OF SPECIMENS: four
BORE DIAMETER: 6/64 (1), 7/64 (3)
TYPE OF BOWL: unknown heeled bowl
COMPARISONS: McCashion (1979: 104) illustrates similar marks as Dutch products, Oswald (1970: 129-130) also illustrates this mark.
CONTEXT: nondiagnostic (4)
MAKER: unknown, possibly Dutch

DATE: 1630-1650 (Oswald 1970: 129-130)

ILLUSTRATION: Figure 11 j

DESCRIPTION: Extremely fragmentary mark composed of a central "T" shaped character (possible hammer?) flanked by initials, "?" and an upper case "P".
NUMBER OF SPECIMENS: two
BORE DIAMETER: 7/64 (2)
TYPE OF BOWL: unknown heeled bowl
COMPARISONS: none
CONTEXT: nondiagnostic (2)
MAKER: unknown
DATE: unknown

ILLUSTRATION: Figure 11 l

DESCRIPTION: Upper case "I R" separated by dots, and with scrolled lines above and below, all specimens of extremely soft paste and worn.
NUMBER OF SPECIMENS: three
BORE DIAMETER: 8/64 (3)
TYPE OF BOWL: unknown heeled bowl
COMPARISONS: Muldoon (1979: 273) illustrates an identical mark on a bowl form dated to circa 1600-1640.
CONTEXT: Phase I (1), nondiagnostic (2)
MAKER: unknown
DATE: 1600-1640 (Muldoon 1979)

BOWL MARKS

ILLUSTRATION: Figure 11 l

DESCRIPTION: Upper case initials "E R" separated by a dot and underlined with a series of three linked ovals.
NUMBER OF SPECIMENS: one
BORE DIAMETER: N.B. (1)
TYPE OF BOWL: unknown
COMPARISONS: Oswald (1975: 86) suggests this may be the mark of Edward Reed, however, Walker (1977: 1479) does not illustrate this mark as one used by Reed.
CONTEXT: nondiagnostic (1)
MAKER: Possibly Edward Reed of Bristol.
DATE: Possibly 1706-1723 (Oswald 1975: 86).

ILLUSTRATION: Figure 11 m

DESCRIPTION: Upper case initial "F" followed by a dot, and a missing initial, the whole mark is surrounded by a scrolled cartouche.
NUMBER OF SPECIMENS: one
BORE DIAMETER: N.B. (1)
TYPE OF BOWL: unknown
COMPARISONS: Oswald (1975: 56-57) illustrates a similar mark and attributes it to Francis Russell II. Walker (1977: 1486) illustrates several Russell marks, of which this specimen is most similar to a mark he attributes to Francis Russell II.
CONTEXT: nondiagnostic (1)
MAKER: Probably Francis Russell II, of Bristol.
DATE: circa 1698

ILLUSTRATION: Figure 11 n

DESCRIPTION: Upper case initials "I T" separated by a star, underlined by three ovals, and framed with a fragmentary, curling cartouche.
NUMBER OF SPECIMENS: one
BORE DIAMETER: N.B. (1)
TYPE OF BOWL: unknown

COMPARISONS: Walker (1977: 1309-1324) lists three Bristol makers with the initials "I T" within the St. John's occupation span, while Oswald (1975: 130-206) lists 32 with these initials. Similar initial marks on pipe heels have been attributed to John Tucker (Jackson and Price 1974: 73,108-109); see also Miller (1986: 85) for examples from St. Mary's City.
CONTEXT: nondiagnostic (1)
MAKER: Possibly John Tucker of Bristol.
DATE: Circa 1662-1671

ILLUSTRATION: Figure 11 d

DESCRIPTION: Upper case initials "? E" with fragmentary scrolled cartouche.
NUMBER OF SPECIMENS: one
BORE DIAMETER: N.B. (1)
TYPE OF BOWL: unknown
COMPARISONS: Walker (1977: 1125-1126) lists 12 Bristol makers with surnames beginning with "E", while Oswald (1975: 130-206) lists 48 pipe makers with surnames beginning with the letter "E".
CONTEXT: nondiagnostic (1)
MAKER: unknown
DATE: unknown

ILLUSTRATION: Figure 11 p

DESCRIPTION: Upper case initials "R T" separated by a dot.
NUMBER OF SPECIMENS: three
BORE DIAMETER: N.B. (3)
TYPE OF BOWL: unknown
COMPARISONS: Walker (1977: 1493) suggests that this is the mark of Robert Tippet II of Bristol.
CONTEXT: nondiagnostic (1)
MAKER: Probably Robert Tippet II of Bristol.
DATE: 1678-1713 (Walker 1977: 1494)

ILLUSTRATION: Figure 11 q

DESCRIPTION: Upper case initial "R T".
NUMBER OF SPECIMENS: three
BORE DIAMETER: N.B. (3)
TYPE OF BOWL: unknown
COMPARISONS: Walker (1977: 1493) suggests that this is the mark of Robert Tippet II of Bristol.
CONTEXT: nondiagnostic (3)
MAKER: Probably Robert Tippet II.
DATE: 1678-1713 (Walker 1977: 1494)

ILLUSTRATION: Figure 11 r

DESCRIPTION: Upper case initials "T"(?) over "P"(?) on a raised boss. Mark appears to be mold imparted.
NUMBER OF SPECIMENS: one
BORE DIAMETER: N.B. (1)
TYPE OF BOWL: unknown

COMPARISONS: Given the fragmentary nature of this specimen, attribution is not feasible. Oswald (1975: 84-85) illustrates other multi-letter bowl marks.
CONTEXT: nondiagnostic (1)
MAKER: unknown
DATE: unknown

ILLUSTRATION: Figure 11 s

DESCRIPTION: Upper case initials "T C" impressed in bowl.
NUMBER OF SPECIMENS: one
BORE DIAMETER: N.B. (1)
TYPE OF BOWL: unknown
COMPARISONS: Walker (1977: 1112) lists Thomas Cullimore as a Bristol maker while Oswald (1975: 130-206) lists 18 other makers with these initials within the St. John's occupation span.
CONTEXT: nondiagnostic (1)
MAKER: unknown
DATE: unknown

ILLUSTRATION: Figure 11 t

DESCRIPTION: Upper case initials "? N" with inter-locking ovals above and below.
NUMBER OF SPECIMENS: one
BORE DIAMETER: N.B. (1)
TYPE OF BOWL: unknown
COMPARISONS: Possibly the mark of Richard Nunney, but Walker (1977: 1466-1467) illustrates only heel marks. Oswald (1975: 130-206) lists 20 makers with surnames beginning with an "N" in this time period.
CONTEXT: nondiagnostic (1)
MAKER: unknown
DATE: unknown

ILLUSTRATION: Figure 11 u

DESCRIPTION: Upper case "M" impressed in bowl.
NUMBER OF SPECIMENS: one
BORE DIAMETER: N.B. (1)
TYPE OF BOWL: unknown
COMPARISONS: Possibly the mark of Thomas Monkes, but the nature of the impressed "M" appears different from illustrated examples (Walker 1977: 1462). Oswald (1975: 130-206)
lists 81 makers with surnames beginning with an "M" in our time period.
CONTEXT: nondiagnostic (1)
MAKER: unknown
DATE: unknown

ILLUSTRATION: Figure 11 v

DESCRIPTION: Upper case initials "W E" with scrolled element separating the initials, entire mark is

surrounded by a circle.
NUMBER OF SPECIMENS: two
BORE DIAMETER: N.B. (2)
TYPE OF BOWL: unknown
COMPARISONS: Walker (1977: 1434-1435) identifies this as the mark of either William Evans I or William Evans II.
CONTEXT: nondiagnostic (2)
MAKER: William Evans (I or II) of Bristol
DATE: 1667-1682, and 1697 (Walker 1977: 1434-1435)

ILLUSTRATION: Figure 11 w

DESCRIPTION: Upper case initials "W E" with a scrolled element below.
NUMBER OF SPECIMENS: one
BORE DIAMETER: N.B. (1)
TYPE OF BOWL: unknown
COMPARISONS: Walker (1977: 1434-1435) identifies this as the mark of either William Evans I or William Evans II.
CONTEXT: nondiagnostic (2)
MAKER: William Evans (I or II) of Bristol
DATE: 1667-1682, and 1697 (Walker 1977: 1434-1435)

ILLUSTRATION: Figure 11 x

DESCRIPTION: Upper case initials "W E" with a scrolled bracket above and below.
NUMBER OF SPECIMENS: two
BORE DIAMETER: N.B. (2)
TYPE OF BOWL: one specimen of a Type M, 1
COMPARISONS: Walker (1977: 1434-1435) identifies this as the mark of either William Evans I or William Evans II.
CONTEXT: nondiagnostic (2)
MAKER: William Evans (I or II) of Bristol
DATE: 1667-1682, and 1697 (Walker 1977: 1434-1435)

ILLUSTRATION: Figure 11 y

DESCRIPTION: Upper case initials "W E" on bowl.
NUMBER OF SPECIMENS: one
BORE DIAMETER: 8/64 (1)
TYPE OF BOWL: Specimen is on a Type M bowl, variety unknown.
COMPARISONS: Walker (1977: 1434-1435) identifies this as the mark of either William Evans I or William Evans II.
CONTEXT: nondiagnostic (1)
MAKER: William Evans (I or II) of Bristol
DATE: 1667-1682, and 1697 (Walker 1977: 1434-1435)

ILLUSTRATION: Figure 11 z

DESCRIPTION: Upper case initials "L E" separated by scrolled decoration. The entire mark is surrounded by a circular cartouche.
NUMBER OF SPECIMENS: 29
BORE DIAMETER: 7/64 (7), 8/64 (2), N.B. (20)
TYPE OF BOWL: one specimen is on a Type M, 2 bowl.
COMPARISONS: Walker (1977: 1428-1431) identifies this as the mark of Llewellin Evans. See Walker (1977: 607, 657) for a discussion of the distribution of "LE" marks from other North American Colonial sites.
CONTEXT: Phase III (1), nondiagnostic (28)
MAKER: Llewellin Evans of Bristol
DATE: 1661-1688/9 (Walker 1977: 1428-1431)

ILLUSTRATION: Figure 11 aa

DESCRIPTION: Upper case initials "L E" on bowl.
NUMBER OF SPECIMENS: 10
BORE DIAMETER: 7/64 (1) N.B. (9)
TYPE OF BOWL: unknown
COMPARISONS: Walker (1977: 1428-1431) identifies this as the mark of Llewellin Evans. See Walker (1977: 607, 657) for a discussion of the distribution of "LE" marks from other North American Colonial sites.
CONTEXT: nondiagnostic (8)
MAKER: Llewellin Evans of Bristol
DATE: 1661-1688/9 (Walker 1977: 1428-1431)

STEM MARKS

ILLUSTRATION: Figure 12 a

DESCRIPTION: Upper case initials "L E" in a band of scrolled diamonds with dots in the center of the diamonds, and two bands of dentate milling above and below.
NUMBER OF SPECIMENS: four
BORE DIAMETER: 7/64 (3)
TYPE OF BOWL: unknown
COMPARISONS: Walker (1977: 1429) illustrates this mark and identifies it as that of Llewellin Evans. See also Walker (1977: 607,657) for a discussion of the distribution of "LE" marks on Colonial North American sites.
CONTEXT: nondiagnostic (4)
MAKER: Llewellin Evans of Bristol
DATE: 1661-1688/9 (Walker 1977: 1428-1429)

ILLUSTRATION: Figure 12 b

DESCRIPTION: Upper case initials "L E" in a band of scrolled diamonds with two bands of dentate milling above and below.

NUMBER OF SPECIMENS: 39
BORE DIAMETER: 7/64 (28), 8/64 (10), N.B. (1)
TYPE OF BOWL: unknown
COMPARISONS: Walker (1977: 1429) illustrates a similar mark and identifies it as that of Llewellin Evans. See also Walker (1977: 607,657) for a discussion of the distribution of "LE" marks on Colonial North American sites.
CONTEXT: nondiagnostic (39)
MAKER: Llewellin Evans of Bristol
DATE: 1661-1688/9 (Walker 1977: 1428-1429)

ILLUSTRATION: Figure 12 c

DESCRIPTION: Small upper case initials "L E" between two bands of dentate milling, below a band of scrolled diamonds with dots in the center of the diamonds, and two bands of dentate milling above.
NUMBER OF SPECIMENS: seven
BORE DIAMETER: 7/64 (3), 8/64 (4)
TYPE OF BOWL: unknown
COMPARISONS: Walker (1977: 1429) illustrates a similar mark and identifies it as that of Llewellin Evans. See also Walker (1877: 607,657) for a discussion of the distribution of "LE" marks on Colonial North American sites.
CONTEXT: nondiagnostic (7)
MAKER: Llewellin Evans of Bristol
DATE: 1661-1688/9 (Walker 1977: 1428-1429)

ILLUSTRATION: Figure 12 d

DESCRIPTION: Upper case initials "W E" in a band of scrolled diamonds with dots in the center of the diamonds, and two lines of dentate milling above and below.
NUMBER OF SPECIMENS: nine
BORE DIAMETER: 7/64 (3), 8/64 (6)
TYPE OF BOWL: unknown
COMPARISONS: Walker (1977: 1434-1435) identifies this as the mark of either William Evans I or William Evans II.
CONTEXT: nondiagnostic (9)
MAKER: William Evans (I or II) of Bristol
DATE: 1667-1682, and 1697 (Walker 1977: 1434-1435)

ILLUSTRATION: Figure 12 e

DESCRIPTION: Upper case characters "WILEVANS" in a band of scrolled diamonds with dots in the center of the diamonds, and two lines of dentate milling above and below.
NUMBER OF SPECIMENS: 10
BORE DIAMETER: 7/64 (9), 8/64 (1)
TYPE OF BOWL: unknown
COMPARISONS: Walker (1977: 1434-1435) identifies this as the mark of either William Evans I or William Evans II.
CONTEXT: nondiagnostic (10)
MAKER: William Evans (I or II) of Bristol
DATE: 1667-1682, and 1697 (Walker 1977: 1434-1435)

ILLUSTRATION: Figure 12 f

DESCRIPTION: Upper case "AGE" followed by an indiscernible character.
NUMBER OF SPECIMENS: one
BORE DIAMETER: 7/64 (1)
TYPE OF BOWL: unknown
COMPARISONS: Oswald (1975: 184) lists William Ager (1706-1713). Obviously this mark could also represent any other name ending in "age".
CONTEXT: nondiagnostic (1)
MAKER: possibly William Ager
DATE: possibly 1706-1713 (Oswald 1975: 184)

ILLUSTRATION: Figure 12 g

DESCRIPTION: Upper case initials "A A" with a fragment of cross hatching to right.
NUMBER OF SPECIMENS: one
BORE DIAMETER: 6/64 (1)
TYPE OF BOWL: unknown
COMPARISONS: Walker (1977: 1042-1054) lists no Bristol makers with the initials "A A", Oswald (1975: 130-206) lists three pipe makers with the initials "A A" (two in London, and one in Yorkshire). Alexander (1979: 52) illustrates very similar marks from the Buck Site on Maryland's Eastern Shore.
CONTEXT: nondiagnostic (1)
MAKER: unknown
DATE: unknown

ILLUSTRATION: Figure 12 h

DESCRIPTION: Upper case "CHRIS ATHARTON" with bands of dentate milling above and below, and scalloped milled lines above and below.
NUMBER OF SPECIMENS: three
BORE DIAMETER: 5/64 (1), 6/64 (2)
TYPE OF BOWL: unknown
COMPARISONS: Oswald (1975: 130-206) lists five Athertons in Liverpool and three in Lancashire, primarily in the 18th century: a very similar mark with the name "THO: ATHARTON" was recovered in the excavations at South Castle Street, Liverpool (Davey 1985: 124).
CONTEXT: nondiagnostic (3)
MAKER: Chris Atharton, probably of Liverpool
DATE: Probably late 17th century or early 18th century. Davey notes (1985: 123) that the Thomas Atharton mark occurs on pipes which must predate 1726.

Figure 12: Stem marks a-k

ILLUSTRATION: Figure 12 i

DESCRIPTION: Upper case initials "I F" (F is fragmentary) in a band of scrolled diamonds with central dots.
NUMBER OF SPECIMENS: three
BORE DIAMETER: 6/64 (2), 7/64 (1)
TYPE OF BOWL: unknown
COMPARISONS: Walker (1971: 26 and 1977: 1438) illustrates an identical mark attributed to James Fox of Bristol. Fox was Llewellin Evans' master (Walker 1977: 608). See also Walker (1977: 656) for a discussion of the distribution of Fox marks on Colonial sites in North America.
CONTEXT: nondiagnostic (3)
MAKER: James Fox of Bristol
DATE: 1651-1669 (Walker 1971: 26)

ILLUSTRATION: Figure 12 j

DESCRIPTION: Upper case initials "I P" in a band of scrolled diamonds with central dots, with two bands of dentate milling above and below.
NUMBER OF SPECIMENS: two
BORE DIAMETER: 7/64 (1), 8/64 (1)
TYPE OF BOWL: unknown
COMPARISONS: Walker (1977: 607) lists three Bristol makers with the initials "I P" within this time period, while Oswald (1975: 130-206) lists 39 makers with these initials. Miller (1983: 76) illustrates an identical mark from the Village Center at St. Mary's City. Given the style of the mark it appears to be most likely a Bristol product (Walker 1977: 607).
CONTEXT: nondiagnostic (2)
MAKER: unknown, probably from Bristol
DATE: unknown

ILLUSTRATION: Figure 12 k

DESCRIPTION: Upper case initials "R(?)S" in a band of scrolled diamonds, with two bands of dentate milling above and below.
NUMBER OF SPECIMENS: one
BORE DIAMETER: 7/64 (1)
TYPE OF BOWL: unknown
COMPARISONS: Walker (1979: 608,1291) lists a Richard Saunders and a Robert Sheppard as Bristol pipe makers, but since Sheppard took apprentices, Walker suggests that it is more likely that this is his mark.
CONTEXT: nondiagnostic (1)
MAKER: Probably Robert Sheppard of Bristol.
DATE: Circa 1690 (Walker 1977: 1291)

ILLUSTRATION: Figure 13 a

DESCRIPTION: Upper case "I S" in a band of scrolled diamonds with central dots, and with two parallel bands of dentate milling above and below.
NUMBER OF SPECIMENS: three
BORE DIAMETER: 7/64 (1), 8/64 (2)
TYPE OF BOWL: unknown
COMPARISONS: Walker (1977: 608,668) lists several Bristol makers with the initials "I S", but favors an association with John Sinderling. Alexander (1979: 53) and Miller (1985: 77) illustrate identical marks.
CONTEXT: nondiagnostic (3)
MAKER: probably John Sinderling of Bristol
DATE: 1666-1699 (Walker 1977: 606)

ILLUSTRATION: Figure 13 b

DESCRIPTION: Upper case initials "I S" inset in rectangles in a band of scrolled diamonds with central dots, and with two bands of dentate milling above and below.
NUMBER OF SPECIMENS: four
BORE DIAMETER: 8/64 (4)
TYPE OF BOWL: unknown
COMPARISONS: Walker (1977: 608,668) lists several Bristol makers with the initials "I S", but favors an association with John Sinderling. Alexander (1979: 53) and Miller (1985: 77) illustrate identical marks.
CONTEXT: nondiagnostic (4)
MAKER: probably John Sinderling of Bristol
DATE: 1666-1699 (Walker 1977: 608)

MOLD IMPARTED BOWL BASE MARKS

ILLUSTRATION: Figure 13 c

DESCRIPTION: Poorly molded upper case initials "I P" on base of stem.
NUMBER OF SPECIMENS: one
BORE DIAMETER: 6/64 (1)
TYPE OF BOWL: Type G bowl
COMPARISONS: Walker (1977: 607) lists three Bristol makers with the initials "I P" within this time period while Oswald (1975: 130-206) lists 39 makers with these initials. See also "I P" stem marks above.
CONTEXT: nondiagnostic (1)
MAKER: unknown
DATE: unknown

ILLUSTRATION: Figure 13 d

DESCRIPTION: Upper case initial "P" molded on left side of bowl, initial on right side may be missing.
NUMBER OF SPECIMENS: one
BORE DIAMETER: N.B. (1)
TYPE OF BOWL: unknown, heeled bowl
COMPARISONS: Walker (1977: 1234-1254) lists 23 Bristol makers with surnames beginning with "P"; Oswald (1975: 130-206) lists 94 makers with

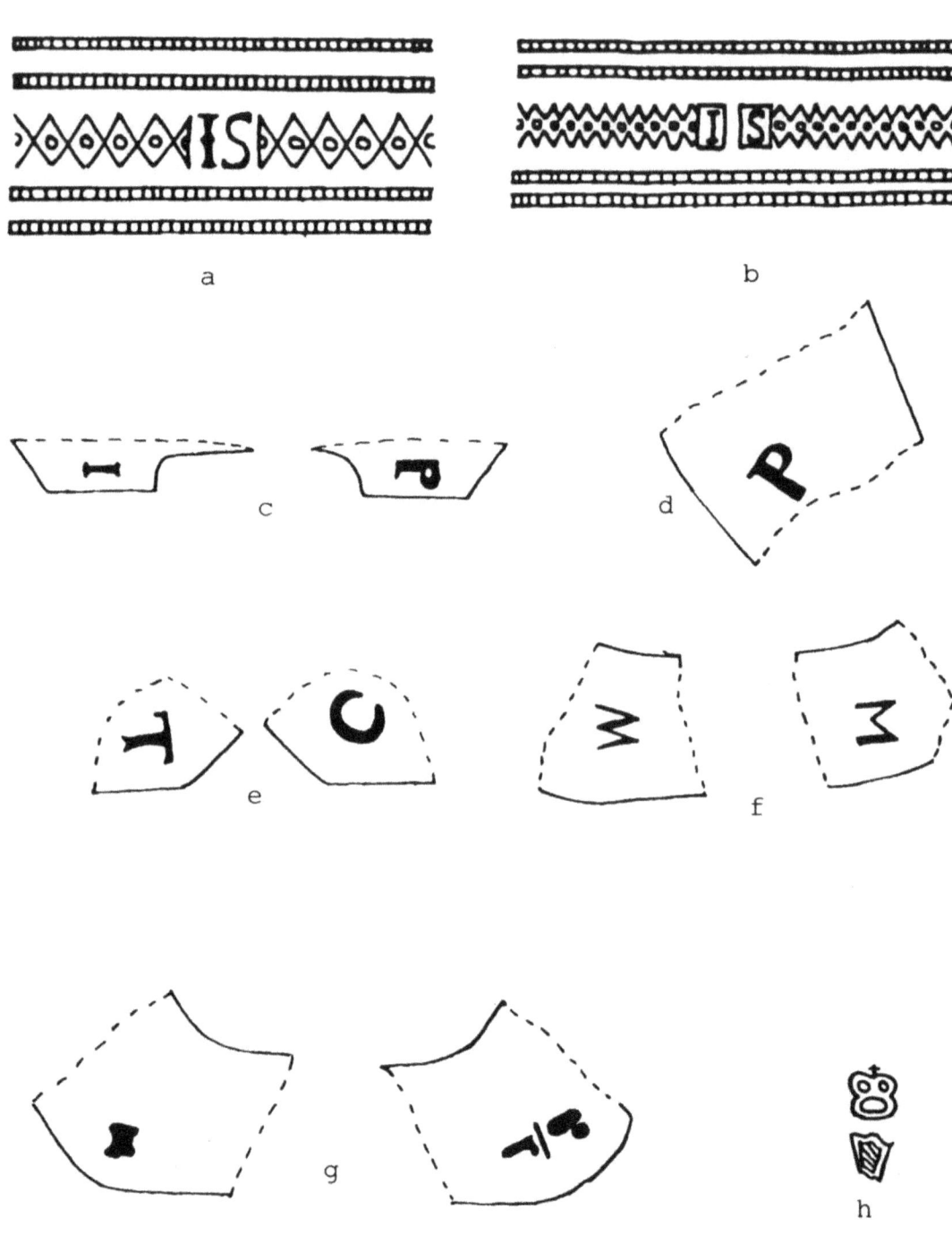

Figure 13: Stem marks: a-b. Mould imparted bowl base marks: c-h

surnames beginning with the letter "P" within this time period. If the "P" stands for a Christian name the list is potentially longer.
CONTEXT: nondiagnostic (1)
MAKER: unknown
DATE: unknown

ILLUSTRATION: Figure 13 e

DESCRIPTION: Upper case initials "T C" molded on sides of base of bowl.
NUMBER OF SPECIMENS: one
BORE DIAMETER: N.B. (1)
TYPE OF BOWL: Fragmentary Type J bowl.
COMPARISONS: Walker (1977: 1112) lists Thomas Cullimore as a Bristol maker while Oswald (1975: 130-206) lists 18 other makers with these initials within this time period. Given the bowl form, this may be a product of Holland.
CONTEXT: nondiagnostic (1)
MAKER: unknown, possibly Dutch
DATE: unknown

ILLUSTRATION: Figure 13 f

DESCRIPTION: Upper case initials "W M" on either side of the base of the bowl.
NUMBER OF SPECIMENS: four
BORE DIAMETER: 6/64 (1), 7/64 (3)
TYPE OF BOWL: unknown, heeled bowl
COMPARISONS: Atkinson and Oswald (1969: 186) illustrate a similar mark and attribute it to William Manby I.
CONTEXT: nondiagnostic (4)
MAKER: Possibly William Manby
DATE: circa 1680-1700 (Atkinson and Oswald 1969: 186)

ILLUSTRATION: Figure 13 g

DESCRIPTION: Poorly molded initial "I"(?) on right of bowl, two indiscernible initials on left of bowl.
NUMBER OF SPECIMENS: two
BORE DIAMETER: 6/64 (1), 7/64 (1)
TYPE OF BOWL: Funnel elbow type (see Type J above).
COMPARISONS: none
CONTEXT: Phase III (1), nondiagnostic (1)
MAKER: unknown, possibly Dutch
DATE: unknown

ILLUSTRATION: Figure 13 h

DESCRIPTION: Harp surmounted by a crown (coronet); mark appears on both sides of base of bowl.
NUMBER OF SPECIMENS: one
BORE DIAMETER: N.B. (1)
TYPE OF BOWL: unknown, heeled bowl

COMPARISONS: Oswald (1975: 74) illustrates this as a mark found in London.
CONTEXT: nondiagnostic (1)
MAKER: unknown
DATE: unknown

DECORATED PIPE BOWLS AND STEMS: RELIEF MOLDED BOWLS

ILLUSTRATION: 14 a

DESCRIPTION: Six raised dots around a central raised dots on either side of the bowl.
NUMBER OF SPECIMENS: three
BORE DIAMETER: N.B. (3)
TYPE OF BOWL: unknown
COMPARISONS: Termed the "Tudor Rose" decoration, Atkinson and Oswald (1972: 176-177) state the Tudor Rose motif began in the early 17th century and lasted for 100 years. Oswald (1970: 140) notes that it was a common Dutch design as well as an English one: NoelHume (1969: 26-28) illustrates a similar design on a bowl of the period 1640-1670, and Faulkner and Faulkner (1987: 169) recovered identical decorations at Pentagoet, in Maine.
CONTEXT: nondiagnostic (3)
MAKER: unknown
DATE: unknown

ILLUSTRATION: Figure 14 b

DESCRIPTION: Five raised dots around a central raised dot on either side of the bowl.
NUMBER OF SPECIMENS: three
BORE DIAMETER: N.B. (3)
TYPE OF BOWL: unknown
COMPARISONS: Termed the "Tudor Rose" decoration, Atkinson and Oswald (1972: 176-177) state the Tudor Rose motif began in the early 17th century and lasted for a 100 years: Oswald (1970: 140) notes that it was a common Dutch design as well as an English one: Noel Hume (1969: 26,28) illustrates a similar design on a bowl of the period 1640-1670, and Faulkner and Faulkner (1987: 169) recovered identical decorations at Pentagoet, in Maine.
CONTEXT: nondiagnostic (3)
MAKER: unknown
DATE: unknown

ILLUSTRATION: Figure 14 c

DESCRIPTION: A series of raised dots forming a triangle with a linear stem below, on either side of the bowl.
NUMBER OF SPECIMENS: eight
BORE DIAMETER: 7/64 (1), 8/64 (1), N.B. (6)
TYPE OF BOWL: One specimen on a Type G bowl, one on a Type B, 1 bowl.

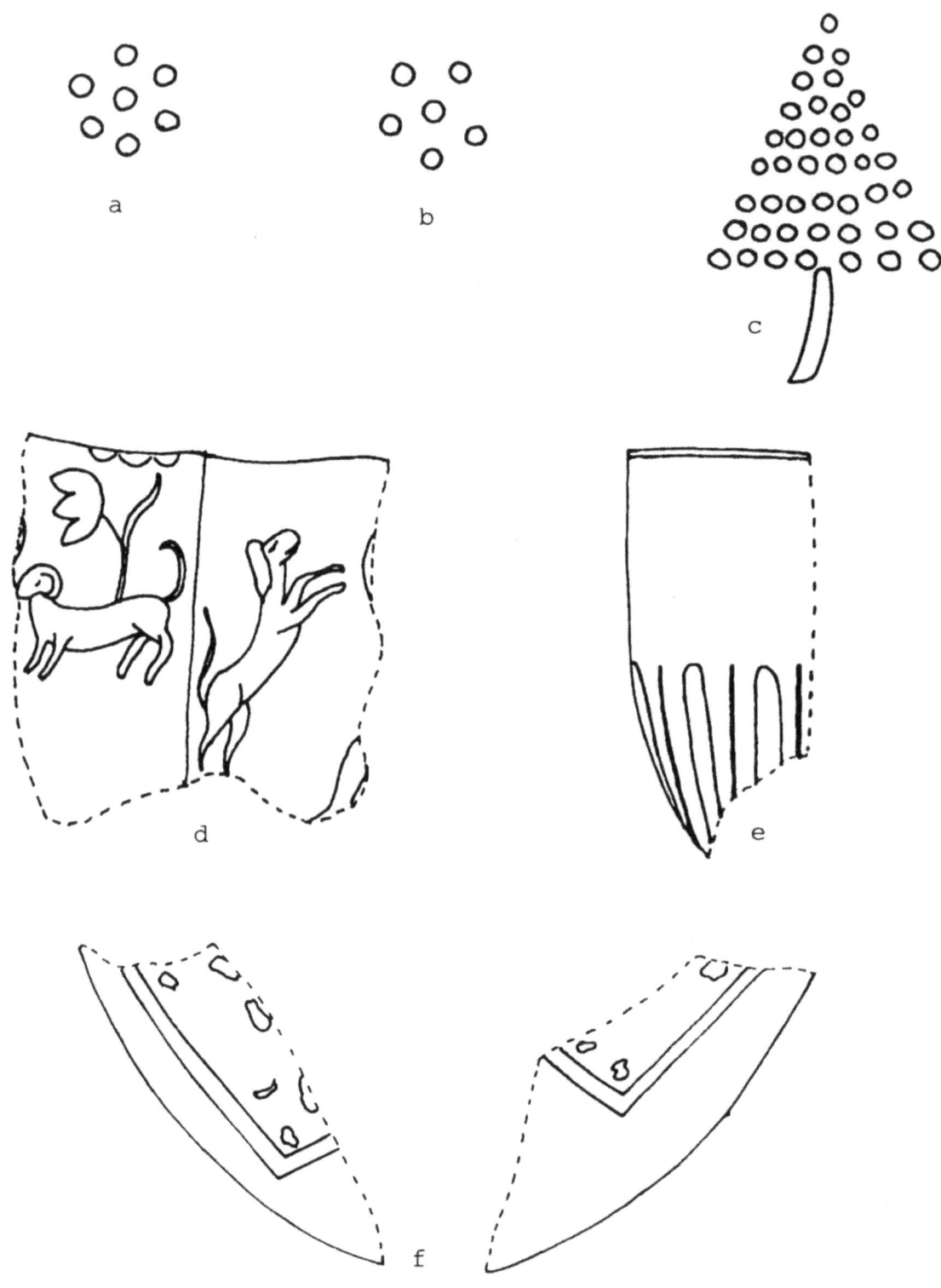

Figure 14: Decorated pipe bowls and stems: relief moulded bowls a-f

COMPARISONS: The so-called "Mulberry Tree" decoration, Oswald (1969: 136-137) illustrates a specimen with this motif dating to circa 1660-1690, similarly decorated bowls were recovered at Pentagoet (Faulkner and Faulkner 1987: 169).
CONTEXT: nondiagnostic (8)
MAKER: unknown
DATE: unknown

ILLUSTRATION: Figure 14 d

DESCRIPTION: Fragmentary bowl with two quadrupeds (dogs?) one standing on hind legs, one standing on four legs. The latter animal has floral element above it.
NUMBER OF SPECIMENS: one
BORE DIAMETER: N.B. (1)
TYPE OF BOWL: unknown
COMPARISONS: Oswald (1975: 116), illustrates a so-called "Crusader and Huntress" pipe; Camp (1975: 59) illustrates a similar decoration from Pemaquid, Maine, while Faulkner and Faulkner (1987: 169) illustrate the best parallel to this specimen.
CONTEXT: nondiagnostic (1)
MAKER: unknown, probably Dutch
DATE: 1670-1700 (Oswald 1975: 116)

ILLUSTRATION: Figure 14 e

DESCRIPTION: Fragmentary bowl with fluted molding extending slightly less than half way up the bowl.
NUMBER OF SPECIMENS: two
BORE DIAMETER: N.B. (2)
TYPE OF BOWL: unknown
COMPARISONS: unknown
CONTEXT: nondiagnostic (2)
MAKER: unknown
DATE: unknown

ILLUSTRATION: Figure 14 f

DESCRIPTION: Fragmentary bowl molded with two shields, poorly molded, decoration is barely discernible.
NUMBER OF SPECIMENS: one
BORE DIAMETER: N.B. (1)
TYPE OF BOWL: unknown
COMPARISONS: unknown
CONTEXT: nondiagnostic (1)
MAKER: unknown
DATE: unknown

DECORATED PIPE BOWLS AND STEMS: ROULETTED AND IMPRESSED STEM DECORATION

ILLUSTRATION: Figure 15 A

DESCRIPTION: Bristol-style rouletting composed of a diamond chain with dots in the center of the diamonds, flanked above and below with two lines of dentate milling.
NUMBER OF SPECIMENS: twenty-one
BORE DIAMETER: 6/64 (2), 7/64 (13), 8/64 (4), 9/64 (1), N.B. (1)
TYPE OF BOWL: unknown
COMPARISONS: Walker (1977: 1428-1495) illustrates a variety of similar rouletted decorations associated with Bristol makers. See also Faulkner and Faulkner (1987) for examples from Pentagoet, Maine.
CONTEXT: nondiagnostic (20)
MAKER: probably Bristol
DATE: unknown

ILLUSTRATION: Figure 15 B

DESCRIPTION: Bristol-style rouletting composed of a diamond chain flanked above and below with two lines of dentate milling.
NUMBER OF SPECIMENS: seven
BORE DIAMETER: 7/64 (6), 8/64 (1)
TYPE OF BOWL: unknown
COMPARISONS: Walker (1977: 1428-1495) illustrates a variety of similar rouletted decorations associated with Bristol makers. See also Faulkner and Faulkner (1987) for examples from Pentagoet, Maine.
CONTEXT: nondiagnostic (6)
MAKER: probably Bristol
DATE: unknown

ILLUSTRATION: Figure 15 c

DESCRIPTION: Bristol-style rouletting with a small diamond chain flanked above and below with two lines of dentate milling.
NUMBER OF SPECIMENS: 12
BORE DIAMETER: 6/64 (1), 7/64 (7), 8/64 (4)
TYPE OF BOWL: unknown
COMPARISONS: Walker (1977: 1428-1495) illustrates a variety of similar rouletted decorations associated with Bristol makers. See also Faulkner and Faulkner (1987) for examples from Pentagoet, Maine.
CONTEXT: nondiagnostic (12)
MAKER: probably Bristol
DATE: unknown

Figure 15: Decorated pipes: rouletted and impressed stem decoration a-k

ILLUSTRATION: Figure 15 d

DESCRIPTION: Bristol-style rouletting with a diamond chain with small diamonds in their centers flanked above and below with two lines of dentate milling.
NUMBER OF SPECIMENS: two
BORE DIAMETER: 7/64 (2)
TYPE OF BOWL: unknown
COMPARISONS: Walker (1977: 1428-1495) illustrates a variety of similar rouletted decorations associated with Bristol makers. See also Faulkner and Faulkner (1987) for examples from Pentagoet, Maine.
CONTEXT: nondiagnostic (2)
MAKER: probably Bristol
DATE: unknown

ILLUSTRATION: Figure 15 e

DESCRIPTION: Bristol-like style rouletting with two lines of dentate milling, flanked above and below with a line of small diamond chains with dots in the centers of the diamonds.
NUMBER OF SPECIMENS: sixteen
BORE DIAMETER: 6/64 (10), 7/64 (4), 8/64 (1), N.B. (1)
TYPE OF BOWL: unknown
COMPARISONS: Walker (1977: 1428-1495) illustrates a variety of similar rouletted decorations associated with Bristol makers. See also Faulkner and Faulkner (1987) for examples from Pentagoet, Maine.
CONTEXT: nondiagnostic (16)
MAKER: unknown, possibly Bristol
DATE: unknown

ILLUSTRATION: Figure 15 f

DESCRIPTION: Dutch-style rouletting with six lines of single-line milling, flanked above and below with oval linked chains.
NUMBER OF SPECIMENS: three
BORE DIAMETER: 6/64 (2), 7/64 (1)
TYPE OF BOWL: unknown
COMPARISONS: Faulkner and Faulkner (1987) illustrate a variety of similar rouletted decorations recovered in the excavations at Pentagoet, Maine.
CONTEXT: nondiagnostic (3)
MAKER: unknown, possibly Dutch
DATE: unknown

ILLUSTRATION: Figure 15 g

DESCRIPTION: Dutch-style rouletting with 10 lines of scalloped, single-line milling flanked above and below with oval linked chains.
NUMBER OF SPECIMENS: two
BORE DIAMETER: 6/64 (2)
TYPE OF BOWL: unknown
COMPARISONS: Faulkner and Faulkner (1987) illustrate a variety of similar rouletted decorations recovered in the excavations at Pentagoet, Maine.
CONTEXT: Phase III (1), nondiagnostic (1)
MAKER: unknown, probably Dutch
DATE: unknown

ILLUSTRATION: Figure 15 h

DESCRIPTION: Dutch-style rouletting composed of small unlinked diamond milling, an oval linked chain, diamond within diamond milling (imperfectly applied), a second oval linked chain, and two lines of dentate milling.
NUMBER OF SPECIMENS: five
BORE DIAMETER: 7/64 (2), 8/64 (2), N.B. (1)
TYPE OF BOWL: unknown
COMPARISONS: Faulkner and Faulkner (1987) illustrate a variety of similar rouletted decorations recovered in the excavations at Pentagoet, Maine.
CONTEXT: nondiagnostic (5)
MAKER: unknown, possibly Dutch
DATE: unknown

ILLUSTRATION: Figure 15 i

DESCRIPTION: Dutch-style rouletting composed of a central area of small diamond and triangle milling, flanked above and below with three lines of evenly spaced scalloped single-line milling, a gap, and one additional line of scalloped single-line milling.
NUMBER OF SPECIMENS: two
BORE DIAMETER: 6/64 (1), 7/64 (1)
TYPE OF BOWL: unknown
COMPARISONS: Faulkner and Faulkner (1987) illustrate a variety of similar rouletted decorations recovered in the excavations at Pentagoet, Maine.
CONTEXT: nondiagnostic (2)
MAKER: unknown, possibly Dutch
DATE: unknown

ILLUSTRATION: Figure 15 j

DESCRIPTION: Dutch-style rouletting composed of an area of small diamond and triangle milling with dots within the diamonds, three lines of scalloped single line milling, an area of small diamond and triangle milling with dots within the diamonds, and a line of scalloped single-line milling.
NUMBER OF SPECIMENS: three
BORE DIAMETER: 7/64 (2), N.B. (1)
TYPE OF BOWL: unknown
COMPARISONS: Faulkner and Faulkner (1987) illustrate a variety of similar rouletted decorations recovered in the excavations at Pentagoet, Maine.
CONTEXT: nondiagnostic (3)
MAKER: unknown, possibly Dutch
DATE: unknown

Figure 16: Decorated pipes: rouletted and impressed stem decoration a-f; mould decorated stems g-h

ILLUSTRATION: Figure 15 k

DESCRIPTION: Dutch-style rouletted decoration composed of three lines of truncated "V" chain milling, a line of "V" chain milling, and a single line of scalloped single-line milling.
NUMBER OF SPECIMENS: three
BORE DIAMETER: 6/64 (2), 7/64 (1)
TYPE OF BOWL: unknown
COMPARISONS: Duco (1980: 246) illustrates an identical decoration while Faulkner and Faulkner (1987) illustrate similar decorations on specimens recovered in the excavations at Pentagoet, Maine.
CONTEXT: nondiagnostic (3)
MAKER: unknown, possibly Dutch
DATE: unknown

ILLUSTRATION: Figure 16 a

DESCRIPTION: Impressed decoration composed of a *fleur-de-lis* within a diamond, repeated.
NUMBER OF SPECIMENS: 46
BORE DIAMETER: 6/64 (14), 7/64 (25), 8/64 (5), N.B. (2)
TYPE OF BOWL: unknown
COMPARISONS: McCashion (1979) and Faulkner and Faulkner (1987) discuss similar decoration.
CONTEXT: Phase III (3), nondiagnostic (43)
MAKER: unknown, possibly Dutch
DATE: unknown

ILLUSTRATION: Figure 16 b

DESCRIPTION: Impresseded decoration composed of four *fleurs-de-lis* within conjoined diamonds, flanked above and below with a single line of dentate milling.
NUMBER OF SPECIMENS: 18
BORE DIAMETER: 6/64 (4), 7/64 (11), 8/64 (2), N.B. (1)
TYPE OF BOWL: unknown
COMPARISONS: McCashion (1979) and Faulkner and Faulkner (1987) discuss similar decoration.
CONTEXT: Phase I (1), nondiagnostic (17)
MAKER: unknown, possibly Dutch
DATE: unknown

ILLUSTRATION: Figure 16 c

DESCRIPTION: Impressed decoration composed of four *fleurs-de-lis* within conjoined diamonds.
NUMBER OF SPECIMENS: six
BORE DIAMETER: 7/64 (1), 8/64 (3), N.B. (2)
TYPE OF BOWL: unknown
COMPARISONS: McCashion (1979) and Faulkner and Faulkner (1987) discuss similar decoration.
CONTEXT: nondiagnostic (6)
MAKER: unknown, possibly Dutch
DATE: unknown.

ILLUSTRATION: Figure 16 d

DESCRIPTION: Rouletted decoration composed of a repeating motif of *fleurs-de-lis* within dot-milled frames, above a line of diagonal reversed "S" curves and a line of dot milling.
NUMBER OF SPECIMENS: two
BORE DIAMETER: 7/64 (1), 8/64 (1)
TYPE OF BOWL: unknown
COMPARISONS: none
CONTEXT: nondiagnostic (2)
MAKER: unknown, possibly Dutch
DATE: unknown

ILLUSTRATION: Figure 16 e

DESCRIPTION: Impressed decoration composed of a repeating motif of a circle with seven wedge-shaped slices, with dots in the center of each wedge; wedges do not coincide in the center, creating a seven-armed central element.
NUMBER OF SPECIMENS: one
BORE DIAMETER: 7/64 (1)
TYPE OF BOWL: unknown
COMPARISONS: none
CONTEXT: nondiagnostic (1)
MAKER: unknown
DATE: unknown

ILLUSTRATION: Figure 16 f

DESCRIPTION: Rouletted decoration consisting of a single line of dentate milling applied at the point where the bowl rises from the pipe stem.
NUMBER OF SPECIMENS: two
BORE DIAMETER: 8/64 (2)
TYPE OF BOWL: Fragmentary Type J bowls.
COMPARISONS: none
CONTEXT: nondiagnostic (2)
MAKER: unknown, possibly Dutch
DATE: unknown

ILLUSTRATION: not illustrated

DESCRIPTION: Rouletted decoration composed of lines of dentate milling, specimens broken at milled lines, decoration probably part of a larger motif or makers' mark.
NUMBER OF SPECIMENS: 61
BORE DIAMETER: 6/64 (7), 7/64 (24), 7/64 (23), N.B. (7)
TYPE OF BOWL: unknown
COMPARISONS: Walker (1977: 1428-1495) illustrates a variety of rouletted decorations associated with Bristol makers. See also Faulkner and Faulkner (1987) for examples from Pentagoet.
CONTEXT: Phase III (4), nondiagnostic (57)
MAKER: unknown
DATE: unknown

DECORATED PIPE BOWLS AND STEMS: MOLD DECORATED STEMS

ILLUSTRATION: Figure 16 g
DESCRIPTION: "Pinched" stem with opposing, offset compressions of the stem.
NUMBER OF SPECIMENS: one
BORE DIAMETER: 7/64 (1)
TYPE OF BOWL: unknown
COMPARISONS: Similar specimens have been recovered from Fort Orange in New York (Huey, Personal Communication 1977).
CONTEXT: nondiagnostic (1)
MAKER: unknown, possibly Dutch
DATE: unknown

ILLUSTRATION: Figure 16 h

DESCRIPTION: Molded decoration composed of an elaborate foliate scrolling with *fleurs-de-lis* at the terminal ends of the foliate scrolls.
NUMBER OF SPECIMENS: 16
BORE DIAMETER: 7/64 (10), 8/64 (6)
TYPE OF BOWL: unknown
COMPARISONS: McCashion (1979) illustrates similar decorations associated with Dutch trade pipes from New York, as do Bradley and De Angelo (1981). See also Faulkner and Faulkner (1987) for similar examples from Pentagoet.
CONTEXT: Phase II (1), nondiagnostic (15)
MAKER: unknown, probably Dutch
DATE: unknown

PIPE BOWLS: DISCUSSION

The white clay tobacco pipes recovered at the St. John's Site fall into two very broad categories: heeled bowls and heel-less bowls. Over half of the specimens are the heel-less or "export" varieties (Type J and Type M above). Given the dates for the Type M pipes, the predominance of the "export" style of pipes may relate to the later use of St. John's as an ordinary. Activities associated with public inns would likely generate a greater deposition of tobacco pipes. This interpretation is also borne out by the makers' marks, which date primarily to the inn period (see below). The heeled pipes represent a wider range of varieties and time periods. It would appear that these include the earliest pipes used at St. John's, but the heeled varieties continue in use throughout the occupation of the site.

The predominate country of origin for the pipe bowls from the St. John's Site is Great Britain. Even if all the Type C pipes within the sample are of Dutch manufacture, when combined with the A, 2 and J Types, they constitute less than 10% of all recovered specimens. The Type M pipes alone represent nearly half of the sample. This is indicative of the strong hold that England maintained on her colonies in reference to matters of trade as the 17th century progressed.

Approximately one-fifth of the recovered pipe bowls are from contexts dated by other artifact classes. Bowls of the A Type occur in Phase I contexts, Types A and C bowls are in Phase III contexts. The greater range and number of types in the Phase III features is probably a result of redeposition rather than curation of earlier pipe forms. Only three specimens within the sample bear makers' marks, and only two are decorated. This indicates that marked or decorated tobacco pipes constitute a very small portion of all recovered pipes, and therefore probably represented an extreme minority among all tobacco pipes in use at the St. John's Site.

PIPE MARKS: DISCUSSION

Stem marks predominate in the sample of white clay tobacco pipe fragments recovered in the excavations at the St. John's Site. Second in popularity to stem marks are bowl marks, while heel marks and base marks represent only a minority of the total (Table 1). Forty-six different varieties of marks occur in the sample, but these constitute the marks of only 34 makers (Table 2). All of the makers with multiple varieties of marks among the recovered specimens are Bristol makers. The pipe maker whose marks predominate within the sample is Llewelin Evans of Bristol. Over half of the recovered marks are his products. Since Evans often marked his pipes on both the stem and bowl, his products within the sample comprise a minimum of 49 pipes. Even with this adjusted figure, Llewelin Evans' products constitute over a third of all recovered specimens. Second in importance to Llewelin Evans is William Evans (I and/or II) with 22 examples. Since William Evans appears to have double-marked some of his pipes, his production represents a minimum of 19 pipes (nearly 15% of the sample). Other Bristol makers are well represented among the recovered fragments. Of all the marked pipe fragments for which a country of origin can be suggested, England predominates with 86.3% of the sample, while Holland (the only other country of origin identified) constitutes only 13.7%. Within the sample from England, Bristol makers make up over 90% of the recovered specimens.

Table 1. Location of marks on specimens.

Location	Number	Percent
Stem	86	50.6
Bowl	55	32.5
Heel	19	11.1
Base	10	5.8
TOTALS	170	100.0

Table 2: White Clay Tobacco Pipe Makers' Marks.

Mark	Number	Maker	Origin	Date
HEEL MARKS (11)				
crowned "A"	1	unknown	Holland?	unknown
"E B"	2	Edward Bird	Holland	1635-1655
"N B"	2	unknown	Holland?	unknown
Crowned "I P"	1	unknown	Holland?	unknown
"L S"	1	Lawrence Starkey	England, Chester (?)	circa 1670
human figural	1	unknown	Holland?	Phase II (c. 1660-1685)
"I D"	1	John Draper	Holland	1630-1645
Tulip (?)	1	unknown	Holland?	unknown
rose mark	4	unknown	Holland?	unknown
"(?) T P"	2	unknown	unknown	unknown
"I R"	2	unknown	unknown	1600-1649 (Phase (II)
	TOTAL 18			
BOWL MARKS (16)				
"E R"	1	Edward Reed	England, Bristol	1706-1723
"F (?)"	1	Francis Russell	England, Bristol	circa 1698
"I T"	1	unknown	unknown	unknown
"(?) E"	1	unknown	unknown	unknown
"RT" variety 1	3	Robert Tippet II	England, Bristol	1678-1713
"RT" variety 2	3	Robert Tippet II	England, Bristol	1678-1713
"R (?) P"	1	unknown	unknown	unknown
"T C"	1	unknown	unknown	unknown
"(?) N"	1	unknown	unknown	unknown
"M"	1	unknown	unknown	unknown
"WE" variety 1	1	William Evans (I or II)	England, Bristol	1667,1682, 1697
"WE" variety 2	2	William Evans (I or II)	England, Bristol	1667-1682, 1697
"WE" variety 3	2	William Evans (I or II)	England, Bristol	1667-1682, 1697
"WE" variety 4	1	William Evans (I or II)	England, Bristol	1667-1682, 1697
"LE" variety 1	10	Llewelin Evans	England, Bristol	1661-1688
"LE" variety 2	29	Llewelin Evans	England, Bristol	1661-1688
	TOTAL 59			
STEM MARKS (13)				
"LE"(variety 1)	3	Llewelin Evans	England, Bristol	1661-1688
"LE"(variety 2)	39	Llewelin Evans	England, Bristol	1661-1688
"LE"(variety 3)	7	Llewelin Evans	England, Bristol	1661-1688
"WE"	9	William Evans (I or II)	England, Bristol	1667-1682, 1697
"WILEVANS"	10	William Evans (I or II)	England, Bristol	1667-1682, 1697
"AGE"	1	William Ager	England, N'amptonshire(?)	1706-1713
"AA"	1	unknown	England, Bristol	unknown
"CHRISATHARTON"	3	Chris Atherton	England, Liverpool(?)	unknown
"IF"	3	James Fox	England, Bristol	1651-1669
"IP"	2	unknown	England, Bristol	unknown
"RS"	1	Robert Sheppard	England, Bristol	circa 1690
"IS"(variety 1)	3	John Sinderling	England, Bristol	1666-1669
"IS"(variety 2)	4	John Sinderling	England, Bristol	1666-1669
	TOTAL 86			
MOLDED BASE MARKS (6)				
"IP"	1	unknown	unknown	unknown
"P"	1	unknown	unknown	unknown
"TC"	1	unknown	Holland ?	unknown
"WM"	4	William Manby I	England, London	1680-1700
"I(?)"	2	unknown	Holland ?	Phase II (c. 1660-1685)
crowned harp	1	unknown	unknown	unknown
	TOTAL 10			

With the overwhelming number of specimens made by Llewelin Evans and William Evans (I and/or II) of Bristol, pipes from the period of the 1660s through 1690s dominate the collection. However, marks within the sample range from the founding of the colony (John Draper and Edward Bird) to the end of the occupation at St. John's (Edward Reed, William Ager, and Robert Tippet II). The predominance of the 1660s through 1690s marks may be indicative of the period at St. John's when it served as an ordinary. One would assume that there would be a greater use and deposition of pipes associated with such a function than when the building was acting as a private residence. The specimens with identifiable Dutch marks appear to date mostly to the earlier periods of the occupation of the site. This may relate to the tightening of the grasp of the British mercentile system, choking off competition as the 17th century progressed. As English control of the supply of finished goods increased, Bristol came to dominate the North American trade in clay tobacco pipes.

Only four of the recovered pipe makers' marks within the sample are from contexts dated by other means. The "I R" and human figural heel marks occur in Phase II contexts while the "I ?" base mark, the William Evans (I or II) bowl mark, and the Llewellin Evans stem mark are represented in Phase III features. The dates of the varieties of Evans marks are well documented, but the human figural and "I R" heel marks and the "I ?" base mark do not appear to have been previously dated by context. Hence their occurrence in datable features at the St. John's Site provides new information concerning their use and chronology.

DECORATED PIPES: DISCUSSION

Decorated white clay tobacco pipes constitute an extreme minority among the recovered specimens from the St. John's Site. Only 18 decorated pipe bowls representing five types of decoration are present. The bulk of these are Tudor Rose and Mulberry Tree decorations. Within the sample of decorated pipe stems, Dutch style rouletting predominates. Nearly 100 specimens bear this style of decoration with variations on the *fleur-de-lis* being the most popular. This prevalence is most likely a result of the Dutch tendency for more elaborate, overall Baroque style decoration (cf. Duco 1981). Approximately half as many specimens have Bristol style rouletting. Rarest of all among the decorated pipe stems recovered from the St. John's Site are mold decorated stems. Occurring as only one motif (foliate scrolling with *fleur-de-lis*) this type of decoration is represented by only 16 specimens. Grouped here for analytical purposes is the one example of a "pinched" stem, which is not truly mold decorated but rather manually modified after molding.

Decorated pipe fragments occur in very few features datable by other means. Probably of most significance is the occurrence of the four-in-one *fleur-de-lis* stamp in a Phase I feature, indicating the use of this decoration in the earliest period of occupation.

THE ST. JOHN'S PIPE ASSEMBLAGE: CONCLUSIONS

The sample of white clay tobacco pipes recovered in the excavations at the St. John's Site provides meaningful insights into intra and inter-site chronology, site function, and trade networks. In general, the dates provided by the pipes correlate well with other independent dating tools. The extreme prevalence of the Llewellin Evans marks is in full agreement with the later tavern/ordinary functions that St. John's provided. A greater deposition of this class of artifact fits well chronologically and functionally with the tavern usage.

The prevalence of the products of Bristol pipe makers within the sample demonstrates the overwhelming dominance of the white clay tobacco pipe trade exercised by the Bristol makers in the latter part of the 17th century. Earlier trade with London and other English pipe making centers and Dutch merchants is evidenced by the attributable pipes and makers' marks in early contexts at the site. However, the relative paucity of such material in the later contexts correlates with the dominance of Bristol and the better developed British mercantile system of the later period which produced the British hegemony in intercontinental trade to the North American colonies. This is mirrored in other Dutch goods which generally occur earlier rather than later on sites in the Colonial Tidewater.

REFERENCES

Alexander, L.T. (1979) Clay pipes from Buck Site in Maryland. *Archaeology of the Clay Tobacco Pipe II: The United States of America*. Edited by P.J. Davey, British Archaeological Reports International Series 60: 37-61.

Atkinson, D. and Oswald, A. (1972). A brief guide to the identification of Dutch clay tobacco pipes found in England, *Post-Medieval Archaeology*, 6: 175-182.

Atkinson, D. and Oswald, A. (1969) London Clay Tobacco Pipes. *Journal of the British Archaeological Association*, 3rd Series, 32: 171-227.

Bradley, J.W. and De Angelo, G. (1981). European clay pipe marks from 17th century Onondaga Iroquois sites Archaeology of Eastern North America, 9: 109-129.

Camp, H.B. (1975). *Archaeological excavations at Pemaquid, Maine*. Maine State Museum, Augusta.

Davey, P. (1981). Clay pipes, in excavations in South Castle Street, Liverpool 1976 and 1977, *Journal of the*

Merseyside Archaeological Society 4: 122-127.

Duco, D.H. (1981). The clay tobacco pipe in 17th-century Netherlands. *Archaeology of the Clay Tobacco Pipe V: Europe 1.* Edited by P.J. Davey, British Archaeological Reports International Series 106(ii).

Faulkner, A. and Faulkner, G. (1987). *The French at Pentagoet.* Maine Historical Preservation Commission, Augusta, Maine.

Gibson, S.G. (1980). Burr's Hill, A 17th century Wampanoag burial ground in Warren, Rhode Island. *Studies in Anthropology and Material Culture* 2, Haffenreffer Museum of Anthropology, Brown University, Providence.

Henry, S. (1979). Terra-cotta tobacco pipes in 17th century Maryland and Virginia: a preliminary study. *Historical Archaeology* 13: 14-32.

Huey, P. (1978). Personal communication, letter on file Historic St. Mary's City.

Keeler, R.W. (1978). The homelot on the 17th century Chesapeake tidewater frontier. Unpublished Ph.D. dissertation, Department of Anthropology, University of Oregon, University Microfilms, Ann Arbor.

King, J.A. (1988). A comparative midden analysis of a household and an inn in St. Mary's City, Maryland. *Historical Archaeology* 22(2): 17-39.

Lawrence, S. (1979). York pipes and their makers. *Archaeology of the clay tobacco pipe 1: Britain, the Midlands and Eastern England.* Edited by P.J. Davey, British Archaeological Reports British Series 63: 67-84.

Mitchell, V. (1983). The history of Nominy Plantation with an emphasis on the clay tobacco pipes. *Clay Tobacco Pipe Studies II.* Sudbury, Editor pp.1-38. Ponca City, OK.

McCashion, J.H. (1979) A preliminary chronology and discussion of seventeenth and early eighteenth century clay pipes from New York State Sites. *Archaeology of the Clay Tobacco Pipe II: The United States of America.* Edited by P.J. Davey, British Archaeological Reports International Series 60: 63-150.

Miller, H.M. (1983). The search for the "Citty of Saint Maries". *St. Mary's City Archaeology Series*, 1.

Muldoon, S. (1979). Marked clay pipes from Coventry. *Archaeology of the Clay Tobacco Pipe I: Britain: the Midlands and Eastern England.* Edited by P.J. Davey, British Archaeological Reports International Series 63: 255-278.

Noel Hume, I. (1970) *Guide to Artefacts in Colonial America.* Knopf, New York.

Noel Hume, I. (1966). Excavations at Clay Bank in Gloucester County Virginia. *Contributions from the Museum of History and Technology*, Paper 52. Smithsonian Institution, Washington, D.C.

Noel Hume, I. (1963). *Here lies Virginia.* Knopf, New York.

Oswald, A. (1975). *Clay Pipes for the Archaeologist.* British Archaeological Reports 14. Oxford, England.

Oswald, A. (1970). The clay tobacco pipe: its place in English ceramics. *Transactions of the English Ceramic Circle* 7: 55-62.

Rutter, J. and Davey, P. (1980). Clay pipes from Chester. *Archaeology of the Clay Tobacco Pipe III: Britain: the North and West.* Edited by P.J. Davey, British Archaeological Reports International Series 78: 41-272.

Stone, G.W. (1977) Dating seventeenth-century white clay tobacco pipe stem groups: a proposal to the seventeenth-century study group. Ms. on file, Historic St. Mary's City.

Stone, G.W. (1974). St. John's archaeological questions and answers. *Maryland Historical Magazine*, 69(2): 146-168.

Walker, I.C. (1977) *Clay Tobacco Pipes with Particular Reference to the Bristol Industry.* (4 vols) Parks Canada, Ottawa.

Walker, I.C. (1971). *The Bristol Clay Tobacco-Pipe Industry.* City Museum, Bristol.

Watkins, G. (1979). Hull Pipes: a typology. *Archaeology of the Clay Tobacco Pipe I: Britain, the Midlands and Eastern England.* Edited by P.J. Davey, British Archaeological Reports British Series 63: 85-122.

Tobacco Pipes from Pope's Fort, St. Mary's City, Maryland: an English Civil War Site on the American Frontier.

Henry M. Miller

INTRODUCTION

Archaeological research at St. Mary's City, the site where the Colony of Maryland was founded in 1634, has revealed the remains of a fortification dating to the year 1645 (Figure 1). Built following an attack on the city by Parliamentary forces, this is the first evidence of the impact of the English Civil War found in America. In this paper, the mold made tobacco pipes from the Fort are described. Dating to 1645-*circa* 1655, this site provides precise temporal control on pipes of this period and helps illuminate the trade relationships which prevailed in the American colonies during the Civil Wars.

SITE HISTORY

In the year 1645, the English Civil Wars reached the shores of America. The newly established capital of the Colony of Maryland, St. Mary's City, founded in 1634, was attacked by the ship *Reformation*, under command of Captain Richard Ingle (Shomette 1985:20-34). Working under privateer papers issued by Parliament, Ingle justified the attack as due to the Royalist leanings of the colony's Proprietor, Cecil Calvert, the Lord Baltimore, and many of the settlers. Personal animosity against the colony's leaders also played a role in Ingle's action. The assault was completely unexpected and there was no time for defensive action by Governor Leonard Calvert. He fled to Virginia for protection and the other leaders were arrested. Ingle and his men pillaged the town, focusing much of their effort on the property of the Catholic settlers. Structures were burned, homes looted, and livestock rustled. Catholic priests in the colony were either arrested or forced to flee. The colonists later described this traumatic period as "The Plundering Time". Ingle departed in May, taking several prominent colonists and two Catholic priests with him to England in chains, and apparently leaving Protestant settler Nathaniel Pope in charge of a garrison. Pope nominally controlled Maryland until January of 1647, when Governor Leonard Calvert returned with troops and recaptured the capital. Calvert died six months later and uncertainty again prevailed in the colony. Not until 1650, with the appointment of William Stone as governor, did conditions seem to finally stabilize. However, the 1650s proved equally unsettled, with Lord Baltimore again losing control of the colony to Puritans in 1655. Only with the restoration of Charles II to the throne did Maryland again experience stability and sustained growth (Dozer 1967).

Pope's Fort was a central element in this drama. Probably built by Ingle's men before their departure, it enclosed the home of Governor Leonard Calvert, the largest structure in the colony. It was garrisoned by the servants of Nathaniel Pope, along with an undetermined number of Protestant sympathizers (Miller 1986:47-48). Archaeological evidence indicates that the fort was defended with artillery and the garrison wore armor and possessed advanced, flint ignition firearms. It remained under the control of Pope until early 1647, when the fortification was captured by troops led by Leonard Calvert. Following this event, the historical record on Pope's Fort falls silent. Archaeological evidence suggests that it did not stand for long afterward and was almost certainly demolished by 1650. Filling of the fort ditch took a few additional years at most. Available evidence therefore indicates that the fort and artifacts associated with it date to the period 1645-*circa* 1655, with many of the artifacts probably deposited during the first half of this span.

ARCHAEOLOGY OF POPE'S FORT

Discovery of the fort came about by accident. While archaeologists were conducting the first season of excavations in the former town center of St. Mary's, the septic tank for a nearby *circa* 1840 house failed and its replacement uncovered an impressive group of early artifacts and remnants of a large feature. Study of the surviving stratigraphic sections permitted the identification of this feature as a fort ditch. Preliminary artifact analysis indicated that it was apparently of pre-1650 date. Further excavations permitted the overall shape and construction methods of the fort to be determined (Miller 1986).

Pope's Fort consisted of a wooden palisade line, an external ditch or moat, and three bastions (Figure 2). The two smaller bastions faced west toward the river while the larger one faced inland. Further excavations also found indications of an extension of the fort wall and ditch on the landward side (not shown in Figure 2), but the date and purpose of this extension is uncertain. It may date to the 1647-1648 period when there was a need for more room to house the troops brought by Leonard Calvert.

Units have been excavated from various sections of the fort ditch to obtain a representative sample of its contents. To date, approximately 15% of the ditch has been excavated and the remainder is being preserved for future research. Most of the artifacts reported here are from stratified contexts. However, installation of the original septic tank had disturbed a section of the fort ditch. Some pipes from this disturbed context have been

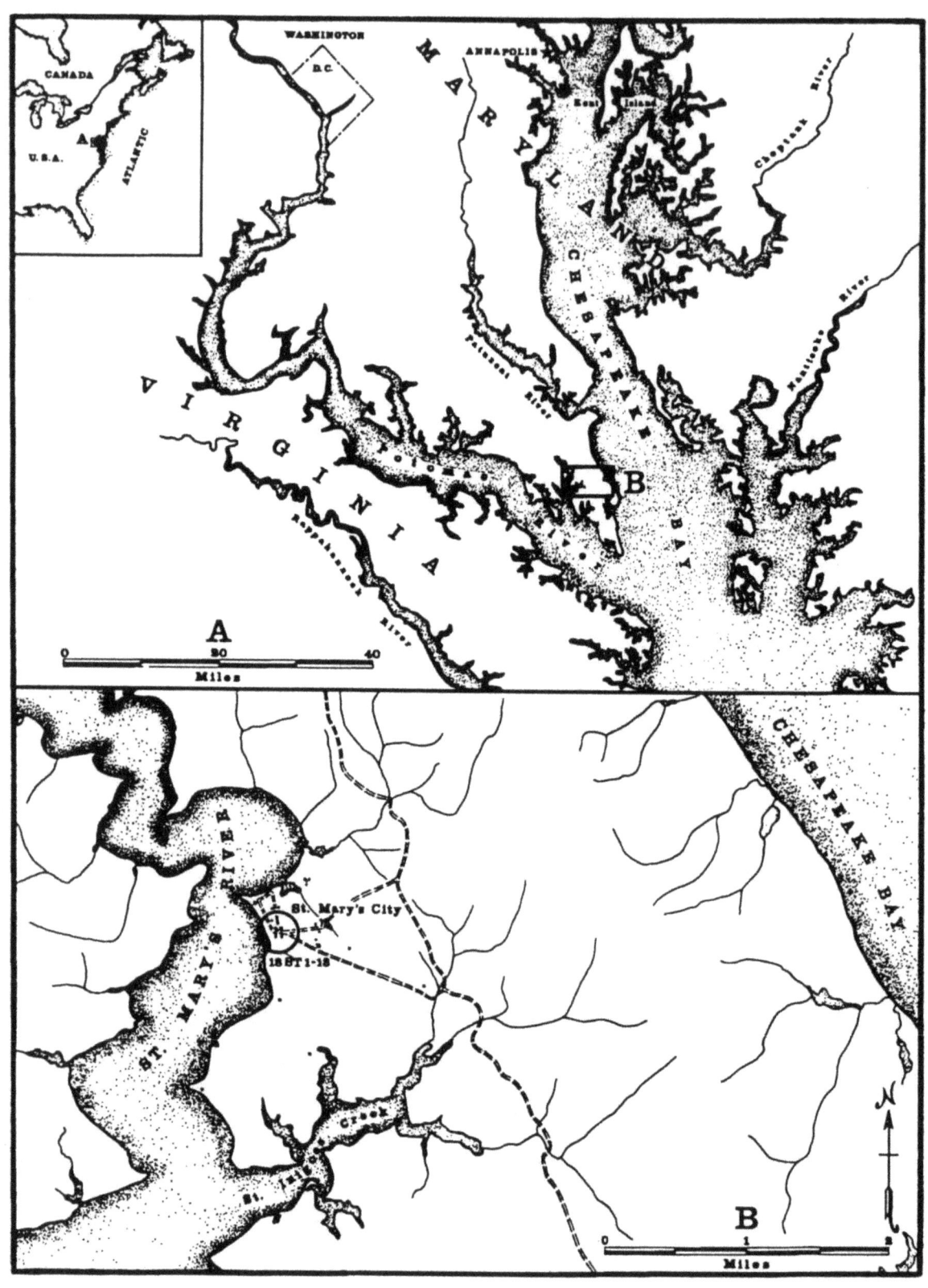

Figure 1: Location of St. Mary's City and Pope's Fort (18ST1-13).

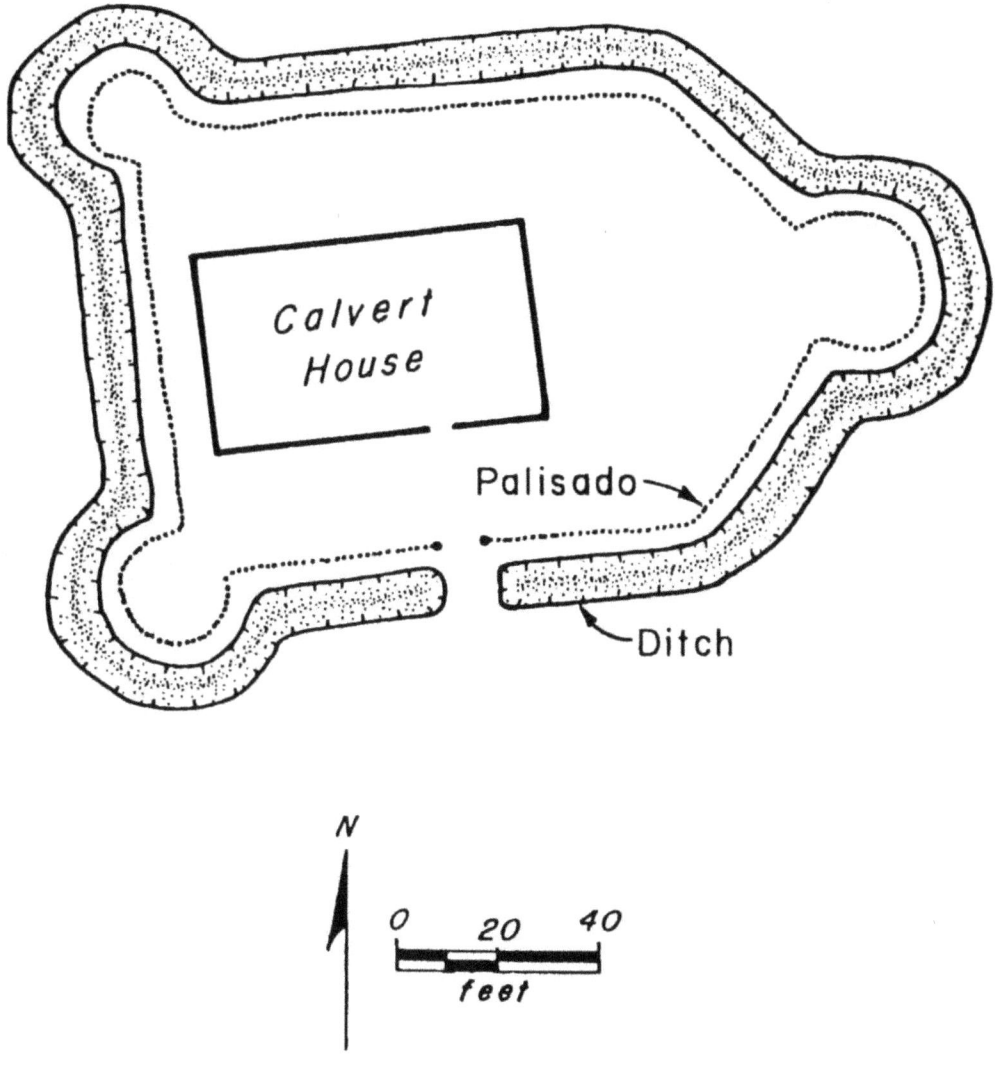

Figure 2: Plan view of Pope's Fort, built in 1645.

included in this analysis, but only where less complete examples of the same type of pipe were recovered from sealed proveniences. A number of pipes were probably associated with the fort occupation but have not been included because of their recovery from mixed contexts.

ANALYSIS OF THE PIPES

The excavations recovered a large quantity of tobacco pipe fragments, representing a minimum of 181 bowls. Both mold-made and handmade pipes are in the collection, but this study focuses only upon the mold-made specimens. Handmade pipes make up 53% of the identified bowls, but since they are not found on European sites, they will be only briefly discussed in this paper. Mold-made pipes occur in two varieties. The first is the white clay pipe of English or Dutch origin, of which there are 54 identified bowls. The second type, known as terra cotta, was produced from non-white clays, and tend to be brown or orange in color. There are 31 of these bowls in the collection. Although no production site for the molded terra cotta pipes is known, most were probably of Colonial manufacture in the Maryland - Virginia area. Types are defined primarily on the basis of bowl form, although maker's marks and decorative devices are also used.

WHITE CLAY PIPES WITH MAKER'S MARKS

In the Pope's Fort collection, there are three maker's marks which occur in six styles on the pipes. All marks occur on heels and the initials are "EB", "MB", and "RW".

EB PIPES - TYPE 1 (Figure 3a):

A medium-sized bowl with central swelling and fine rouletting below the mouth, also known as a "belly-bowl" form. The heel is cut at a slight angle to the stem axis and has a small tail of clay extending along the stem, a remnant of the mold joint. The heel is not regular in shape due to trimming, but is generally oval. An impressed mark consists of large EB letters in relief, within a circular depressed area. It is shallowly impressed on most specimens. The mark is usually centered on the heel but placement varies. Total specimens: five. Bore diameters: four (8/6ths, 3.4 mm.), one (9/64ths, 3.6 mm.). Minimum number of pipes: five.

EB PIPES - TYPE 2 (Figure 3b):

Similar bowl to Type 1 but slightly larger. The small heel is also cut at a slight angle to the stem axis. A distinctive characteristic is a straight cut at the base of the heel, running generally perpendicular to the stem. The mark consists of smaller EB letters in relief, within a depressed oval area. The mark consistently appears slightly off center on the heel. The bowls and stems display burnishing.

Total Specimens: 11. Bore diameters: two (9/64ths, 3.8 mm.), seven (10/64ths, 4.0 mm.), two (not measurable). Minimum number of pipes: 11.

EB PIPES - TYPE 3 (Figure 3c):

A smaller, more slender form, still of bulbous shape, with a heel that is more rectangular in form. The mark consists of small raised shallowly impressed, EB letters within a solid ring.

Total specimens: two. Bore Diameters: both 7/64ths, 2.8 mm. Minimum number of pipes: two.

Discussion:
These are probably the products of Edward Bird, an expatriot Englishman, who worked in Amsterdam from 1635 to 1665 (Duco 1981:399, 463; McCashion 1979:92). Similar specimens have been found at the St. John's site in St. Mary's City, and at numerous sites in New York State (McCashion 1979; Huey 1985). Indeed, an identical Type 2 mark is illustrated in McCashion (1979: 92-93, Plate 14) and the Type 3 mark is also shown (1979:99 Plate 18). The bowl forms are also similar to the New York examples. An identical Type 3 mark was also recovered from excavations in Amsterdam (Bart 1985:97). Although these can all be dated to the period 1645-circa 1655, the Type 1 pipes occur consistently in the lower strata of the fort ditch while the Type 2 pipes tend to be found in higher layers. Hence, the stratigraphic evidence from Pope's Fort suggests that the Type 1 specimens may be slightly earlier than Type 2.

MB PIPES - TYPE 1 (Figure 3d):

This is a medium-sized, bulbous pipe with regularly applied rouletting near the mouth of the bowl. Evidence of burnishing is apparent on the bowls and stems. The heel is large and the impressed mark occupies most of its surface. The circular mark consists of the letters MB in relief within a wreath. The "M" is poorly formed and resembles an "H" on the more ill-defined examples. One stem-heel section was recovered which indicates these pipes had relatively short stems, measuring perhaps five inches (130 mm.) from the bowl.

Total specimens: six. Bore diameters: five (9/64ths, 3.8 mm), one (10/64ths, 4.0 mm.) Minimum number of pipes: six.

MB PIPES - TYPE 2 (Figure 3e):

This type is represented by heel and stem fragments only. The heels are large and are similar in size and appearance to the Type 1 heels. Unlike the first variety, the mark on these pipes has larger, better formed initials within a round to slightly oval serrated line. A sword or dagger appears between the letters.

Total Specimens: two. Bore diameters: both 9/64ths, 3.6 mm.). Minimum number of pipes: two.

Discussion:
A maker for these pipes has not been identified, although Type 1 could be Dutch. The Type 1 specimens were found in the middle layers of the fort ditch while the Type 2 specimens occur at the top. Thus, it is possible that Type 2 is slightly later in time. A specimen with a similar Type 2 mark was recovered in London (Atkinson and Oswald 1969, Figure 3, #11; Le Cheminant 1981:132, #33). The bowl of the London specimen was dated 1660-1680. In the Chesapeake, Type 2 marks have been excavated from the Clay Bank Site (Noel Hume 1966:28), the Green Spring Plantation Site, and at several other sites in the Jamestown area of Virginia (Crass 1988: 86-87).

RW PIPES (Figure 3f):

These fragmentary specimens have heels that are large and circular in form. The impressed mark consists of the raised initials RW within a raised beaded circle. A six-pointed hollow star and the two flanking dots occur above and below the letters. Placement of the mark on the heel varies.

Total specimens: three. Bore diameters: one (8/64ths, 3.2 mm.), two are not measurable. Minimum number of pipes: three.

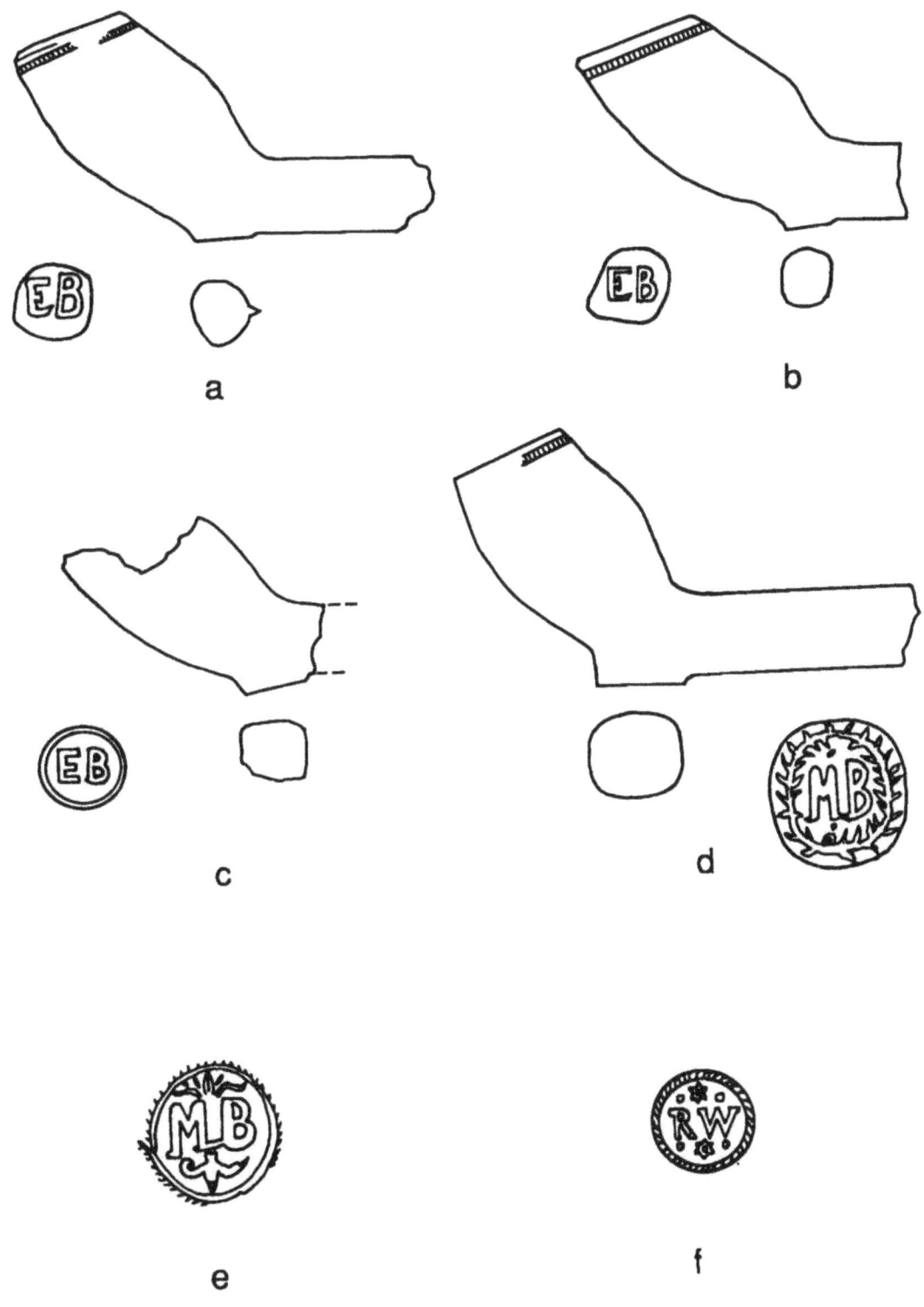

Figure 3: White clay tobacco pipes with maker's marks (bowls 1x, Marks 2x).

Discussion:
Maker uncertain, possibly Dutch. Three Amsterdam makers have these initials but marks attributed to them are not similar (Duco 1981: 400-401). A Robert Wiggins was listed as a pipe-maker in London in 1646, but his mark is apparently unknown (Oswald 1975:148).

PLAIN WHITE CLAY PIPES

Excavators recovered eight types of tobacco pipes without maker's marks. These are of two basic forms: bulbous shaped pipes with heels, and funnel shaped pipes without heels.

BULBOUS BOWL - TYPE 1 (Figure 4a):

A slender, medium-sized bowl with swelling on the back side. The heel is shallow and of medium size. Rouletting occurs around the mouth. Distinctive features include a prominent mold seam on the front of the bowl and a small clay knob just above the heel along this seam, probably due to an imperfection in the mold. Both bowl and stem have highly polished surfaces. The bowl size is similar to that of the EB pipes.

Total specimens: four. Bore Diameters: all 8/64ths, 3.4 mm. Minimum number of pipes: four.

BULBOUS BOWL - TYPE 2 (Figure 4b):

Larger bowl than Type 1 but of similar form. Heel also larger with the edges frequently flattened and misshapened by handling during production. Overall, less well made than Type 1 with little surface polishing.

Total specimens: four. Bore diameters: all 8/64ths, three (3.2 mm). and one (3.4 mm). Minimum number of pipes: four.

Discussion:
Probably Dutch in origin (McCashion 1979; Duco 1981), although similar bowl shapes have been recovered in London (Le Cheminant 1981: 132, 158, 162).

BULBOUS BOWL - TYPE 3 (Figure 4c):

A large "belly bowl" pipe with a pronounced forward thrust. Small, high heel of oval shape. Rouletting at mouth only occurs on the back side of the bowl. Surfaces display some burnishing.

Total specimens: six. Bore diameters: four (7/64ths, two 2.8 mm. and two 3.0 mm.), two (8/64ths, one 3.0 mm., one 3.2 mm.).

Discussion:
Probably of Dutch origin, this bowl form is like that illustrated by McCashion (1979:83) who identifies it as a Dutch Pipe dated *circa* 1640-1650. It is also similar to other Dutch pipes illustrated by McCashion (1979:80-81), who calls them "early Dutch Belly Bowls", dated 1635-1645. The Dutch settlement of Fort Orange also yielded a similar bowl form (Huey 1985:77b).

SMALL BULBOUS PIPES - TYPE 1 (Figure 4d):

The smallest bowl from Pope's Fort it has a very pronounced forward lean. The constricted mouth has rouletting just below it. Small oval heel has a possible mark but it is illegible.

Total specimens: one. Bore diameter: 7/64ths, 3.0 mm.

Discussion:
Possibly English, it is similar to Oswald's (1975) General Type 5, dated 1640-1660, and a specimen illustrated in Walker (1977:1547, #6), which is dated 1620-1660. The St. Mary's pipe also bears a resemblance to a specimen from Chester, England (Rutter and Davey 1980:60-61, Figure 4, #1) which is identified as a South West England bowl form.

SMALL BULBOUS PIPES - TYPE 2 (Figure 4e):

Bowl section only; probably had heel originally. Incurving mouth encircled by a groove rather than a rouletted line. Surface polished.

Total specimens: one. Bore diameter: not measurable.

Discussion:
Possibly a Dutch pipe it is similar to a pipe illustrated by Noel Hume (1979:20-21, #5), who identifies it as Dutch, *circa* 1620-1630 in date. Also similar to a London pipe find described by Le Cheminant (1981: 158, #166) who dates the bowl as *circa* 1650-1660.

PIPES WITH VERY LARGE HEELS (Figure 4f):

These all are incomplete specimens; the heel is the largest of any pipe in the collection. Cut flush with the stem and approximately square in shape, measuring 12 mm. on a side. Bowl form uncertain but probably bulbous.

Total specimens: two. Bore diameters: one measurable (7/64ths, 2.8 mm.). Minimum number of pipes: two.

Discussion:
Probably of English origin.

FUNNEL BOWL PIPES - TYPE 1 (Figure 5a):

Bowl expands from the stem junction, with sides straight and no heel. Bowl is at a very steep angle to the stem at approximately 70 degrees. Bowl and portions of the stem polished.

Total specimens: three. Bore diameters: one (6/64ths, 2.8. mm), two (7/64ths, one 2.8 mm., one 3.0 mm.). Minimum number of pipes: three.

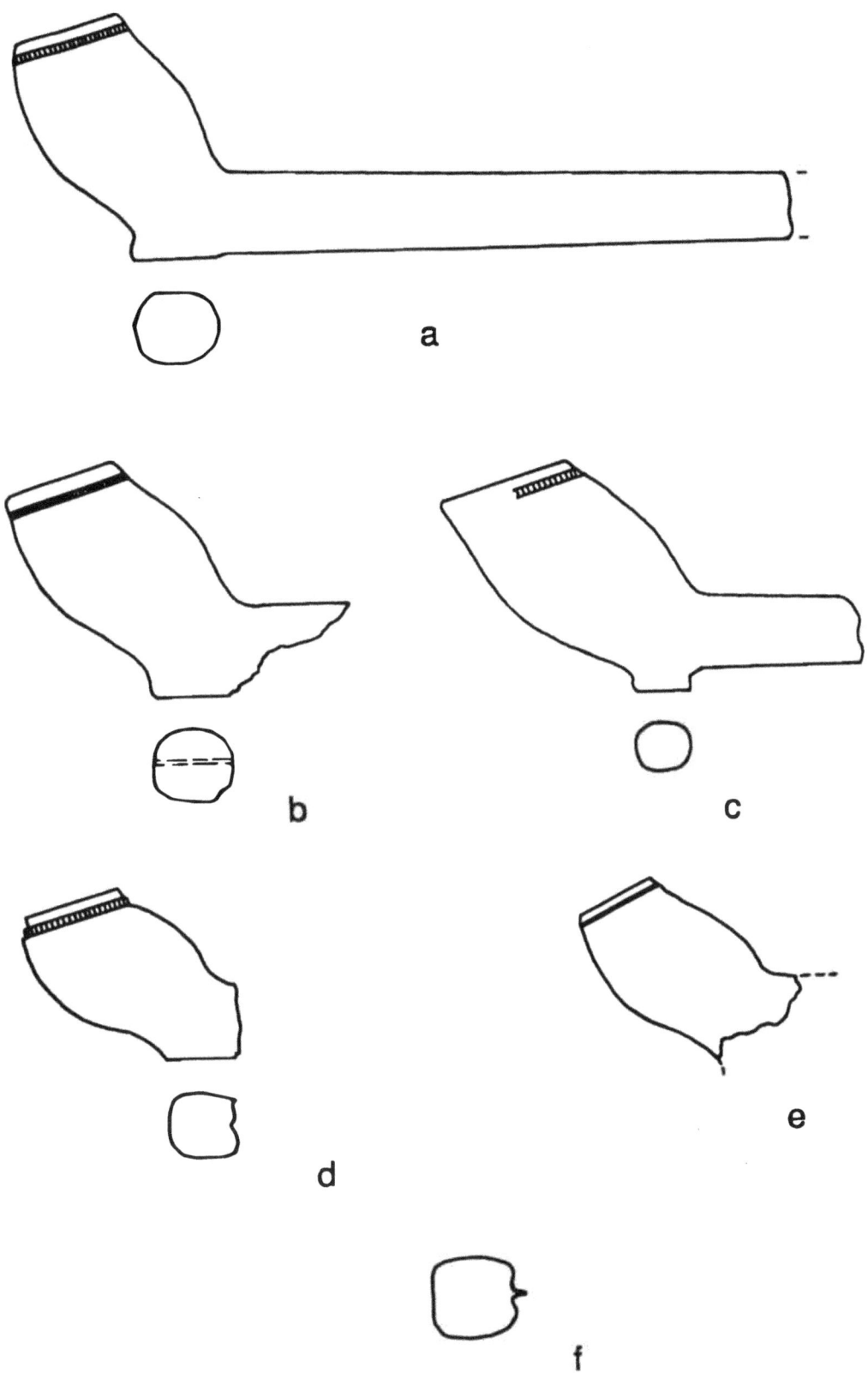

Figure 4: Unmarked white clay pipes from Pope's Fort.

FUNNEL BOWL PIPES - TYPE 2 (Figure 5b):

Also funnel form but the bowl-stem angle is much less, approximately 50 degrees. Mold seam very prominent on the bottom of the stem. Less well finished than Type 1.

Total specimens: three. Bore diameters: One (6/64ths, 2.6 mm.), one (8/64ths, 3.2 mm.), one (not measurable). Minimum number of pipes: three.

Discussion:
These are Dutch "export" pipes. Similar bowls are illustrated in McCashion (1979). However, the very high angle of the Type 1 pipes is unusual. McCashion illustrates none that are similar. This variety is apparently rare in the Netherlands (cf. Duco 1981), but they have been recovered on Dutch sites in America (McCashion 1979; Huey 1985:77; Baker (1985:23).

DECORATED WHITE CLAY PIPES

TUDOR ROSE PIPES:

Fragment only. This form of pipe displays a cluster of molded dots on opposite sides of the bowl and has been the Tudor Rose type. The Pope's Fort specimen consists of a small bowl fragment with five raised dots.

Total specimens: one. Bore Diameter: not measurable.

Discussion:
This was a popular Dutch mark (Duco 1981) which ranges in date from *circa* 1630-1670, but it also appears on English products. Other examples have been found at the St. John's, Van Sweringen, and Smith's Ordinary Sites in St. Mary's City; in *circa* 1635-1654 contexts at the Pentagoet site in Maine (Faulkner and Faulkner 1987:71); at the Clark and Lake Company Site (Baker 1985:24) in Maine; and at Fort Orange in Albany, New York (Huey 1978: personal communication).

ELABORATELY MOLDED STEMS (Figure 5c):

These stems have a raised molded decoration sometimes called the "vine and leaf" motif. The decoration extends for approximately 90 mm. along the top side of the stem and begins and ends with large *fleur-de-lies*. In addition to lines and dots, this decoration includes the following elements: flowers, leaves, small *fleur-de-lies* and birds, probably doves.

Total specimens: 10. Bore diameters: six (7/64ths, 3.0 mm.), three (8/64ths, 3.2 mm.), one (not measurable).

Discussion:
These are Dutch pipes (Atkinson and Oswald 1972:179; Duco 1981). Other decorated examples are illustrated by Duco (1981:251, #132-136), who notes that this style of decoration was common during the 1635-1660 period (1981:384). Identical specimens have been found in America at the St. John's and Chapel Sites in St. Mary's City, at Jamestown, Virginia and at Fort Orange in New York (Huey 1978: personal communication). Oswald (1979:115) reports another from Plymouth, England.

FLEUR-DE-LIS STAMPED STEMS - TYPE 1 (Figure 5d):

These stems display a large quadruple *fleur-de-lis* mark between two rouletted lines. The mark is 20 mm. in length and approximately 14 mm. in width. Distance between the rouletted lines is 23 mm. Some polishing is apparent on one of the stems.

Total specimens: three. Bore diameters: All 7/64ths, 2.8 mm.

FLEUR-DE-LIS STAMPED STEMS - TYPE 2 (Figure 5e):

A smaller quadruple *fleur-de-lis* mark within a plain border. Rouletted lines also appear above and below this mark. It measures 13.5 mm. by 9 mm. and the distance between the rouletted lines is 25 mm.

Total specimens = one. Bore diameter: 7/64ths, 2.8 mm.

FLEUR-DE-LIS STAMPED STEMS - TYPE 3 (Figure 5f):

Another small quadruple *fleur-de-lis* mark, but within a dashed border. Multiple marks occur along the stem with no evidence of the rouletted lines, as seen on Types 1 and 2. These are sharp, clear marks, more deeply impressed than those on the above specimens.

Total specimens: two. Bore diameters: both 7/64ths, 3.0 mm.

FLEUR-DE-LIS STAMPED STEMS - TYPE 4 (Figure 5g):

A large four-on-diamond *fleur-de-lis* mark. Shallowly impressed on the stem and portions obliterated through abrasion. The mark appears twice on the stem.

Total specimens: one. Bore diameter: 7/64ths, 3mm.

Discussion:
The quadruple *fleur-de-lis* marks are generally recognized as being of Dutch origin and a variety of styles are known (Atkinson and Oswald 1972; McCashion 1979; Duco 1981). These are not maker's marks, and instead serve as decoration. Similar specimens have been recovered at the St. John's, Smith's Ordinary and Van Swearingen Sites in St. Mary's City, at Martin's Hundred in Virginia (Noel Hume 1979), in New York State where they are dated *circa* 1630-1650 (McCashion 1979:84-85), at Fort

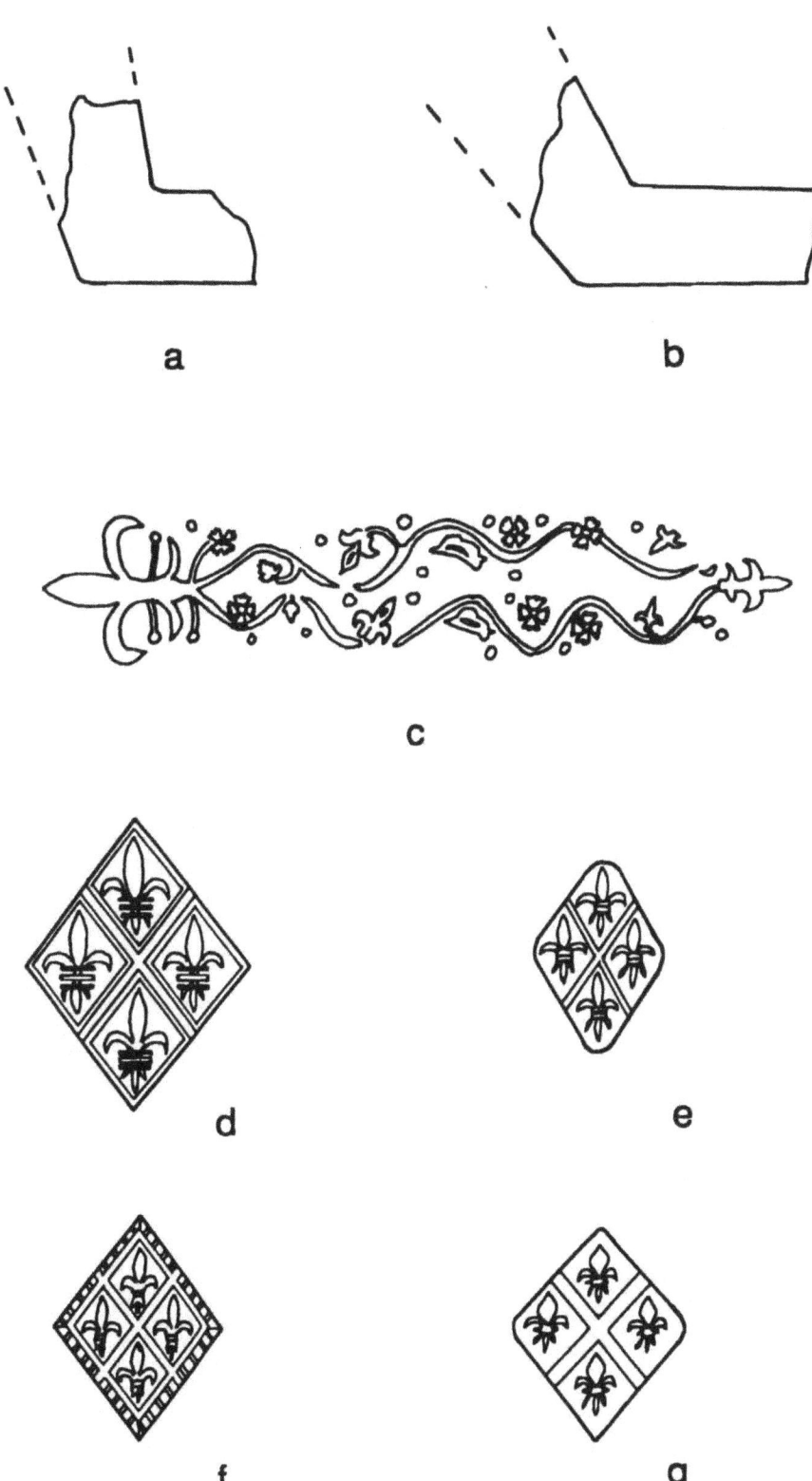

Figure 5: White clay funnel pipes and stem decorations of likely Dutch origin.

Orange (Huey 1978: personal communication), and at the Pentagoet Site in Maine, where they were found in *circa* 1635-1654 contexts (Faulkner and Faulkner 1987:176). Use of rouletted lines with the *fleur-de-lis* marks are also known on pipes in the Netherlands (Duco 1981:249). It is notable that no stems with single *fleur-de-lis* marks were recovered from Pope's Fort; all are four-on-diamond types. Single marks are found on pipes from middens surrounding Governor Calvert's House, and at other St. Mary's City sites.

MOLDED TERRA COTTA PIPES

The Pope's Fort ditch yielded a large number of tobacco pipe fragments and the majority are not of white clay. Over 70% of the pipe bowls in the collection were produced from non-white clays. Of the 127 identified terra cotta bowls, 31 (24.4%) were produced in European style molds. In the following section, the various forms of these molded pipes are described. The molded pipes occur in a wide range of colors, but most tend to be dark brown to light orange. There is little consistency in color within a given type. Indeed, a single pipe may be of several colors, due to firing imperfections. Hence, detailed color descriptions are not considered appropriate.

TERRA COTTA PIPES - TYPE 1 (Figure 6a):

A large "belly bowl" style pipe with a prominent heel that flares slightly at its base. The bowl is not round but somewhat flattened on the sides. Instead of rouletting, a band of elaborate decoration occurs around the mouth. However, this impressed band was so shallowly applied that much of it is no longer visible.

Total specimens: eight. Bore diameters: three (7/64ths, two 2.8 mm., one 3.0 mm.), two (8/64ths, 3.4 mm.), three not measurable. Minimum Number of Pipes: eight.

Discussion:
A very distinctive pipe due to numerous imperfections in the mold. This type has also been found at the St. John's Site (Henry 1979:21, Figure 2f). No maker is known.

TERRA COTTA PIPES - TYPE 2 (Figure 6 b,c):

A large bulbous pipe with shallow rouletting at the mouth, and a large heel with a Tudor Rose mark impressed on it. There are two bowl forms associated with this mark and they are of generally similar shapes, although Variety 1 (Figure 6b) is slightly smaller and more rounded. Variety 2 (Figure 6c) is a larger bowl and it curves in prominently at the mouth. However, the Tudor Rose marks are identical on both varieties, implying two pipe molds used by the same maker.

Total specimens: five. Bore diameters: two (9/64ths, one 3.6 mm., one 3.8 mm.), one (10/64ths, 3.8 mm.), two not measurable. Minimum Number of Pipes: five.

Discussion:
Bowls with this mark have been found at the St. John's Site in St. Mary's City (Henry 1979:21) and at Jamestown, Virginia. This bowl shape is similar to Oswald's (1975:39) Type 5 (1975:39), dated 1640-1660. An English pipe bowl without the Tudor Rose mark that is very similar in shape to Variety 1 was recovered from the Martin's Hundred site in Virginia, where it was dated to the 1640-1670 period (Noel Hume 1979:24, Figure 6, #5). The maker of these pipes is unidentified.

TERRA COTTA PIPES - TYPE 3 (Figure 6d,e):

A bulbous form with a low heel which is cut nearly flush with the stem on some examples. Rouletting appears below the mouth. Perhaps the most distinctive feature is a rouletted line at the bowl-stem junction. On one specimen (Figure 6e), rouletting encircles the heel and appears on the heel itself. This pipe also displays another unusual feature as it has grooves cut into the top and bottom of the stem, at the broken end. This was apparently to facilitate holding the pipe with the teeth while smoking, perhaps to free the hand for other activities.

Total specimens: four. Bore diameters: one (8/64ths, 3.4 mm.), one (9/64ths, 3.6 mm.), one (164ths, 4.2mm), one not measurable. Minimum Number of Pipes: four.

Discussion:
Of unknown origin but probably from the Chesapeake region. These have not been identified at other sites. Bowls with similar rouletting at the bowl-stem junction were found at Jamestown, but their shapes are different.

TERRA COTTA PIPES - TYPE 4 (Figure 7a,b):

A slender bowl with curving sides and a small, low heel. The rim displays a decorative band consisting of triangles alternately pointing up and down. Trimming of the pipe removed much of this decoration on several specimens.

Total specimens: 12. Bore Diameters: one (8/64ths, 3.4 mm.), one (10/64ths, 4.0 mm.), two (11/64ths, 4.2 and 4.4 mm.), eight not measurable. Minimum Number of Pipes: 12.

Discussion:
This pipe also occurs at the St. John's site and the design has been illustrated by Henry (1979:28, Figure 8e and 30, Figure 9a). A pipe with similar form and decoration was also found at the Martin's Hundred site (Noel Hume 1979: 15, Figure 3, #4).

TERRA COTTA PIPES - TYPE 5 (Figure 7c):

Incomplete specimen. Large bulbous bowl with a maker's mark on a medium-sized heel. However, this mark was obscured during manufacture. All that can be made out is a single large letter, possibly an "R", within a dashed circle.

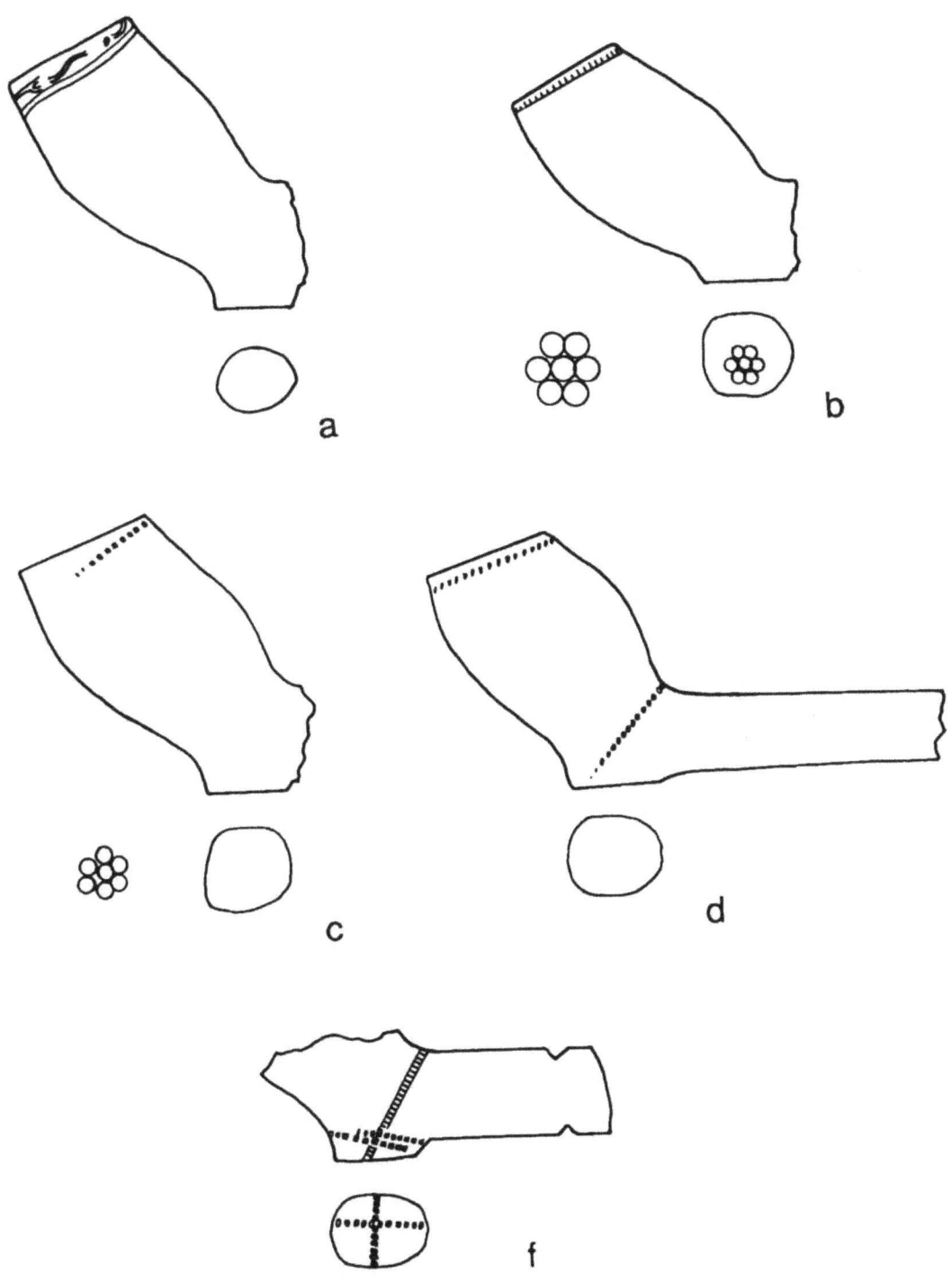

Figure 6: Molded terra cotta pipes.

Total specimens: one. Bore diameter: not measurable.

Discussion:
Unknown maker.

TERRA COTTA PIPES - TYPE 6 (Figure 7 d,e,f):

A slender bowl form with a beveled rim at the mouth and apparently without a heel. Elaborately decorated with stamping and rouletting on the bowl and stem. A band of rouletting occurs below the bowl mouth (7d,f). This band includes various design elements, including rows of dots, a star-like device, and a grid. Below this, eight stamped petalled rosettes are irregularly spaced around the bowl. These apparently also occur near the base of the bowl. Additional rouletting occurs just past the bowl-stem junction and continues along the stem. This begins with three closely spaced rouletted lines (7e). The first is a double-dentate line, followed by the same decorative band that was used on the bowl, and then another double dentate line. Following this is an area from 25 to 35 mm. in length where the rosettes are stamped in columns running down the stem. After this the same three-line pattern used above is repeated. This decorative design appears to occur only once on the stem. The total stem length of this type of pipe is approximately 125 mm. A number of these specimens are made from a mixture of buff and red clays to produce an agate-like appearance. Several of the specimens are also well polished.

Total specimens: 21. Bore diameters: Five (all 10/64ths, three 4.0 mm., two 4.2 mm.), 16 not measurable. Minimum number of pipes: six.

Discussion:
This type of pipe is found on a number of early sites. It was recovered from the St. John's excavations in St. Mary's City (Henry 1979:21 Figure 2h,i), and at Jamestown, Virginia. Similar specimens were reportedly found at the Mathews Manor Site in Virginia and an identical pipe was recovered from Martin's Hundred (Noel Hume 1979: 17, Figure 4, #7).

HANDMADE TERRA COTTA PIPES

Although this report does not include a full analysis of the handmade terra cotta pipes, a brief discussion of them is appropriate because they form the majority of the brown clay pipes in the collection.

A thorough analysis of similar handmade pipes from the St. John's Site in St. Mary's City has been published (Henry 1979). Preliminary study of the Pope's Fort specimens has identified a minimum of 96 pipes made by hand. Figure 8 illustrates several of the bowl forms and decorations used on them. The bowls tend to be funnel or tubular shaped and display a variety of decorative motifs. The most popular decoration is the so called "Running Deer" motif, although geometric designs are also common. Of the entire group, the most unusual specimens are human face effigy pipes (Figure 8, Bottom). These elaborate specimens, which were probably manufactured by Indians, have not been previously reported from the Chesapeake region.

PIPE MAKING WASTE

A small group of artifacts also was recovered from the Fort ditch which appear to be waste from pipe production. These include unfinished bowls, flattened or warped stems, trimming waste, and small clumps of fired clay with fingerprints. This evidence indicates that handmade pipes were being produced at the site. Manufacture of molded pipes is also possible, but this cannot be determined with the available data.

THE POPE'S FORT PIPE ASSEMBLAGE

Besides of its short period of deposition, this collection of pipes is notable in several respects. One is the predominance of Dutch products compared to those from England. Very few bowls in the assemblage are of definite English origin. Of the 54 white clay pipes identified, 49 (90.7%) are of Dutch or probable Dutch origin. In comparison, only three pipes (5.5%) are of definite English origin. The likely place of manufacture for two pipes could not be determined. Another unusual feature is the large quantity of terra cotta pipes. The molded and handmade terra cotta pipes together account for 70% of the collection and some were made at the site. Such a pipe assemblage on an English colonial site requires explanation.

Although objects from a variety of countries typically are found on 17th-century English colonial sites in America, the high proportion of Dutch pipes is unusual. The paucity of English pipes and plethora of Dutch specimens is probably a direct result of the English Civil Wars. Colonists in the Chesapeake were dependent upon the annual fleet of ships which came to collect tobacco. Tobacco was the sole economic basis of the Maryland and Virginia colonies, and in exchange for the annual crop, the tobacco planters received essential manufactured goods, liquor and other supplies such as tobacco pipes. The Civil Wars disrupted normal business activities and reduced the volume of shipping to the Chesapeake. As the number of English ships declined, the planters suffered serious shortages. Dutch merchants took advantage of this situation and rapidly expanded their trading activities in the Chesapeake region (Bruce 1895:310; Menard 1975:297). By offering a better exchange rate than the English merchants the Dutch quickly became a major force in the tobacco economy and helped keep crop prices high for the planters (Craven 1970:240; Morgan 1975:147). It is noteworthy that when Ingle attacked St. Mary's City in 1645, a Dutch merchant ship, the *Speagle*, was engaged in trading at the city (Shomette 1985:28).

The importance of the Dutch merchants to the Chesapeake colonists during the period of the Civil Wars and in the years directly afterward is suggested by the response of the Governor of Virginia to Cromwell's proposal to bar Dutch ships from the Chesapeake. He

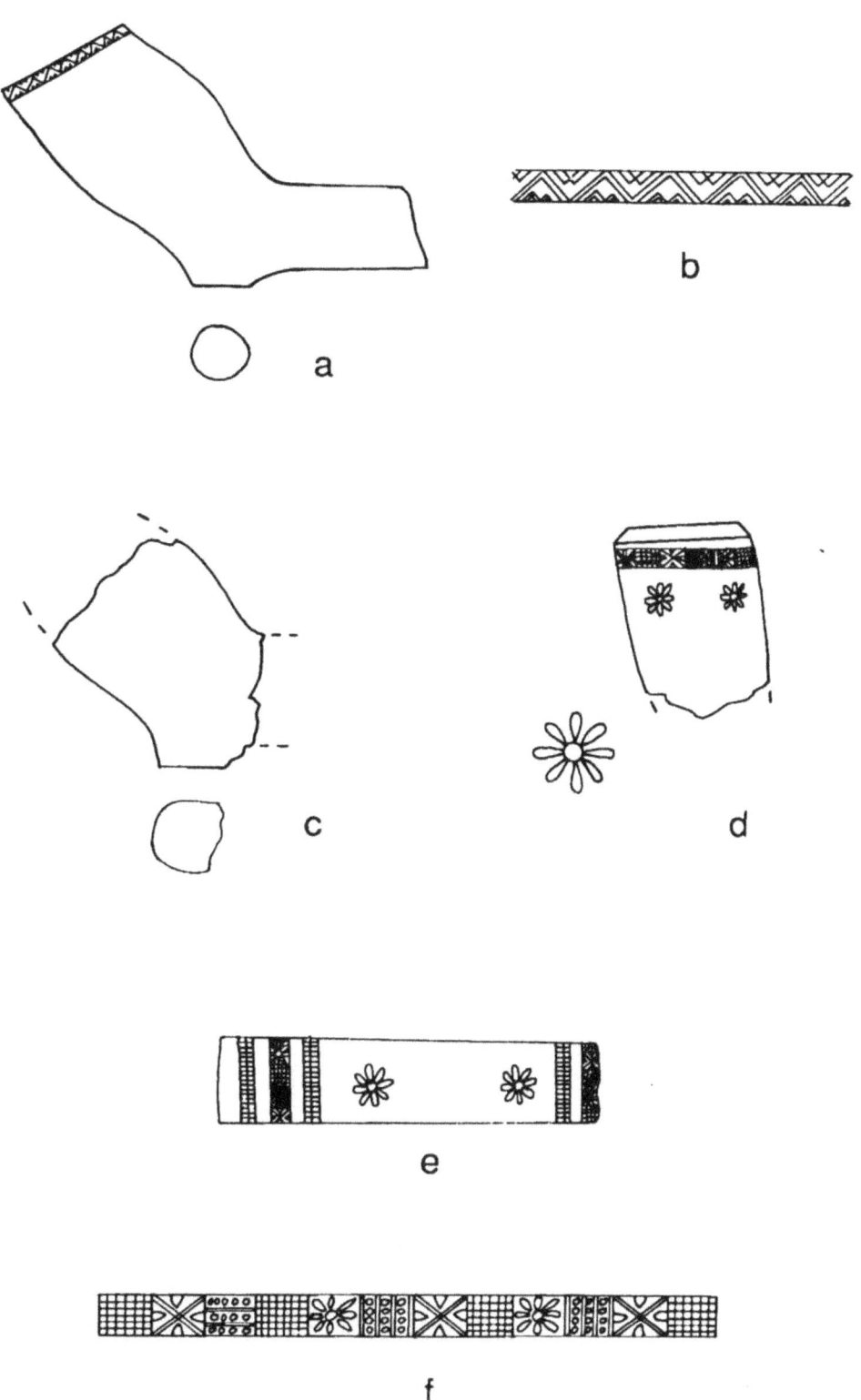

Figure 7: Molded terra cotta pipes from Pope's Fort.

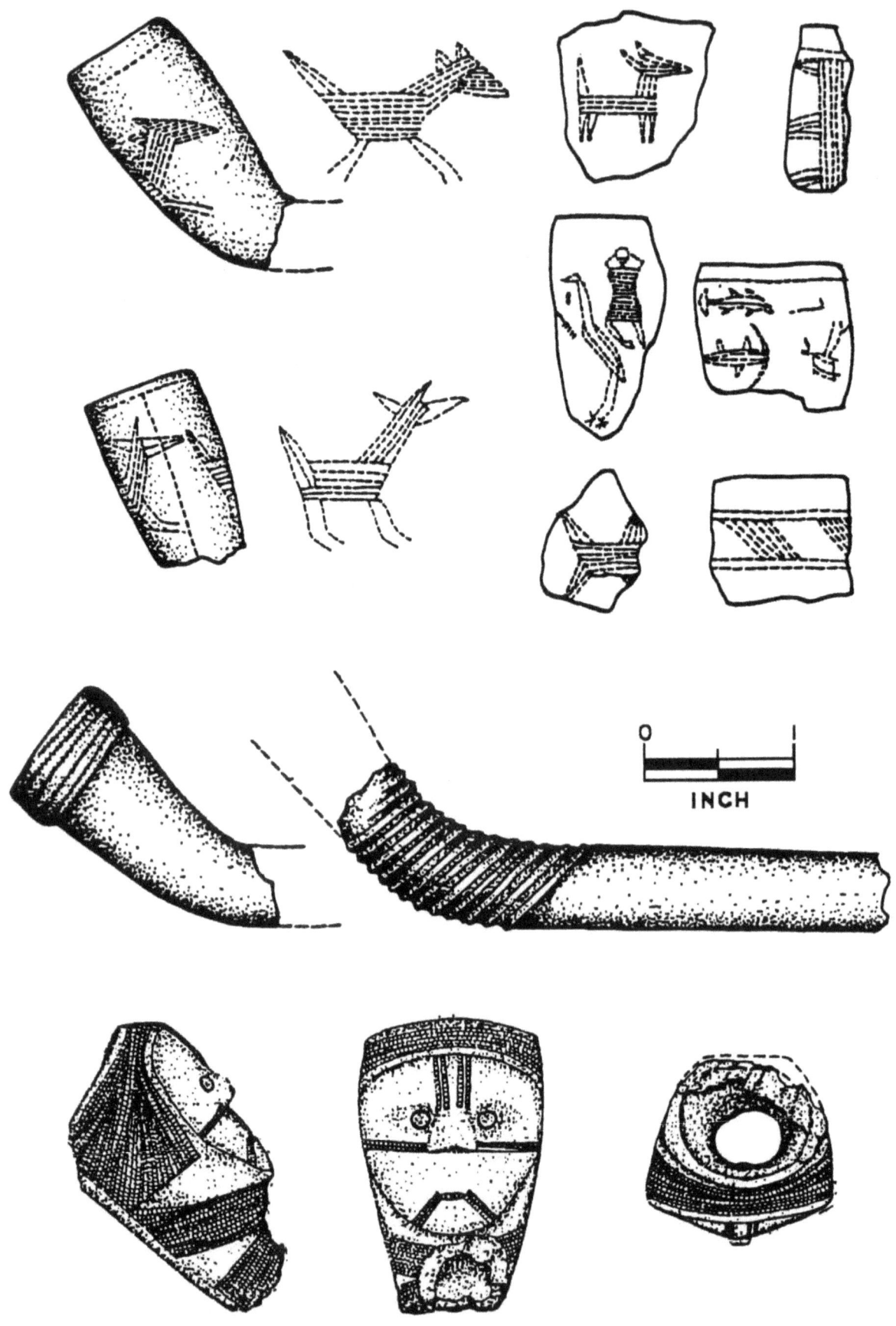

Figure 8: Handmade terra cotta pipes from Pope's Fort; probably of American Indian manufacture.

stated that this would create serious difficulties and mean a return to "...the same poverty wherein the Dutch found and relieved us" (Morgan 1975:147). Parliament nevertheless prohibited the Dutch trade in 1651, at the request of the London merchants. Not surprisingly, reports of severe shortages of manufactured goods were heard by 1653 (Menard 1975:298). Documents indicate that there continued to be insufficient shipping to transport much of the tobacco crop to market during the latter 1650s as well (Beer 1922:395). Dutch tobacco pipes at Pope's Fort are thus understandable given the economic environment of the time. Indeed, given the near absence of English pipes at the fort, it is possible that the Maryland colonists relied even more heavily on the Dutch than did the Virginians.

The effects of the English Civil Wars may also help explain the large numbers of terra cotta pipes at the fort. As noted, over 70% of the pipes are terra cotta. Henry (1979) has proposed that the production of terra cotta pipes in the Chesapeake is directly related to the status of the economy. She hypothizes that "The colonists in 17th century Tidewater Maryland and Virginia made their own tobacco pipes of local clay during economic depressions, i.e., at times of low tobacco prices, decreased availability of English manufactured goods, and increased costs of these goods" (Henry 1979:15). According to this hypothesis, the proportion of terra cotta pipes should fall during periods of prosperity and increase during depressions, as planters attempted to cut costs.

This argument does not seem to be supported by the Pope's Fort data. The 1645-1655 period was one of relatively good tobacco prices (Menard 1975) and yet the terra cotta pipes predominate. The Pope's Fort data may indicate that the general condition of the tobacco economy is not the crucial variable in spurring local manufacture. Instead, it may be the availability of manufactured goods. A basic problem for most colonial societies is that of supply (c.f. Craven 1970:240), and this certainly was a recurring problem in the Chesapeake during the 17th century. The Dutch helped ease this supply shortage during the 1640s, although shipping still probably was not sufficient to meet all needs. After the Dutch were forbidden to trade in the Chesapeake, the historical evidence suggests that the supply problem again became serious. Demand for items like tobacco pipes remained stable or even increased as the population grew, but the supply decreased. Thus, the plethora of handmade and molded pipes at Pope's Fort and other sites may well be a response to shortages. Production of local pipes may still have occurred during periods of depression, but not because planters were attempting to cut costs. Rather, depressions, like wars, tended to restrict market activity, reduce the volume of shipping coming to the Chesapeake, and thus produce shortages (Menard 1975:290). The hypothesis put forward by Henry seems basically sound, but should be amended to focus specifically on supply rather than tobacco prices or costs as the critical factor in the local production of pipes. If further research confirms the hypothesis, then the proportion of terra cotta to white clay pipes could serve as an important measure of the overall supply situation in the Chesapeake.

Where the molded terra cotta pipes were produced is not certain, although it is likely that some were made at Pope's Fort. It is of relevance to note that some of the specimens (Types 2, 4, and 6) are found on Maryland sites as well as those along the James River in Virginia. These pipes seem to have a pan-Chesapeake distribution while other varieties (Types 1, 3, and 5) only occur on sites in St. Mary's City. Study of pipes in the collection at Jamestown, Virginia has revealed a number of other varieties which do not appear on Maryland sites. Thus, the various terra cotta pipes exhibit very different distributional patterns, the reasons for which are not yet clear. It seems likely that pipe production generally occurred on a small scale. Some of the major merchant/planters, on the other hand, may have attempted to produce on a larger scale and market the pipes throughout the Chesapeake. These molded pipes may be the earliest physical evidence for the development of local marketing networks in the Chesapeake region.

CONCLUSION

Excavations at Pope's Fort have provided new information on the tobacco pipes used in Maryland during the period 1645 - *circa* 1655. They indicate that the majority of the pipes derived from Dutch rather than English sources. This situation is explained by the severe disruptions in English business activity and marketing caused by the Civil Wars. As a result, the Dutch were provided with an excellent opportunity to capture the tobacco market and the archaeological evidence indicates that they quickly took advantage of this situation. The presence of numerous terra cotta pipes suggests that the colonists were responding to the shortage of imported materials by producing molded pipes and obtaining handmade pipes from local Indians.

REFERENCES

Atkinson, D. and Oswald, A. (1972). A brief guide to the identification of Dutch clay tobacco pipes found in England. *Post-Medieval Archaeology* 6:175-182.

Atkinson, D. and Oswald, A. (1969). London clay tobacco pipes. *Journal of the British Archaeological Association*, Third Series, 32:171-227.

Baker, E.W. (1985). *The Clarke and Lake Company: the historical archaeology of a seventeenth-century Maine settlement*. Occasional Publications in Maine Archaeology 4. The Maine Historic Preservation Commission, Augusta.

Baart, J. (1985). Ho-De-No-Sau-Nee and the Dutch,

interaction in material culture between Autochthons and Allochthons in 17th-century New Netherlands. NEW NETHERLAND STUDIES. *Bulletin KNOB* 84(2-3):89-99.

Beer, G.L. (1922). *The Origins of the British Colonial system, 1578-1660*. MacMillan, New York.

Bruce, P.A. (1895). *Economic History of Virginia in the seventeenth century* (two volumes). MacMillan, New York.

Le Cheminant, R. (1981). Clay tobacco pipes from London and the south east. *The archaeology of the clay tobacco pipe VI: pipes and kilns in the London region*. Edited by Peter Davey, British Archaeological Reports 97: 127-172.

Crass, D.C. (1988). The clay pipes from Green Spring Plantation (44JC9), Virginia. *Historical Archaeology* 22(1):83-97.

Craven, W.F. (1970). *The southern colonies in the seventeenth century, 1607-1689*. Louisiana State University Press.

Dozer, D.M. (1967). *Portrait of the Free State: a history of Maryland*. Tidewater Publishers, Cambridge, Maryland.

Duco, D.H. (1981). The clay tobacco pipe in 17th-century Netherlands. *The Archaeology of the Clay Tobacco Pipe, V Europe 2*. Edited by Peter Davey, British Archaeological Reports International Series 106. Oxford.

Faulkner, A. and Faulkner, G. (1987). *The French at Pentagoet*. Occasional Publications in Maine Archaeology 5. Maine Historic Preservation Commission, Augusta, Maine.

Henry, S.L. (1979). Terra-Cotta tobacco pipes in 17th century Maryland and Virginia: a preliminary study. *Historical Archaeology* 13:14-37.

Huey, P. (1985). Archaeological excavations in the site of Fort Orange: a Dutch West India Company trading fort built in 1624. NEW NETHERLAND STUDIES. *Bulletin KNOB* 84(2-3):68-79.

Huey, P. (1978). Personal communication.

McCashion, J.H. (1979). A preliminary chronology and discussion of seventeenth and early eighteenth century pipes from New York State sites. *The Archaeology of the Clay Tobacco Pipe II: The United States of America*. Edited by Peter Davey, British Archaeological Reports International Series 60:63-150.

Menard, R.R. (1975). Economy and Society in Early Colonial Maryland. Ph.D. Dissertation, University of Iowa. University Microfilms, Ann Arbor.

Miller, H.M.(1986). *Discovering Maryland's First City: A Summary Report on the 1981-1984 Archaeological Excavations in St. Mary's City, Maryland*. St. Mary's City Archaeology Series 2. St. Mary's City.

Morgan, E.S.(1975). *American Slavery American Freedom: The Ordeal of Colonial Virginia*. W.W. Norton and Company. New York.

Noel Hume, A. (1979). Clay Tobacco Pipes Excavated at Martin's Hundred, Virginia 1976-1978. *The Archaeology of the Clay Tobacco Pipe II. The United States of America*. British Archaeological Reports International Series 60. Oxford.

Noel Hume, I. (1966). *Excavations at Clay Bank in Gloucester County, Virginia, 1962-1963*. Contributions from the Museum of History and Technology. U.S. Government Printing Office, Washington, D.C.

Oswald, A. (1979). The clay pipes in St. Andrews Street, Plymouth Excavations: 1976. Edited by Graham Fairclough. *Plymouth Museum Archaeological Series* No. 2:114-119.

Oswald, A. (1975). *Clay Pipes for the Archaeologist*. British Archaeological Reports 14, Oxford.

Rutter, J. and Davey, P. (1980). Clay Pipes from Chester. *Archaeology of the Clay Tobacco Pipe III: Britain; the North and West*. Edited by Peter Davey. British Archaeological Reports International Series 78, 41-272.

Shomette, D.G. (1985). *Pirates of the Chesapeake*. Tidewater Publishers. Centerville, Maryland.

Walker, I.C. (1977). *Clay Tobacco Pipes with Particular Reference to the Bristol Industry*. History and Archaeology Series 11. Parks Canada. Ottawa.

Seventeenth-Century Clay Tobacco Pipes from Smith's Townland, St. Mary's City, Maryland

Timothy B. Riordan

INTRODUCTION

Smith's Townland was a three-acre tract in St. Mary's City, Maryland, leased to William Smith in 1666. By 1670, four buildings were built on the property. One of these, Smith's Ordinary, burned in 1678 and was not replaced. Excavations conducted on this site by Historic St. Mary's City yielded almost 200 marked or identifiable pipes. This sample is important because it provides a unique insight into pipe availability in the Chesapeake during the third quarter of the 17th century. It also demonstrates the continued dominance of Dutch pipes in this period.

HISTORY OF THE SITE

Smith's Townland, located in the center of the 17th-century town of St. Mary's City, Maryland (Figure 1), was a three-acre tract leased to William Smith for 31 years by the Proprietary government in 1666 (Miller 1986:67-68). Prior to this lease there had been no domestic occupation within the Smith's Townland tract. The lease was granted to Smith on the condition that he build and operate an ordinary or public inn. The Ordinary was not complete when William Smith died in 1668. His will revealed that he had built two dwelling houses (one almost certainly was the Ordinary) and had added a hog house, a stable, an orchard and a pasture. The public inn was apparently finished in the same year by Daniel Jennifer, who married Smith's widow and who built two other houses on the property. By 1669, Garrett van Sweringen, a Dutch immigrant, leased the Ordinary from Jennifer. He later testified that he spent a great deal of money "fitting up" the inn to accommodate travellers. He must have been successful at his trade because in 1672 he was able to purchase the lease of Smith's Townland from Jennifer. Van Sweringen operated the inn for several years, but by 1678 he was renting it to another ordinary keeper. Late one night, the Ordinary caught fire and was totally destroyed. After this fire, no other building was erected in this part of the three-acre tract.

While the Ordinary was never replaced, occupation of the other buildings on Smith's Townland continued

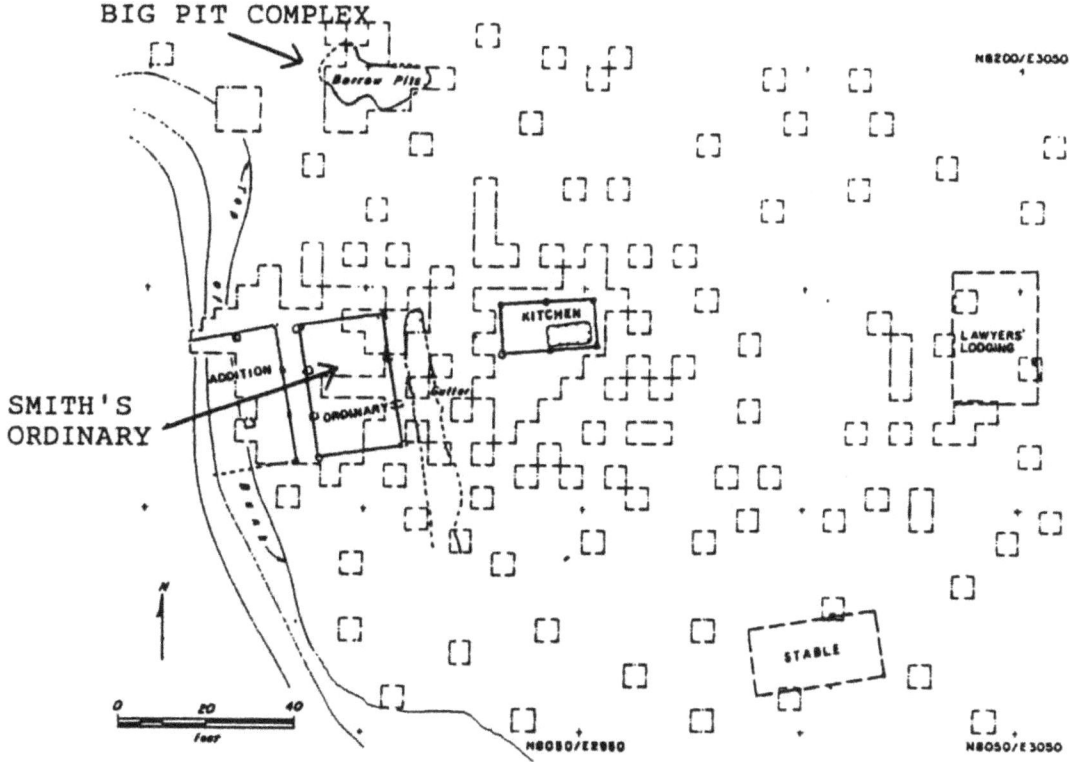

Figure 1: Distribution of excavation squares on Smith's Townland and the major structures found there.

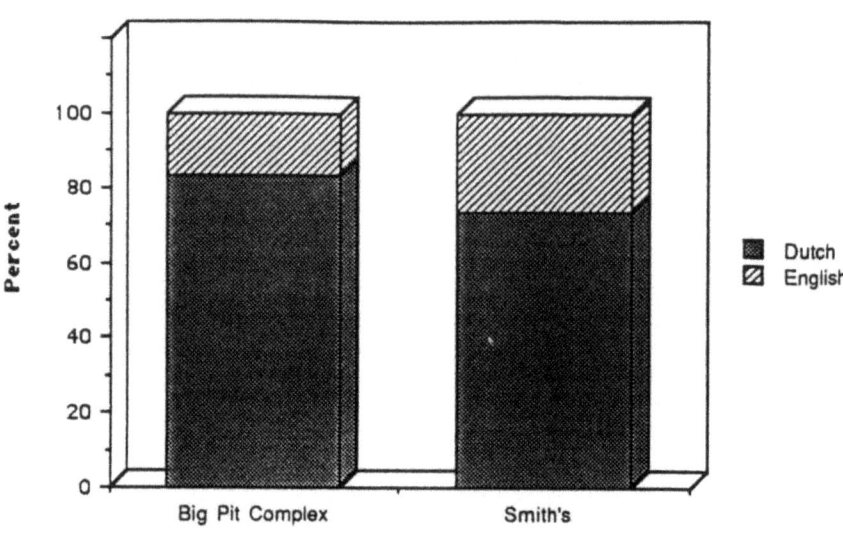

Figure 2. Pipes by country of origin.

through the late 17th century. The last reference was in 1692 when the buildings were said to be in poor repair. The moving of the provincial capital from St. Mary's City to Annapolis in 1695 probably meant the end of any occupation on this tract. The land became part of a succession of plantations and was plowed repeatedly (Miller 1986:4).

THE EXCAVATIONS

Between 1981-1984, Historic St. Mary's City (HSMC) conducted archaeological excavations on Smith's Townland which identified all of the major buildings and uncovered a number of 17th-century features. Two areas were excavated in greater detail and produced important collections of pipes from relatively well dated contexts. The first of these was the public inn known as Smith's Ordinary (Miller 1986:68-104). There was little question that the discovered features related to the Ordinary. Layers of charcoal and ash, part of a burned plaster wall, and part of a tile floor that showed scorch marks from the fire of 1678 all were revealed. Although the upper layers of this site have been plowed in later years, there appeared to be little mixture with earlier or later materials. The sample was therefore assigned a date of 1666-1678.

The second area investigated in detail was not strictly on the Smith's Townland tract but was north of it in an area identified as the town green (O'Connor 1985). Originally this complex of features was thought to be a cellar hole, but excavation revealed it to be a series of seven borrow pits. While these borrow pits, known as the Big Pit complex, cannot be definitely associated with the building of Smith's Ordinary, they are in close enough proximity to have been dug for this purpose and the artifacts included in them are roughly contemporary to the construction of Smith's Ordinary. Whatever their association, the pits were apparently filled in rapidly. Based on the artifacts in the pits, this complex appears to date to *circa* 1670 (O'Connor 1985:19). This would coincide with van Sweringen's "fitting up" the ordinary.

The differences between the deposition of the Smith's Ordinary and Big Pit samples will be important in the pipe analysis and so need to be further explored. The deposition of the sample from Smith's Ordinary could have begun as early as 1666 but more likely it began in 1668 when Daniel Jennifer finished the building. It continued until the fire destroyed the structure in 1678. The sample represents the accumulation of a decade. The deposition of the Big Pit complex probably coincided with van Sweringen's repairs to the building in 1669 and was sealed fairly rapidly. It most likely dates *circa* 1669-1670. While the initial date of the deposition of the sample from Smith's is slightly earlier than that from the Big Pit area, it also lasted much longer. This is important in considering comparisons between the two samples.

THE PIPES

The excavations produced a large sample of artifacts which are currently under analysis. Included in this sample are 172 marked or identifiable pipes. Most of the pipes were recovered from plowzone above the features, but more than a third (N=67) were recovered from within feature contexts. Even in the plowzone, however, mixture with earlier or later materials did not seem to be great. There are no pipes with an initial date of manufacture after the Ordinary was burned in 1678 and only 31 pipes (18%) that have a suggested terminal date before the construction of Smith's Ordinary in 1666. All of these early pipes are in

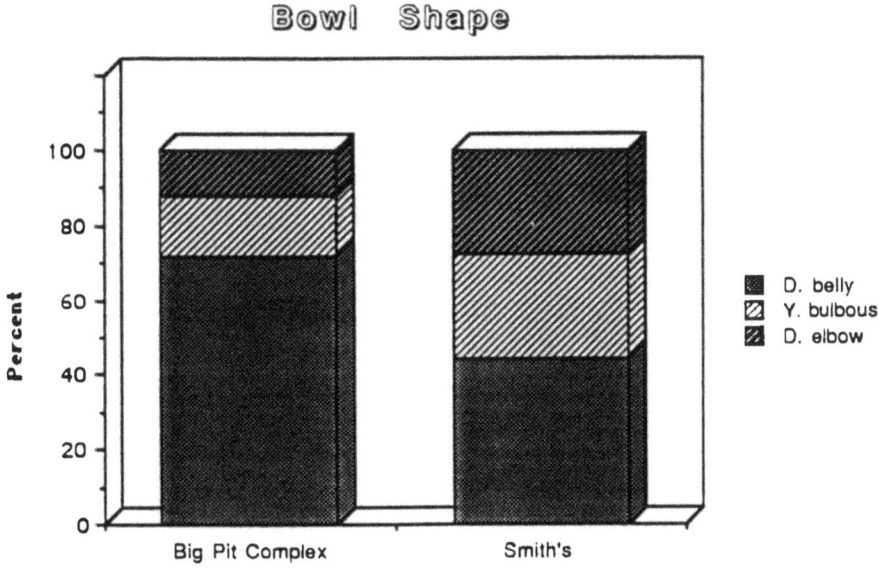

Figure 3. Graph of bowl shape types.

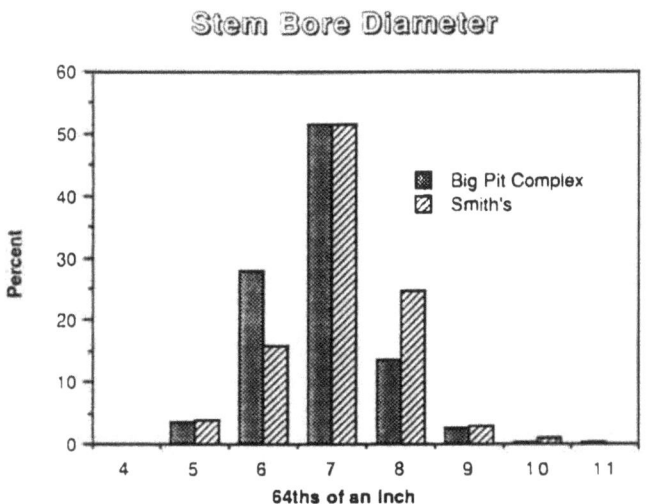

Figure 4. Stem bore diameter from plowzone.

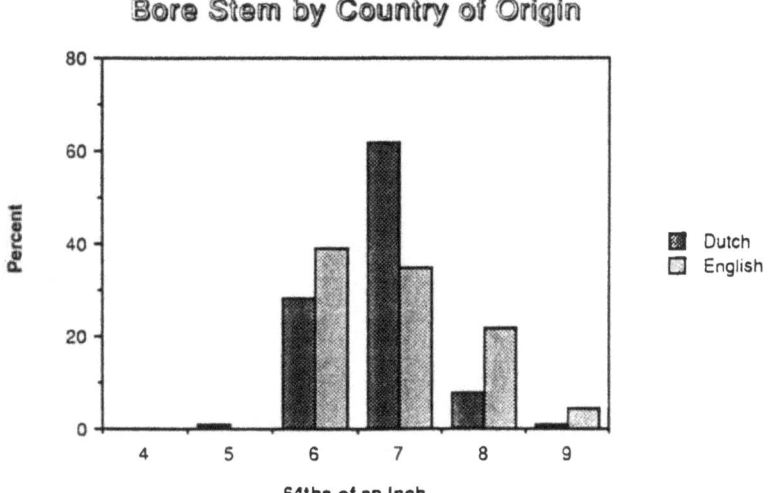

Figure 5. Bore stem diameter by country of origins.

loosely-dated decorative styles that could have extended several years to as much as a decade after their suggested terminal date. Thus, both samples appear to retain significant temporal integrity. The significance of these narrowly dated samples lay in what they may demonstrate concerning trade relations and pipe availability in the Maryland during the third quarter of the 17th century. The samples represent two overlapping periods and comparison of the two samples suggest several trends in pipe availability.

The most striking characteristic of both groups of pipes is the presence of an overwhelming number of Dutch pipes. The Big Pit complex has 83.5% that were identified as Dutch (N=86), while the slightly later Smith's Ordinary pipes are 73.6% (N=39) Dutch (Figure 2). The 10% drop in the proportion of Dutch pipes may be related to a continuing restriction of trade with the Netherlands caused by the Navigation Acts and the second (1664-67) and third (1672-74) Anglo-Dutch wars. It is interesting that despite such strong pressure against trade with the Dutch, the percentage of Dutch pipes is still very high, even in the later Smith's Ordinary sample. It could be argued that the presence of a Dutch immigrant, Garret van Sweringen, on the site was a factor in this high proportion of Dutch pipes, but other sites in St. Mary's City, while not as tightly dated, show a similarly high proportion of Dutch-made pipes (Hurry, this volume; Miller, this volume).

Both Dutch and English pipes in the samples show a narrow geographic origin. Not surprisingly, the majority of the Dutch pipes are from pipe makers in Gouda. The English pipes that could be attributed to a specific maker or city show the overwhelming influence of the Bristol pipe industry. A total of 10 pipes were identified as to specific English pipe makers and all of these are from Bristol. In addition, 11 stems are decorated in the Bristol style.

Bowl shape was another feature that differs significantly between the two samples. Of the identified bowl shapes noted, there are three that make up the majority of the sample: Yorkshire bulbous (Lawrence 1979:69), Dutch belly bowl (Duco 1981:245), and Dutch funnel elbow (McCashion 1979:124-5). These three forms accounted for 96.4% of all of the recognizable bowls. Bowl shape shows the same trend in its distribution as that of manufacturer. The most numerous bowl type recovered from the Big Pit complex is the Dutch belly bowl, accounting for 72% (N=18) of the sample. Yorkshire bulbous and Dutch funnel elbow bowls account for 16% (N=4) and 12% (N=2) respectively (Figure 3). This profile is in contrast to that of the Smith's Ordinary bowls, where Dutch belly bowls make up only 44.4% (N=8) of the sample and the other types each represent 27.7% (N=5). As with the identified pipes, the proportion of Dutch bowl shapes declined approximately 10% between the two samples. There was also a slight shift in the style of the available Dutch bowl shape. The funnel elbow shape increased between the two samples, from 12% to 27.7%. Given the small

Table 1. Bore diameters of plowzone stems

64ths"	Big Pit Complex		Smith's Ordinary	
	No.	%	No.	%
4	0	0.0	0	0.0
5	19	3.5	11	4.0
6	150	27.9	43	15.8
7	277	51.6	141	51.6
8	74	13.8	67	24.5
9	14	2.6	8	2.9
10	2	0.4	3	1.1
11	1	0.2	0	0.0
TOTALS	537	100.0	273	99.9

Table 2. Formula dates of samples. (Source: O'Connor (1985)

Formula	Big Pit Complex	Smith's Ordinary
Binford (1962)	1671.00	1660.24
Hanson (1969)	1672.44	1664.29
Heighton & Deagan (1971)	1688.59	1681.19

Table 3. Pipe stems by bore diameter and country.

64ths"	Dutch		English	
	No.	%	No.	%
9	1	0.9	1	4.3
8	8	7.8	5	21.7
7	63	61.7	8	34.8
6	29	28.4	9	39.1
5	1	0.9	0	0.0
TOTAL	102		23	

sample of identified bowls at Smith's Ordinary, these conclusions are tentative but they point to the continued dominance of Dutch pipes in the Chesapeake in the 1670s.

Pipe stems marked with one or several *fleur-de-lis* make up a significant proportion of both samples. Overall, 40% of the pipes considered in this paper have some form of the *fleur-de-lis* mark. This style of decoration was declining during the last half of the 17th century. Duco (1981:248) suggests that the end date of this style was *circa* 1670. The data from the two samples in St. Mary's City support this decline. The earlier Big Pit complex has 42.9% of the sample so marked but by the time of the Smith's Ordinary sample, the proportion is only 39.7%. It would be dangerous to generalize on such small samples and so slight a decrease, but such a general decline seems probable. These data also suggest that the year of 1670 is too early to mark the end of that decorative practice in the Chesapeake, with 1675 or 1680 being more likely.

Finally, because of the narrow time range represented by these samples, it is important to consider the usefulness of some of the dating methods suggested for pipe analysis. The total number of pipe stems, marked and non-marked, from both samples were analyzed by O'Connor as part of the initial report on this site (O'Connor 1985:14-15). The data are presented in Table 1 and in Figure 4. A comparison of Figure 4 with the chart of pipe bore proportions prepared by Harrington (Noel Hume 1972:298) shows that these samples fit well into the 1650-1680 time range. O'Connor calculated the mean bore diameter of the samples using several of the proposed formulas and these results are shown in Table 2. For the Smith's Ordinary sample, two of the suggested mean dates are well before any deposition could have taken place and the other is three years after the building was torn down. The results for the Big Pit area are somewhat better, with two of the dates being only a year or two off. There is no pattern in these data and suggests that even with samples of 300 and 600 pipe stems, random variation can play an important role.

It has been suggested that the reason these methods seem less applicable to early 17th-century pipes is due to Dutch and English bore diameters changing at different rates. The samples from Smith's Ordinary and from the Big Pit area seem to be ideal to test this hypothesis. The data on bore diameter and country of origin are shown in Table 3. Because of the small number of measurable, identified English pipes (N=23) the two samples were combined for analysis. If we look at the actual distribution of bore diameters (Figure 5), it appears that the English pipes are more variable than the Dutch and occur in greater numbers on both sides of the Dutch mean. This sample of English pipes is much too small to draw conclusions, but this could prove a useful line of future research.

PIPE DESCRIPTIONS

SMPZ	=	Smith's Ordinary Plow Zone
SMF	=	Smith's Ordinary Features
BPPZ	=	Big Pit Complex Plow Zone
BPF	=	Big Pit Features

IDENTIFIED AND MARKED BOWLS

1. Yorkshire bulbous; burnished; poorly rouletted along back of rim only; *circa* 1660-1680 (Lawrence 1979:69 #10); Figure 6a.
   SMPZ 3
   SMF 2
   BPPZ 3
   BPF 1

2. Dutch belly bowl; medium size; *circa* 1650-1670 (Duco 1981:245 #39,41); Figure 6b.
   SMPZ 6
   SMF 2
   BPPZ 3
   BPF 5

3. Dutch funnel elbow pipe; straight sided bowl; no heel; rouletted rim-back of bowl; *circa* 1665- 1685 (McCashion 1979:124-5); Figure 6c.
   SMF 5
   BPPZ 1
   BPF 2

4. Spurred bowl; slightly bulbous; burnished; very forward leaning; English; *circa* 1640-70 (Oswald 1975:41 #17); Figure 6d.
   SMPZ 1

5. Marked "LE" on bowl; Llewellin Evans, Bristol 1661-86 (Walker 1977:1431 #G); Figure 6e.
   SMPZ 2
   BPPZ 3

6. Marked "...E" on bowl; either Llewellin Evans or William Evans, Bristol; *circa* 1660-1697; not illustrated.
   SMPZ 3

7. Tudor rose without sepals; on side of bowl above heel; seven dots; west Dutch *circa* 1640-70 (Duco 1981:244 #31-34); Figure 6f;
   BPF 10

8. Dutch Baroque pipe; leaf fragment; marked "WT"; *circa* 1635-55 (Duco 1981:253 #151-154); Figure 7a.
   SMPZ 1

9. Heel marked "OA" in beaded circle: Ouwen Andriesz, Gouda 1669-70 (Duco 1981:259 #227), 1660-1671 (Duco 1982:74); Figure 7b.
   BPPZ 1
   BPF 1

10. Marked "A" with crown in beaded circle on heel; Dutch belly bowl; Figure 7c.
    BPPZ   3

11. Marked with a crowned Tudor Rose on heel; six dots; with sepals; Dutch belly bowl; c. 1630-1660 (Duco 1981:247 #51, 249#116); Figure 7d.
    BPPZ   5
    BPF   1 (with sepals)

12. Marked with *fleur-de-lis* in diamond on heel; Dutch belly bowl; *circa* 1625-1650 (Duco 1981:249 #121); Figure 7e.
    BPF   1

13. Heel marked "WTW"; Dutch *circa* 1650-60 (McCashion 1979:107); Figure 7f.
    BPF   4

14. Heel marked with crown and cross in beaded circle; Figure 7g.
    BPF   1

15. Unidentified loop mark on bowl; not illustrated.
    SMPZ   1

16. Unidentified embossed molding on bowl; not illustrated.
    SMPZ   1

17. Incised running deer motif; terra cotta pipe; Figure 7h.
    SMPZ   1
    BPPZ   1
    BPF   1

18. Swirled white and red clay bowl; not illustrated.
    SMPZ   1

19. Marked "...R" on bowl; Figure 7i.
    BPPZ   1

20. Marked "...W" on bowl; not illustrated.
    BPF   1

21. Unidentified circle mark on bowl; not illustrated.
    SMPZ   1

MARKED STEMS

22. Multiple *fleur-de-lis* in a line; bordered; possibly Gouda; *circa* 1640-1670 (Duco 1981:248 #107); Figure 7j.
    SMPZ   11
    SMF   2
    BPPZ   16
    BPF   8

23. Multiple *fleur-de-lis*, not in a line; unbordered; possibly Gouda; *circa* 1625-1660 (Duco 1981:249 #122); not illustrated.
    SMPZ   1
    BPPZ   7
    BPF   4

24. Four *fleur-de-lis* arranged in a diamond; bordered; rouletting; possibly Gouda; *circa* 1645-1665 (Duco 1981:249 #118); Figure 8a.
    SMPZ   1
    BPPZ   1
    BPF   3

25. Single *fleur-de-lis* extant; bordered; not illustrated.
    SMPZ   8
    SMF   2
    BPPZ   4
    BPF   5

26. Marked "WE" and rouletted with dots and diamonds; William Evans, Bristol 1660-97 (Walker 1977:1435 #G); Figure 8b.
    SMPZ   1
    BPF   1

27. Rouletted with lattice diamonds and dots; Gouda c. 1660-95 (Duco 1981:250 #5 125-26); Fig. 8c.
    SMPZ   1

28. Marked with rows of "/s"; Gouda *circa* 1670-80 (Duco 1981:246 #44); Figure 8d.
    SMF   1
    BPPZ   1

29. Marked with large dots in diamonds and rouletting; Bristol 1661-89 (Alexander 1979:54-55); Figure 8e.
    SMPZ   1
    SMF   1
    BPPZ   7
    BPF   2

30. Terra cotta pipe stem marked with "WD" or "WID" monogram in circle with three dots above; Figure 8f.
    SMPZ   1

31. Terra cotta stem marked with rouletting; Fig. 8g.
    BPPZ   1

32. Marked with vine and flower motif; Dutch 1625-65 (Duco 1981:251 #132-137); Figure 8h.
    BPPZ   2

33. Marked with "teardrop" shapes below dots; possibly incised tulip; Figure 8i.
    BPPZ   1

34. Marked with "Xs" and rouletting; Gouda 1660-80 (Duco 1981:250 #127); Figure 8j.
    BPF   1

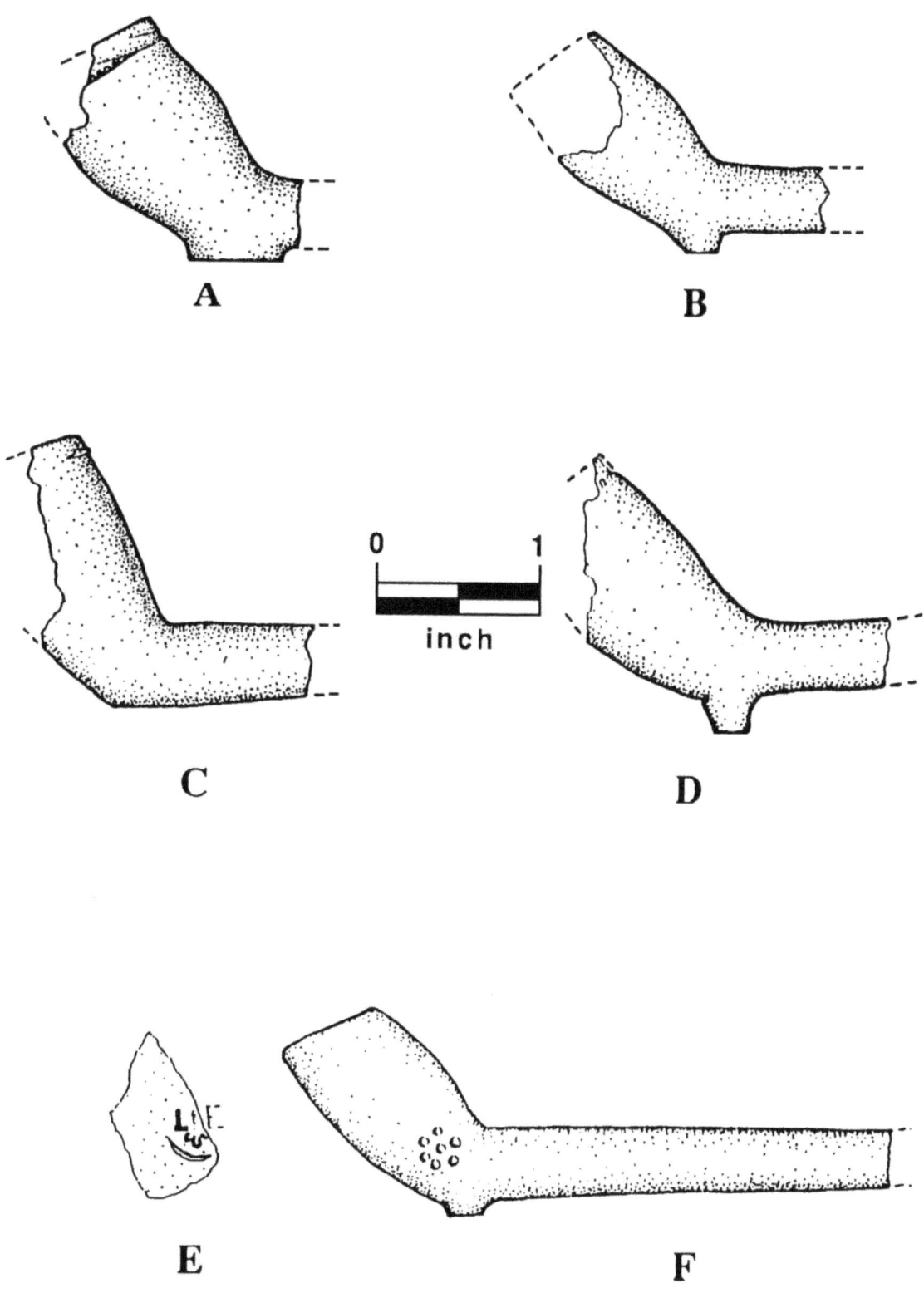

Figure 6: Smith's Townland pipes, identified and marked bowls A-F.

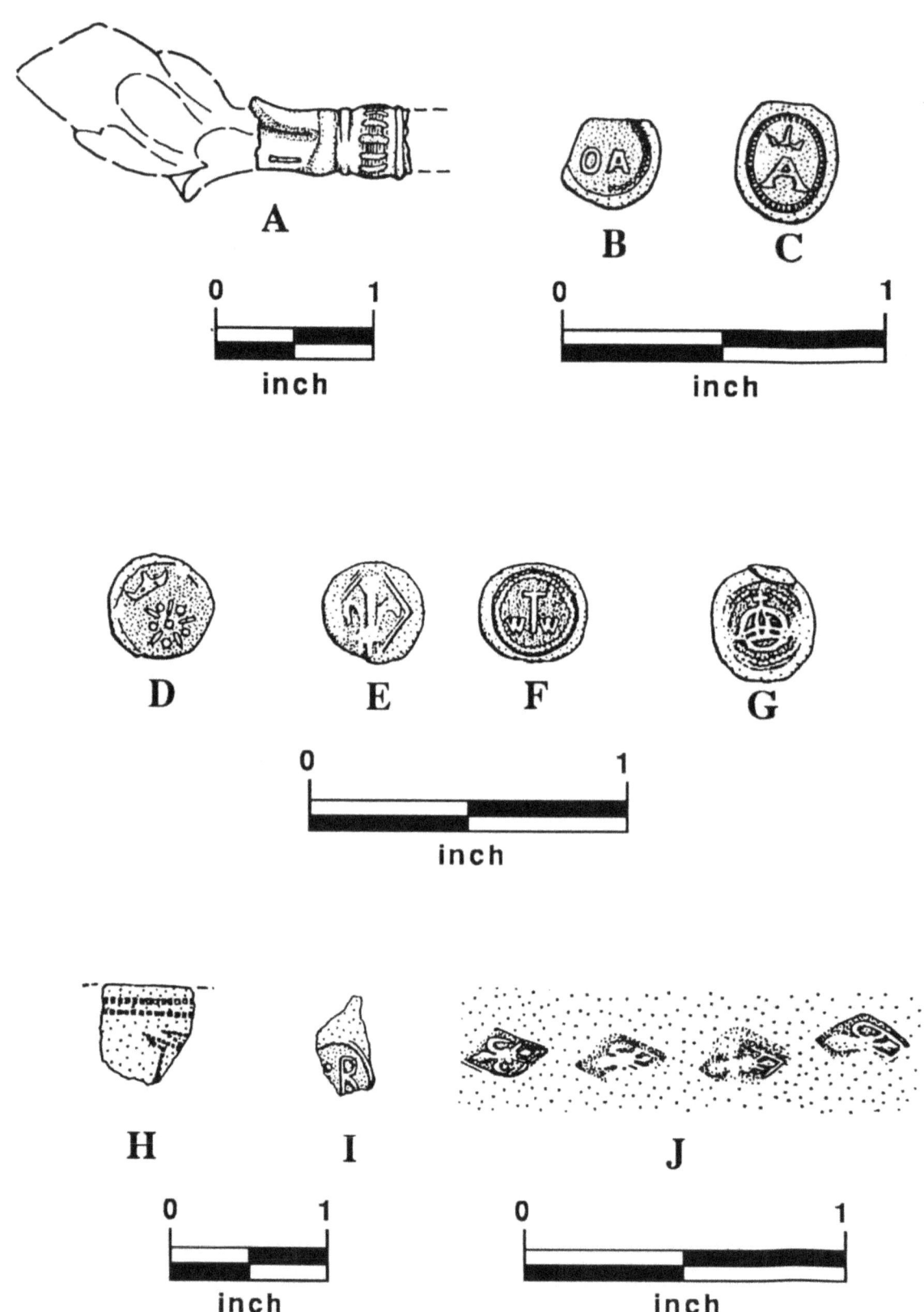

Figure 7: Smith's Townland pipes, identified and marked bowls A-I; marked stem J.

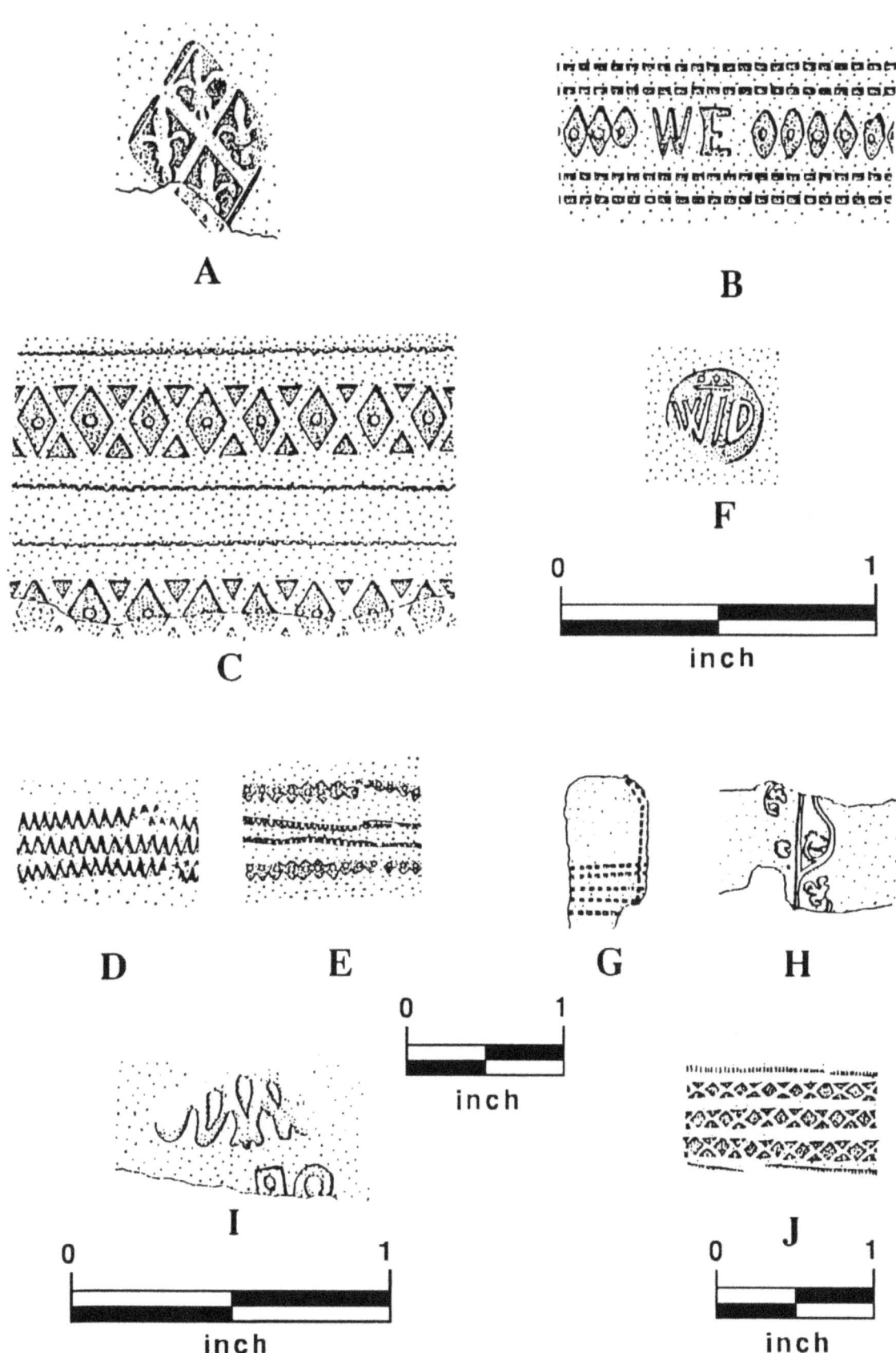

Figure 8: Smith's Townland pipes, marked stems A-J.

CONCLUSIONS

The samples considered in this paper, while small, point out some significant trends in pipe availability in the late 17th-century Chesapeake. The continuing dominance of Dutch-made pipes is obvious, but their decline is foreshadowed by the difference between the two samples. It seems that the decade of the 1670s is the turning point in the Dutch-to-English pipe ratio for Maryland. There is, at the same time, a significant change in the common bowl shape available. The Dutch belly bowl, which made up three-fourths of the earlier sample, declined to one-half of the later sample. In part, this is due to an increase in the availability of English-made pipes but it is also related to a shift in the style of the Dutch pipes being exported to Maryland. There is a real and significant increase in the number of Dutch funnel elbow pipes in the two samples. The reason for this shift is an interesting topic for future research. Finally, the St. Mary's City data suggests that *fleur-de-lis* marked pipes continue to be exported to the Chesapeake in significant numbers throughout the decade of the 1670s, indicating that this style lasted longer than previously reported.

REFERENCES CITED

Alexander, L.T. (1979) Clay pipes from the Buck Site in Maryland. *The Archaeology of the Clay Tobacco Pipe II: The United States of America.* Edited by P.J. Davey, British Archaeological Reports International Series 60: 37-61.

Binford, L.R. (1962) A new method of calculating dates from kaolin pipe stem fragments. *Southeastern Archaeological Conference Newsletter* 9(1):19-21, Cambridge, Mass.

Duco, D.H. (1981). The clay tobacco pipe in 17th-century Netherlands. *The Archaeology of the Clay Tobacco Pipe V:Europe 2.* Edited by P.J. Davey, British Archaeological Reports International Series 106(ii).

Duco, D.H. (1982). *Merken van Goudse Pijpenmakers.* Uitgeversmaatschappij Di Tijdstroom Lochen/ Poperinge.

Hansen, L.W. (1969) Kaolin pipe stems - boring in on a fallacy. *Conference on Historic Site Archaeology Papers* 4:2-15, Columbia, South Carolina.

Heighton, R.F. and Deagan, K.A. (1971) A new formula for dating kaolin clay pipestems. *Conference on Historic Site Archaeology Papers* 6:220-229, Columbia, South Carolina.

Lawrence, S. (1979). York Pipes and their Makers. *The Archaeology of the clay tobacco pipe 1: Britain, the Midlands and Eastern England.* P.J. Davey, editor, pp.67-84. British Archaeological Reports British Series 63, Oxford.

McCashion, J.H. (1979) A preliminary chronology and discussion of seventeeth and early eighteenth century clay pipes from New York State sites. *The Archaeology of the Clay Tobacco Pipe II: The United States America.* Edited by P.J. Davey, British Archaeological Reports International Series 60:63-150.

Miller, H.M. (1986). Discovering Maryland's first city. *St. Mary's City Archaeology Series 2.* Noel Hume, I. (1972). *A guide to artifacts of Colonial America.* A.A. Knopf, New York.

O'Connor, J. (1985). Neither a borrower nor a lender be: findings from a feature in the 17th-century village green of St. Mary's City. Ms. on file, Historic St. Mary's City, Maryland.

Oswald, A. (1975) *Clay pipes for the Archaeologist* British Archaeological Reports 14, Oxford, England.

Walker, I.C. (1977). Clay tobacco pipes with particular reference to the Bristol Industry. *History and Archaeology Series* 11, Parks Canada, Ottawa.

Watkins, G. (1979). Hull pipes: a typology. *Archaeology of the Clay Tobacco Pipe 1: Britain, the Midlands and Eastern England.* Edited by P.J. Davey, British Archaeological Reports British Series 63: 95-122.

Tobacco Pipes from the Abell's Wharf Site (18 ST 53), St Mary's County, Maryland

Michael E. Humphries

INTRODUCTION

The Abell's Wharf Site (18 St 53) is located approximately 50 miles south of Washington, D.C., on a tributary of the Potomac River, in St. Mary's County, Maryland (Figure 1). The site includes both prehistoric Indian remains dating to circa 10,000 years ago, and extensive evidence of a Colonial period habitation spanning the last quarter of the 17th and first quarter of the 18th centuries. Initial investigations at the site were undertaken by the Archeological Society of Maryland in 1975. Intensive excavations were conducted from 1975 to 1978 under the supervision of the Maryland Geological Survey Division of Archeology and the George Washington University, and in cooperation with the St. Clement's Island-Potomac River Museum. In addition to numerous structural features associated with a residence, the major historic feature excavated was a trash-filled pit that contained large quantities of domestic refuse. This includes a total of 446 measurable pipe stems, and 29 largely complete bowls and 120 bowl fragments. The collection has been analyzed through measurement of the stem bores and computation of the Binford mean date, and the analysis of bowl shapes, decorations, and maker's marks.

SITE HISTORY

In 1641 the area now including Abell's Wharf was patented by Randall Revel and named "Revel's". By 1657 the 300-acre tract evidently had passed to the ownership of Henry Fox and his partner, Dr. Luke Barber. With the death of Fox the following year, his interest in the property was transferred to his widow and then to a son. This resulted in a dispute with Dr. Barber, Henry Fox's original partner, over clear title to the land. The 300 acres in question then were divided, with Barber "receiving that parcel of cleared ground with the appurtenances lying next to his dwelling house". In 1673 Dr. Luke Barber's will was probated, with his eldest son receiving 180 acres of Revel's (Humphries 1977). Unfortunately, it is not possible to discern whether the Abell's Wharf Site was included in this portion.

The remaining 120 acres of the Revel's tract are believed to have been split into two parcels owned by James Tant and his spouse. Over the ensuing decades, it appears that these parcels changed hands many times, with the 70-acre portion owned by James Tant, Jr. at the time of his death in 1717. Tant's widow, Mary,

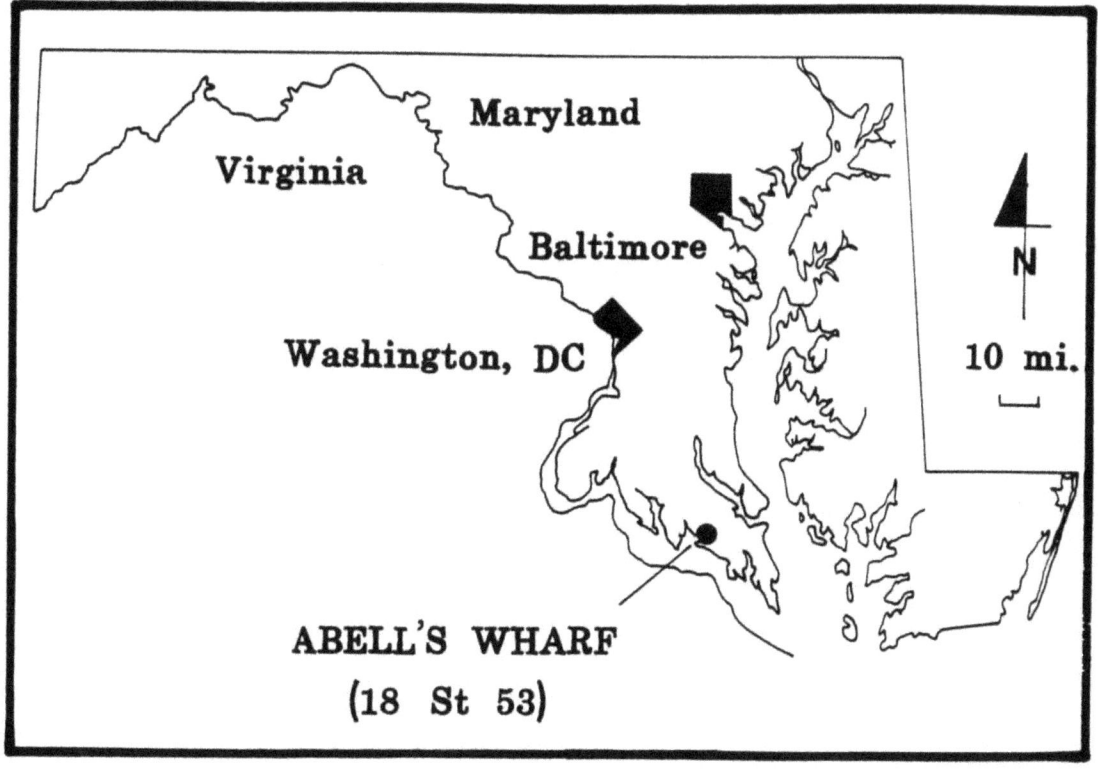

Figure 1. Location of Abell's Wharf Site (18 St 53), St Mary's County, Maryland.

remarried to Robert Ford, who in 1729 purchased a neighboring parcel that alsohad been part of Revel's. Robert Ford, Jr. also obtained more of the original tract, and ultimately appears to have been in possession of at least 120 acres of what had been Revel's. Upon Robert Ford's death in 1753, a sizeable estate valued at more than 1,000 pounds sterling was left to his heirs (Humphries 1977).

No conclusive evidence has been found to link any of these owners with the Abell's Wharf archaeological site. However, the chronology of ownership indicates that the area was inhabited from the third quarter of the 17th century through the first half of the 18th century. This period spans the apparent occupation of the Abell's Wharf Site. During this period, the property owners were several members of the Tant and Ford families, who, therefore, may have been the occupants of Abell's Wharf.

THE PIT

The trash-filled pit was oblong in shape and measured more than 4-by-5 feet in dimension and more than three feet in depth below the plowzone. Its gently sloping sides and the absence of either interior structural supports or any post holes nearby suggests a function other than a cellar. "Borrow pits," excavated to obtain clay required for building, and then repairing, wattle and daub chimneys are commonly found on sites of this period in Maryland and Virginia. Once dug, the borrow pit would have served as a handy trash receptacle. Twenty-three separate strata were identified, including several almost completely comprised of ash, charcoal, and shell, interspersed with sand and clay lenses. This evidence suggests that the pit was mostly filled through purposeful deposition from the residence nearby, but was open long enough for soils to be deposited naturally.

A wide range of common household items were recovered, such as ceramics, wine bottle and tableglass fragments, a pewter spoon, brass pins, and a thimble. Food remains, such as oyster shells and animal bone, were recovered along with structural materials, including nails, brick, and mortar. And of special interest, a farthing bearing the image of Charles II and the date 1673 also was recovered near the bottom of the pit. The coin is worn and suggests that it had been in circulation for some time.

THE PIPES

A total of 446 measurable pipe stems were recovered from the pit, with 42% 7/64ths-inch, 24% 6/64th, and 21% 8/64th (Table 1). In comparison with the histograms for stem bore percentages prepared by Harrington (1954), this distribution suggests an occupation in the circa 1670-1700 range. The relatively broad distribution of bore diameters over 6-8/64ths-inch points to an extended period of deposition. Computation of the Binford (1962) pipe stem formula based on the 446 stems resulted in a mean date of 1674.05.

Table 1: Distribution of measurable bore sizes.

Diameter	Number	Percentage of Total
4/64	1	.0022421 (00%)
5/64	55	.1233183 (12%)
6/64	105	.235428 (24%)
7/64	188	.4215248 (42%)
8/64	92	.206278 (21%)
9/64	5	.0107295 (01%)
TOTAL	446	100%

Figure 2 (opposite): Representative pipes from Abell's Wharf.

A. Locally-made, molded, red clay pipe bowl; probably made by Colonists (6/64);
B. American Export type bowl, with rouletting around rim (7/64);
C. American Export type bowl, with rouletting around rim (8/64);
D American Export type bowl, with vestigial rouletting around rim, "RT" stamped on rear of bowl (7/64);
E. American Export type bowl, with rouletting around rim (7/64);
F. Heeled pipe bowl, with rouletting around rim (7/64);
G. Heeled pipe bowl, with incised line below rim (7/64);
H. Heeled pipe bowl, with incised line below rim (6/64);
I. Heeled pipe bowl, with rouletting around rim, and stamped "Tudor Rose" design on bottom of heel (not shown) (7/64); possibly Dutch;
J. Heeled pipe bowl, with rouletting around rim, and stamped "EB" mark on bottom of heel (8/64); probably Dutch; from plowzone.
K. American Export type bowl, with vestigal rouletting around rim, and stamped "EB" mark on bottom (8/64); probably Dutch; from plowzone.

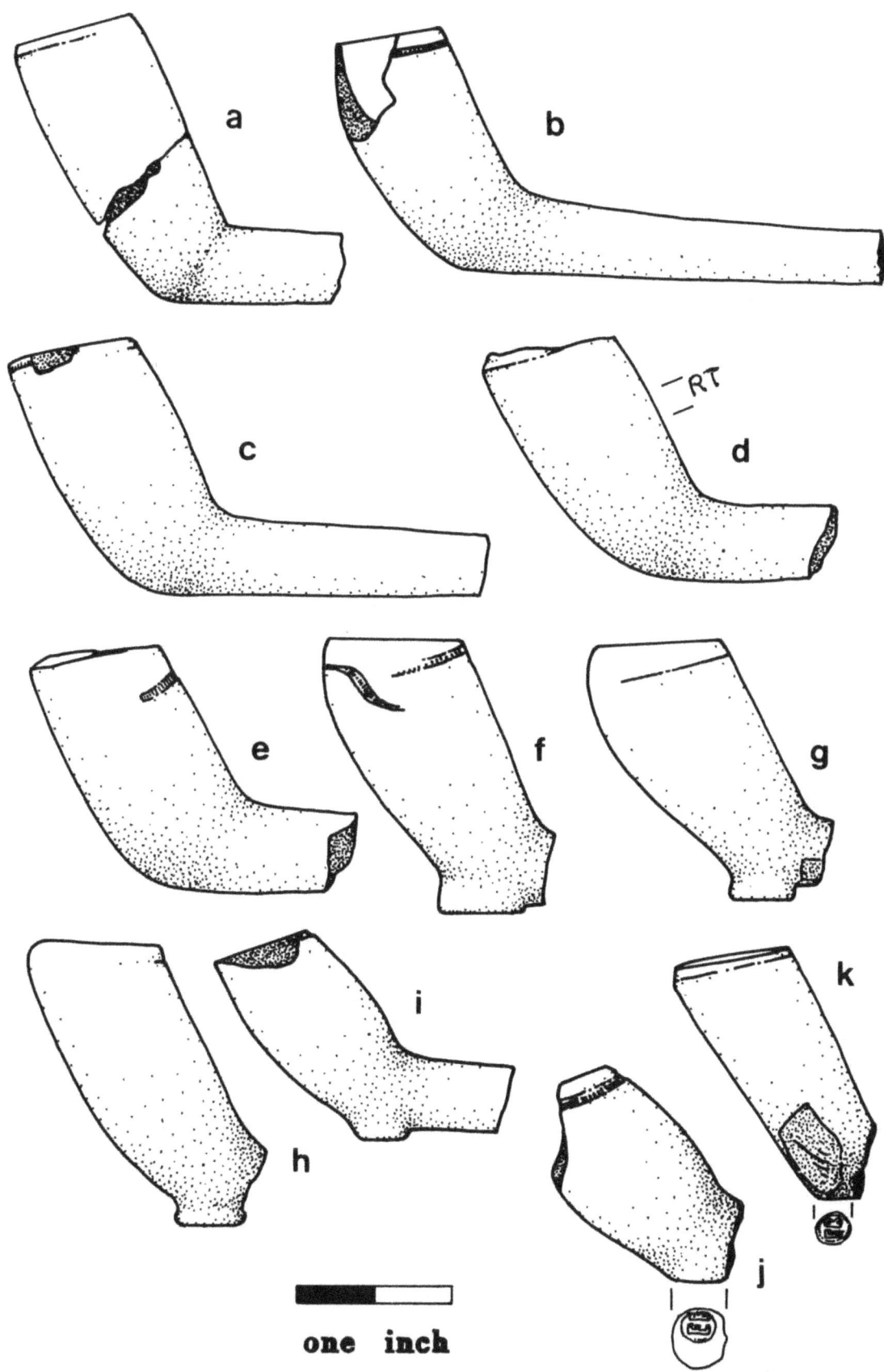

Figure 2: Representative pipes from Abell's Wharf.

Based on a comparison with the total artifact assemblage and the results of the Harrington analysis, the pipe mean date is much too early. The presence of the farthing dated 1673 provides a terminus post quem for the filling of the feature as that year, and makes the 1674 date virtually impossible. Finally, sherds of English brown salt-glazed stoneware also were excavated, which could not have been deposited before circa 1690. Therefore, the combined evidence points to the pit's being filled during the last decade of the 17th century, and serves to reinforce the generally accepted finding that the Binford formula is untrustworthy when the total number of bores calculated is less than approximately 1000.

In addition to the stem fragments, 120 pipe bowl fragments and 29 bowls were recovered. This includes one bowl composed of a reddish-brown clay, which seems to have been mold made (Figure 2:a). As such, it most likely was produced by Colonists rather than local Indians. A second locally-made bowl features a rouletted design, consisting of three incised concentric bands around the rim and two similar bands mid-way down the bowl, and with two large stars (1.4 cm. in length) and one small star (8 mm. in length) in between. Indian-made pipes with almost identical decorations have been recovered in quantity from Chesapeake sites in contexts before circa 1670; after that year, local pipes apparently made by Colonists using imported molds become more common (Miller 1983:83).

Twenty-two of the 28 imported, white clay bowls are of the heel-less, spurless, American Export type, while six are heeled. None of the bowls in this collection have spurs. The prevalence of the American Export bowl type may support a late 17th-century period of deposition. Only two of the bowls exhibit maker's marks. One is a partial "Tudor Rose" design stamped on the bottom of a heeled pipe (Figure 2:i). The RT mark is one of the more commonly found marks on American sites from the Colonial period and is well known as that of one of the three Robert Tippetts of Bristol, England. Unfortunately, it has proven to be virtually impossible to separate the products of the three Tippetts, who together made pipes from circa 1660 until 1720 (Walker 1977(C):1316-1318). This mark consists of the stamped initials on the back of a bowl fragment (Figure 2:d).

In addition to these marked specimens, three identifiable marks were recovered from plowzone. One of them is another extremely common mark that of Llewellin Evans, another Bristol pipe maker who exported great quantities of pipes to North America from 1661 to circa 1689 (Walker 1977(C):1132). This example is similar to many others that have been excavated elsewhere in North America (cf. Walker 1977), and consists of the simple, stamped initials on the bowl back.

Three pipes were recovered exhibiting the initials EB. The initials EB most likely are those of Edward Bird, a manufacturer of trade pipes from 1636 to 1665. A Bristol maker with the same initials, Edward Battle, also produced pipes from circa 1660 to 1669. However, no pipes have been directly attributed to his manufacture (Walker 1977(C):1406). Bird, an expatriate from England, settled in Amsterdam, where his influence in the Dutch trade with the New World is evident from the regularity with which his marked pipes have been found on sites throughout the eastern seaboard. This includes the Chesapeake Bay area, with numerous examples excavated at nearby St. Mary's City (Miller 1983:78). Both examples from Abell's Wharf are marked on the bowl bottoms (Figure 2:i and k).

The other marked pipe is a stem fragment with the name "CHRIS ATHERTON" running around the stem and within two incised lines. Stems with virtually identical marks have been recovered at two other 17th-century sties in St. Mary's County, at St. Mary's City and at St. Inigoes (King and Pogue 1985). No pipe maker with that name has been identified to date, but several named Atherton are known to have been making pipes in Liverpool in the 18th century (Oswald 1975:176-177).

CONCLUSION

While limited in size, the Abell's Wharf pipe collection derives from a restricted context, and therefore provides insight into pipe use in one late 17th-century Maryland household. The contents of the pit appear to have been deposited during the circa 1690-1710 period, and in general the pipes reflect that fact. The predominance of American Export-type bowls and the presence of the Bristol-made mark, RT, supports that period of deposition. The majority of the pipe data, therefore, supports the other artifact evidence. However, the presence of the possible Edward Bird pipe, dating circa 1636 to 1665, and the Indian-made bowl at the same site suggest that the site had been occupied beginning substantially earlier than 1690.

REFERENCES CITED

Binford, L.R. (1962). A new method of calculating dates from kaolin pipe stem samples. *Southeastern Archaeological Conference Newsletter* 9(1):19-21.

Harrington, J.C. (1954). Dating stem fragments of seventeenth and eighteenth century clay tobacco pipes. *Quarterly Bulletin of the Archaeological Society of Virginia* 9(1):9-13.

Humphries, M.E. (1977). Frequency and dating of white clay tobacco pipes from a trash pit at Abell's Wharf, Maryland (18 St 53). *Occasional Paper Number One*, St.Clement's Island and Potomac River Museum, Colton Point, Maryland.

King, J.A. and Pogue, D.J. (1985). *Archaeological investigations at the Antenna Field, St. Inigoes, Maryland*. St. Inigoes, Maryland.

Miller, H.M. (1983). A search for the "Citty of Saint Maries": report on the 1981 excavations in St. Mary's City, Maryland. *St. Maries City Archaeology Series* No. 1.

Oswald, A. (1975). *Clay pipes for the archaeologist*. British Archaeological Reports 14.

Peck, D.W. (1976). Abell's Wharf: a preliminary report. *Maryland Geological, Survey, Archaeological Miscellaneous Series 1*.

Walker, I.C. (1977). *Clay tobacco pipes, with particular reference to the Bristol industry* (4 Vols.). Parks Canada, Ottawa.

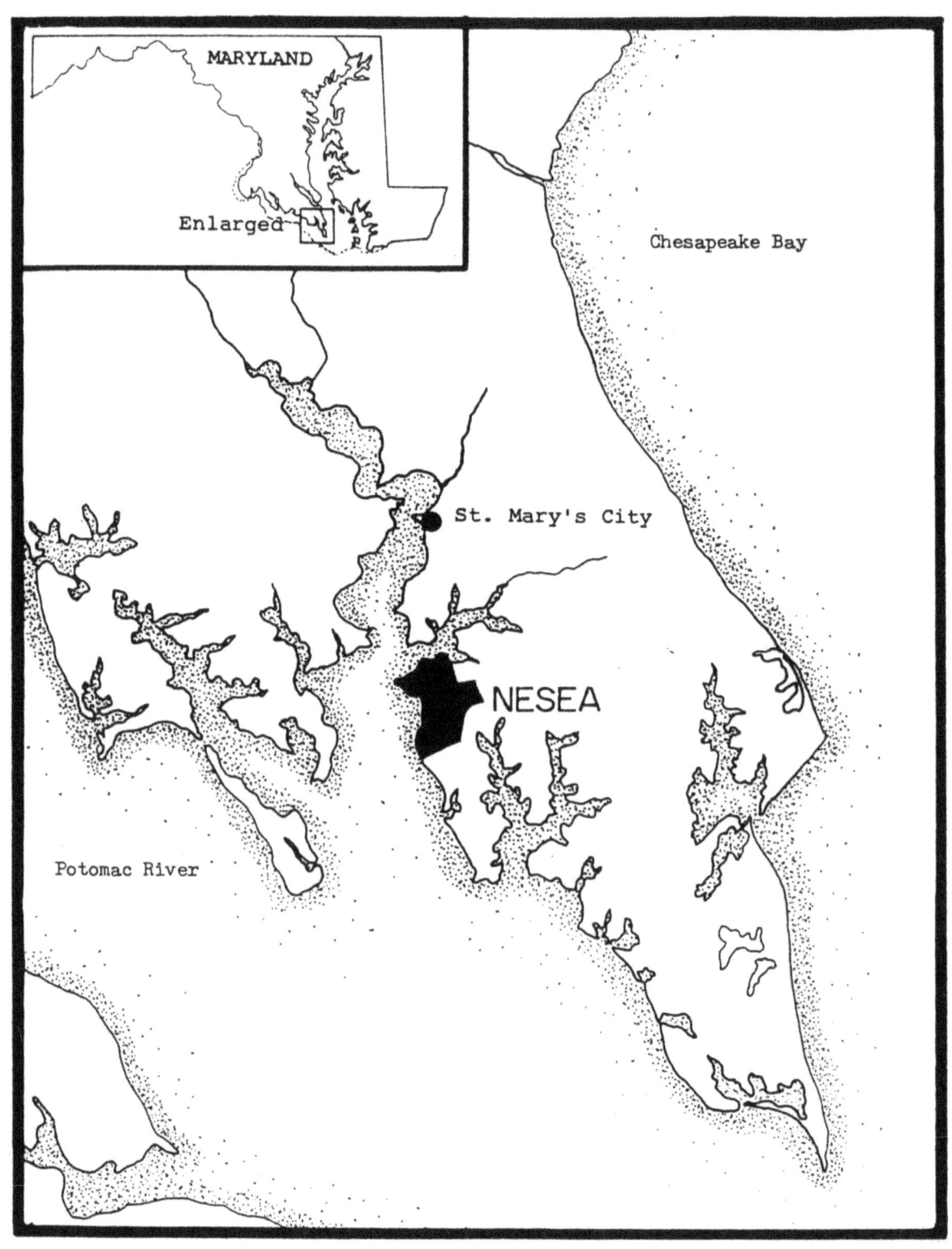

Figure 1: The Location of the Naval Electronics Systems Engineering Activity (NESEA)

Clay Tobacco Pipes from Two Early Colonial Sites at St. Inigoes Manor, Maryland.

Julia A. King.

INTRODUCTION

This paper presents a descriptive analysis of an assemblage of white clay tobacco pipes recovered from two Colonial domestic sites on the Jesuit holding of St. Inigoes Manor, Maryland. The majority of tobacco pipe fragments were retrieved from a two-acre field through the combination of controlled surface collection conducted under the direction of the author, and a random collection by a local informant. Although all the pipe stem and bowl pieces described in this paper were recovered from the surface of a plowed field, and many are provenienced only to the field itself, significant information on the specific site date, and on patterns of pipe availability during the second half of the 17th century, is provided.

HISTORICAL BACKGROUND

St. Inigoes Manor was patented in 1634 by Richard Gerard, one of the investors in Lord Baltimore's New World venture. Gerard soon tired of life in frontier Maryland, however, and, in 1637, he sold his 2000-acre tract of land to the Society of Jesus to serve as the headquarters of their mission effort as well as a major tobacco plantation. A church farm had been established at St. Inigoes by 1637, and large crops of corn and tobacco were being produced in that year. Small tenant farms were present on the manor by 1639 (Beitzell 1976:8, 19-20). St. Inigoes Manor continued to operate as a farm with tenants and remained in the possession of the Jesuits until 1942. At that time, the Society sold the northern 773 acres of the original tract to the United States Navy (Beitzell 1976: 244). The property is now maintained as the Naval Electronics Systems Engineering Activity (NESEA).

Since 1980, the Navy has funded six systematic archaeological investigations in order to protect cultural resources located |there(cf. King and Pogue 1985a). Despite relatively extensive survey, no evidence for historic occupation prior to *circa* 1660 has been recovered, and one investigator has suggested that the earliest sites have been lost to erosion (Smolek et al 1983). The possibility also exists that these resources are situated on land still owned by the Jesuits.

To date, only one 17th-century site has been discovered on that part of St. Inigoes Manor now owned by the Navy (Figures 1, opposite, and 2). The Fort Point Site is located in an approximately two-acre field used to house antennae (Figure 3). The Spence Site, dating to the early 18th century, is also located in the same field, approximately 400 hundred feet northeast of the Fort Point Site (Figure 3).

FIELD METHODS

The survey strategy used in the Antenna Field consisted of a controlled surface collection of plowed areas, with limited subsurface testing in an area which could not be plowed. Grid units of 10 by 10 feet were used in the surface collection and units of 5 by 5 feet were used for subsurface testing. All recovered artifacts were bagged by provenience, washed, catalogued and labelled and, along with field and laboratory records, deposited with the Southern Maryland Regional Center of the Maryland Historical Trust/Jefferson Patterson Park and Museum (King and Pogue 1985b:5-6).

The survey of the Antenna Field revealed evidence for two Colonial sites. The earlier site, the Fort Point Site (18 ST 386), was occupied *circa* 1660-1690, and represents the earliest Colonial archaeological site discovered on the Navy's property to date. The second site, the Spence Site (18 ST 541), dates to the first quarter of the 18th century and possibly as early as *circa* 1690 (King and Pogue 1985b).

Prior to the archaeological survey, an employee of the Naval facility at St. Inigoes had randomly collected artifacts exposed on the Antenna Field's surface. The archaeologists were fortunate to have access to this sizable collection, known as the Spence Collection. Although the artifacts lack the specific provenience information provided by the controlled surface collection, analysis of the assemblage provides further data on occupation in the Antenna Field vicinity.

THE ANTENNA FIELD TOBACCO PIPE ASSEMBLAGE

The clay pipe collection from the Antenna Field totals 810 fragments, including stem and bowl pieces. For the purposes of this discussion, the assemblage has been divided into four categories: the Fort Point Site collection, the Spence Site collection, the Spence artifact collection and the Isolated Pipe Stem Find.

THE FORT POINT SITE:

The controlled surface collection of the Fort Point Site (*circa* 1660-1690) yielded 90 white clay tobacco pipe fragments. Unfortunately, no bowl complete enough to date precisely were recovered. Thirty bowl fragments,

105

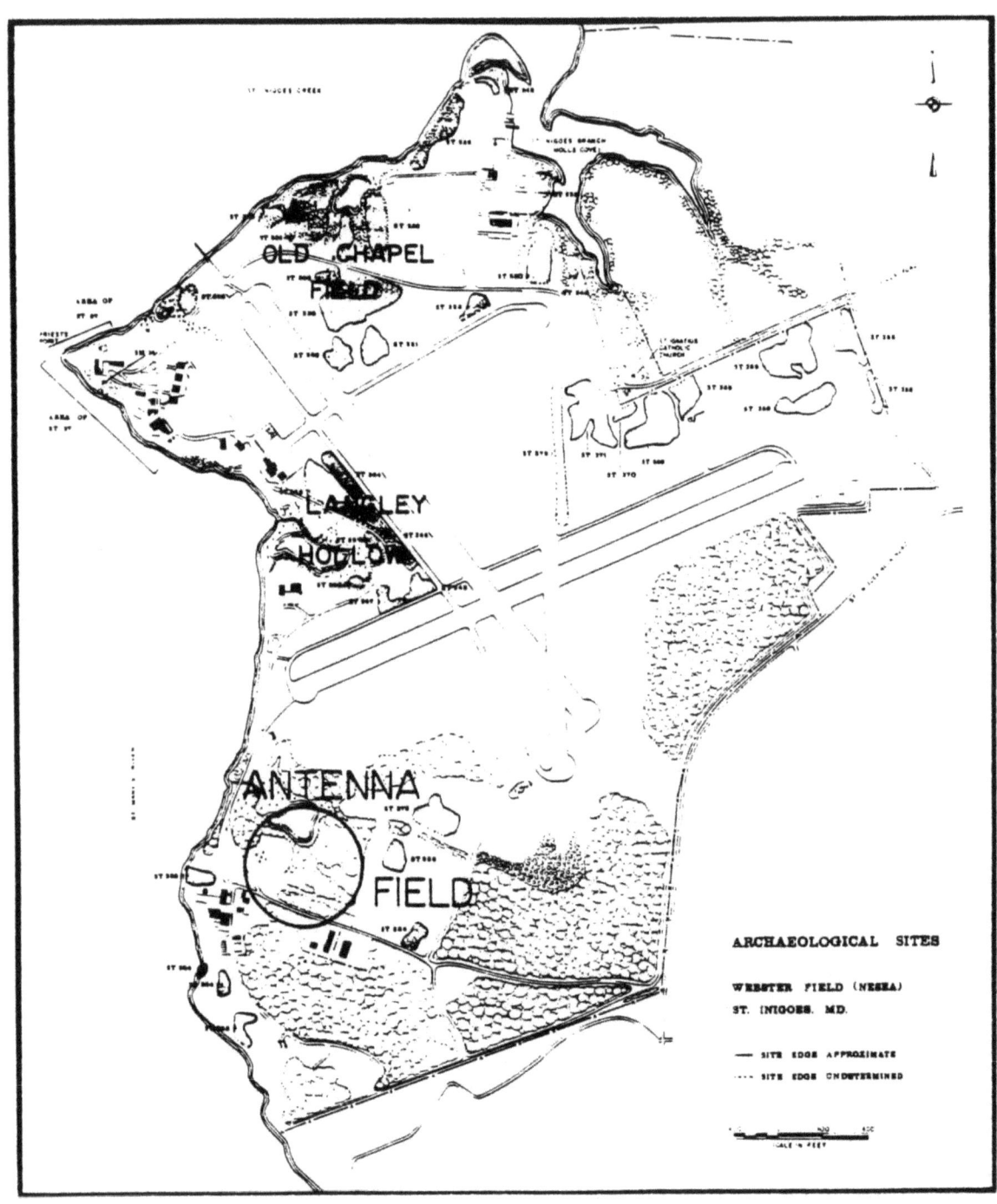

Figure 2: NESEA facility map showing location of Antenna Field.

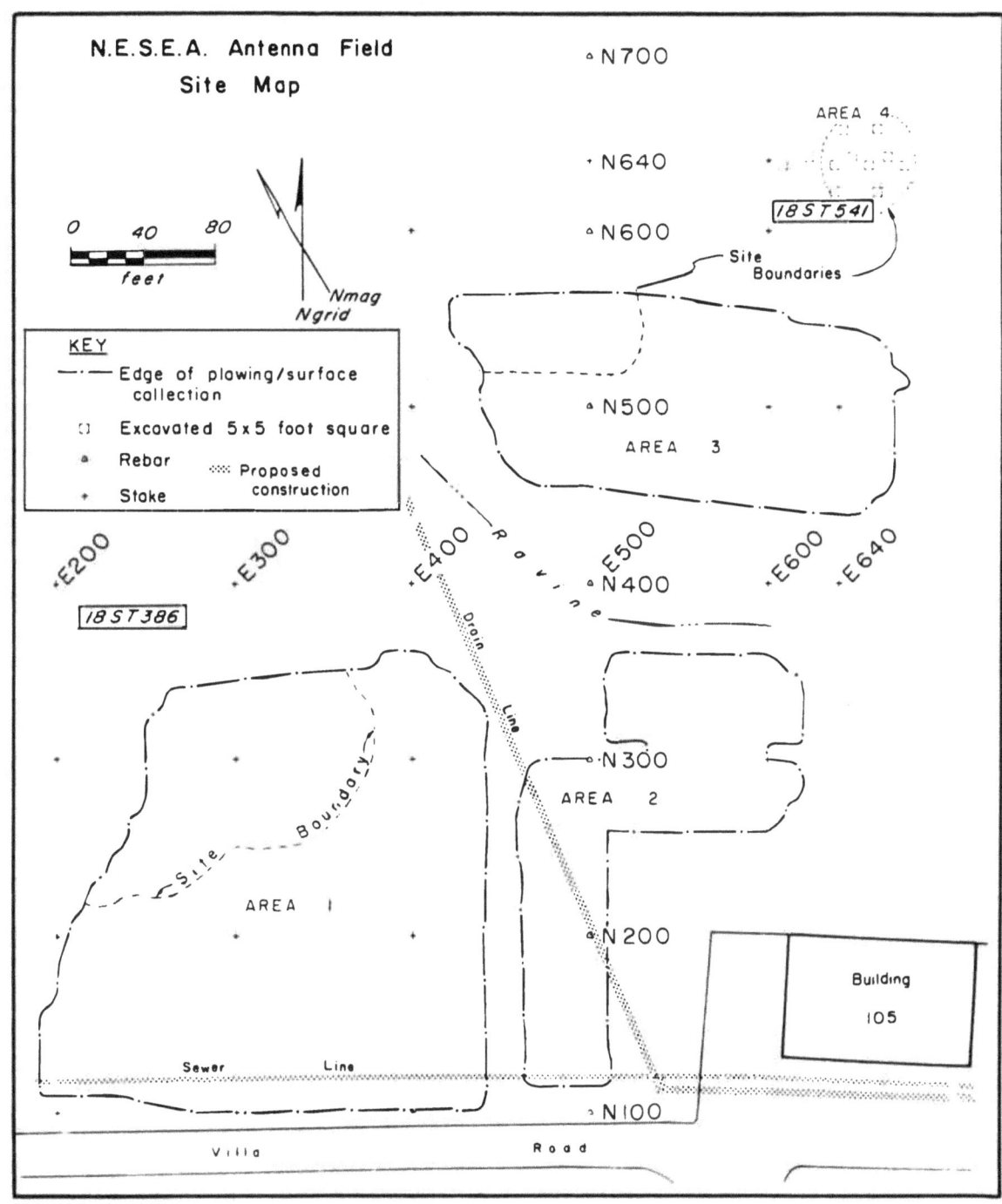

Figure 3: The Fort Point (18 ST 386) and the Spence (18 ST 41) sites in the Antenna Field.

however, are present in the collection, and identifiable attributes are 17th-century in date. Five surviving rim fragments have evidence of rouletting, and one has incising, traits common to 17th-century pipe bowls. Further, two stems have identifiable maker's marks. One stem is marked "LE," and similar marks have been observed on pipes recovered from nearby St. Mary's City (Miller 1983:76-77). This mark is attributed to Llewelin Evans, a pipe maker known to be working in Bristol from *circa* 1661-1688 (Oswald 1975:152). The second marked stem contains the name "WIL EVANS," probably one of two William Evanses (1660-1696), also pipe makers in Bristol (Oswald 1975:152-153).

White clay tobacco pipe stem bore diameters are often used for dating colonial sites. As tobacco decreased in cost throughout the 17th and 18th centuries, tobacco pipe stems lengthened and stem bore diameters necessarily grew smaller. The pipe bores of 56 stem fragments from the Fort Point site were measured and their relative frequency is shown in the histogram in Figure 4. Although this is an admittedly small sample, the distribution most closely resembles that for *circa* 1650-1680 suggested by Harrington (1954). Ceramic and other artifact evidence from the Fort Point Site surface collection, however, strongly suggest a date of occupation of *circa* 1660-1690. The Fort Point pipe stem distribution is also similar to that observed for the pipes recovered from Smith's Townland in St. Mary's City. Smith's Townland was occupied some time during the 1660s until the early 1690s. The stems derived from the plow zone over Smith's Ordinary and a nearby lawyer's house (Miller 1983: 134-135). Ceramic and other artifact evidence from the Fort Point Site surface collection strongly suggest a date of occupation of *circa* 1660-1690.

THE SPENCE SITE

The Spence Site (*circa* 1700-1725) was identified through a combination of surface collection and limited subsurface testing in an area where plowing was not feasible. Eighty-eight tobacco pipe fragments are included in the assemblage, including 44 bowl and 44 stem pieces. None of the bowl fragments are complete enough to identify, nor are any of the stems marked or decorated. The absence of rouletting and incising on surviving rim fragments supports an 18th-century date.

The measurable pipe stem bores are small and also point to an 18th-century date. Forty stem fragments are measurable and more than three-fourths (32) have bore diameters of 5-64ths-inch (Table 1). The distribution is somewhat similar to the histogram used by Harrington (1954) indicating a *circa* 1710-1750 date. The Spence Site pipe stem distribution is more steep than that shown in the Harrington chart, however, and may indicate a shorter term of occupation than that suggested by Harrington. The other artifact evidence from the site points to an occupation beginning no earlier than *circa* 1690, and probably as late as *circa* 1700. The absence of dipped white salt-glazed stonewares suggests an ending date of occupation no later than *circa* 1725. However, little is known about tenant farmers in the 17th and 18th centuries, and the absence of dipped white salt-glazed stonewares may not be simply a temporal phenomenon.

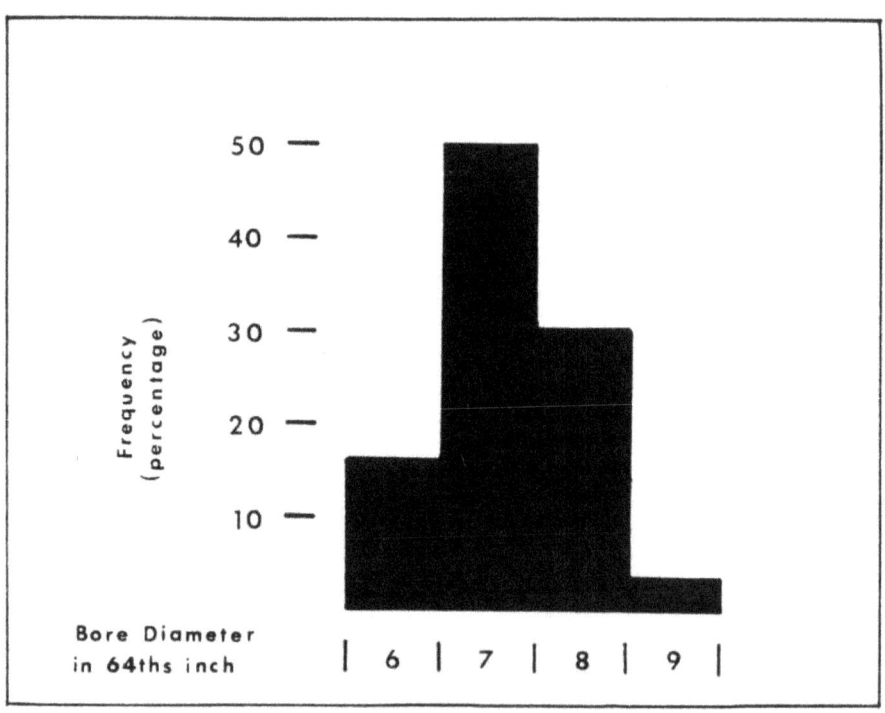

Figure 4: Relative frequency of tobacco pipe bore diameters at the Fort Point site.

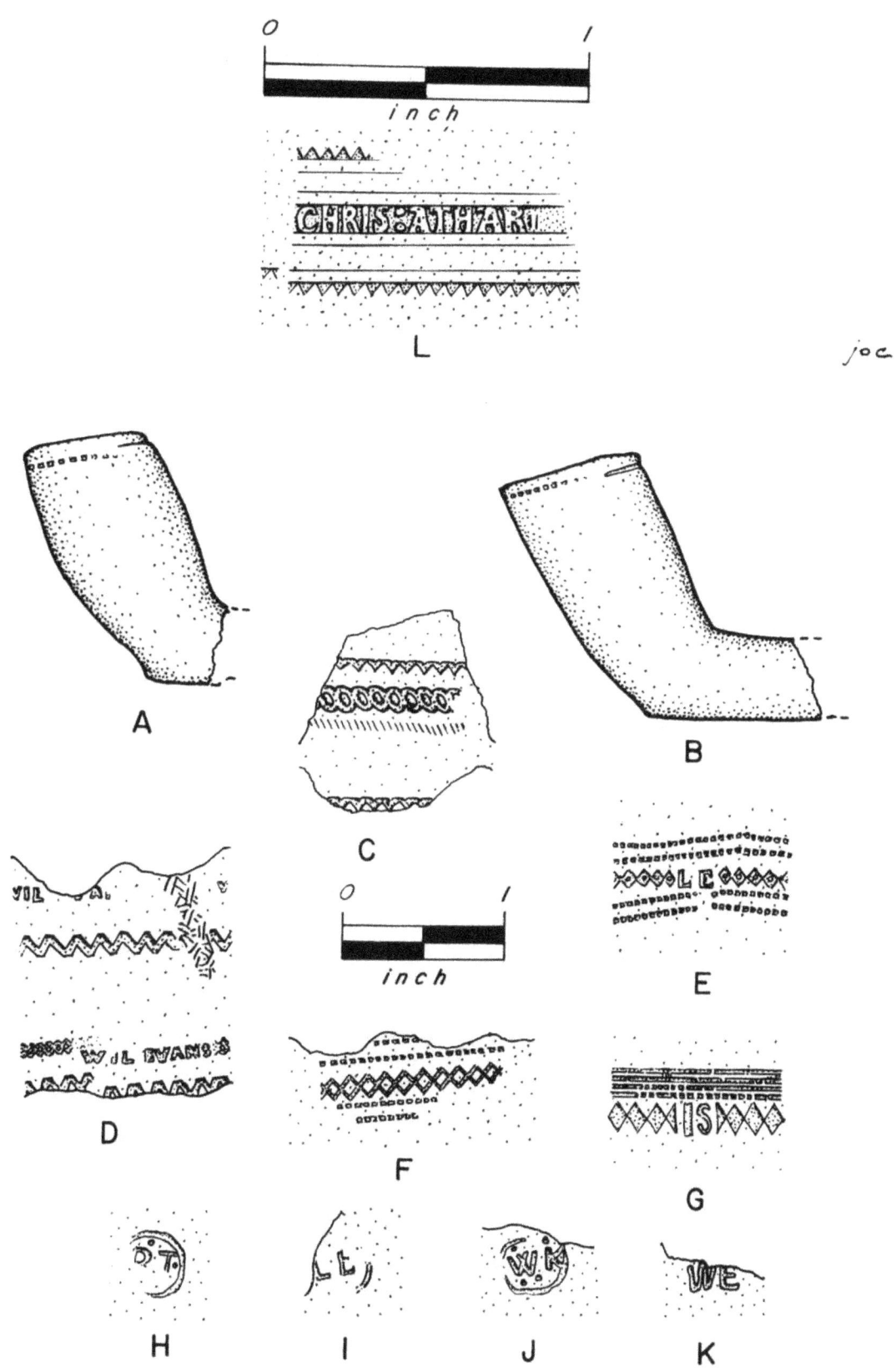

Figure 5: White clay tobacco pipes from the Spence collection.

THE SPENCE COLLECTION:

The unprovenienced surface collection in the possession of the Navy employee contained over 1,000 Colonial artifacts, including 632 white clay pipe fragments. The assemblage represents the results of random surface collecting from the field containing the two sites and, not surprisingly, the artifacts date *circa* 1660 through the first quarter of the 18th century. According to the collector, all but one of the pipe fragments were recovered in the vicinity of the Fort Point Site, although this cannot be completely verified through an analysis of the collection.

Two pipe bowls in the collection are complete enough to suggest a late 17th century date. The first example (Figure 5a) has a slightly forward leaning bowl with a slightly rounded midsection. A flat, un-marked heel is present on the base and the rim is rouletted. The second pipe bowl (Figure 5b) is nearly straight-sided at a slightly forward leaning angle. The rim of the bowl is rouletted and the pipe is heel-less. This unmarked bowl is similar in form to a pipe bowl recovered in St. Mary's City and marked "LE," attributed to Llewellin Evans (*circa* 1661-1688) (Miller 1983:76-77).

Of the 632 pipe fragments, 28 are marked bowl or stem fragments, and nine of these are positively identified. Nine pipes exhibit marks which can be identified as to maker, and all were produced in Bristol, England (Figure 5, d-k). Identified marks range in date from *circa* 1650 to 1720, and all but one are available in the *circa* 1660-1680 range (Figure 6). These include one bowl and two stem fragments attributed to one or both of the William Evanses (1660-1696) (Figure 5 d, k), a stem associated with one of the Robert Tippetts (1660-1720) (Figure 5, h), four stems attributed to Llewellin Evans (1661-1688) (Figure 5, e, i), and one stem of John Sinderling (1668-1699) (Figure 5, g). A tenth bowl fragment is marked "WK," possibly William Kinton (*circa* 1657-1700) or William King (late 17th century) (Figure 5, j) (Oswald 1975:155). Eight bowl rim fragments and one stem are rouletted, a treatment common on tobacco pipes of the 17th century.

Other patterns include a dot and diamond arrangement with rouletting around the stem, sometimes called a "Bristol pattern" (Figure 5, f). Pipes with this design have been found on sites of the second half of the 17th century at St. Mary's City (Miller 1983: 76-77) and on the Eastern Shore of Maryland (Alexander 1979:59).

A stem was also found with an almost complete but

Table 1. Relative frequency of tobacco pipe bore diameters at the Spence Site.

Diameter	Number	Percent
4/64" stem	3	7.5
5/64" stem	32	80.0
6/64" stem	4	10.0
7/64" stem	1	2.5
TOTAL	40	100.0
Unmeasurable	48	

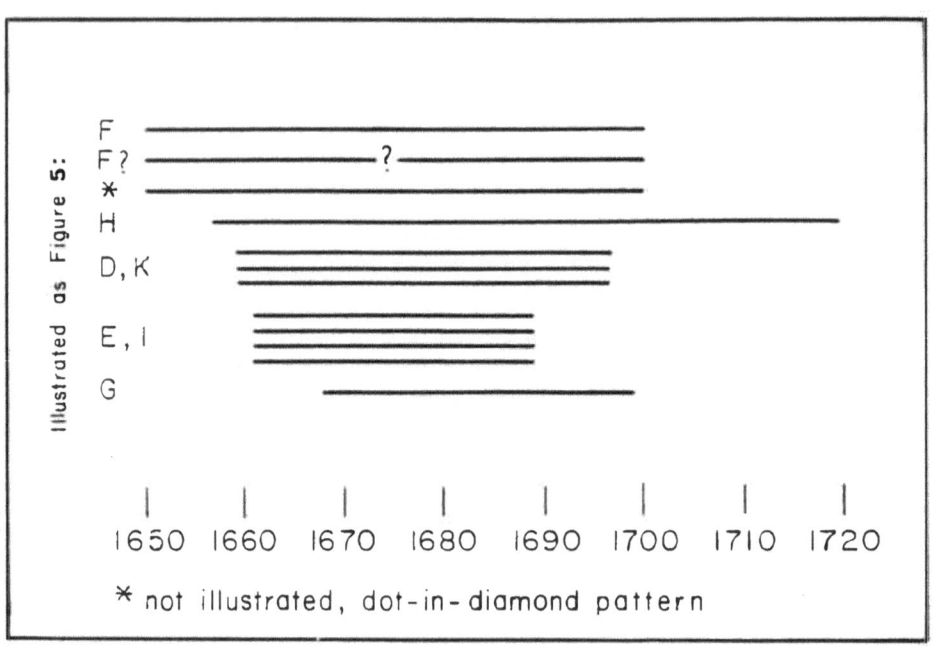

Figure 6: Temporal range of dated pipe marks and decorations from the Spence collection.

unidentified name: "CHRIS:ATHAR-" (Figure 5, l). The stem probably derives from a pipe manufactured by one Chris Atharton, apparently unknown in Bristol since his name is not found listed among pipe makers there. Similar marked pipes have been recovered in undated contexts at both the St. John's (Keeler n.d.) and the van Sweringen sites (King n.d.) in St. Mary's City. A number of pipe makers named Atherton were working in Liverpool, England in the 18th century, but none are recorded for the 17th century (Oswald 1975:176-177). Several Athertons are also listed for Rainford, northwest of Liverpool, all dating to the 18th century, and none is listed as "Christopher," "Christian," or any other variant of "Chris" (Davey et al. 1982:254-255). A Christopher Atherton was baptized in 1666 in the parish of Wigan, Lancashire, and another Christopher was married in 1692 in Standish in Lancashire. No information has been found concerning either of these individuals' occupation (International Geneaological Index n.d.).

Only two possible Dutch marks have been identified in the collection. The two stems have contiguous open circles bordered by incising in a style typical of Dutch decoration (Figure 5, c) (Walker and Wells 1979:34, Fig. 2). The relative paucity of identified Dutch material contrasts with pre-1660 sites in the Southern Maryland region, which often contain large amounts of pottery and tobacco pipes from the Netherlands (Miller 1983; Outlaw 1989).

Bore diameters of 629 stem fragments were measured in 64ths of an inch and their distribution is presented in Figure 7. Comparison of the distribution with that produced by Harrington (1954) indicates an approximate date range of *circa* 1650 to 1680.

ISOLATED FIND

During the survey of the Antenna Field, an unusual and significant pipe stem find was recovered which was not in association with either the Fort Point or the Spence Sites (cf., King and Pogue 1987). Two inscribed white clay pipe stem fragments were recovered on the surface of the plowed field under survey. The more informative stem is marked with the name "JOHN LEWIS" and with an accompanying date of "1666" (Figures 8 and 9). The second stem bears the initials "D.R.," in slightly neater handwork, each letter followed by a period. Both stems, along with a third unmarked stem, were recovered from the same 10-by-10-foot survey unit. All three stems have bore diameters of 5/64ths-inch.

These artifacts and their archaeological provenience are very unusual. The three pipe stems are located at least 120 feet southeast of the early 18th century Spence Site and even farther from the late 17th century Fort Point Site. No other Colonial domestic or architectural artifacts were associated with the find. Both the inscribed pipes and the plain stem have bore diameters of only 5/64ths-inch. Stem diameters of that size are relatively rare on 17th-century sites in Maryland, particularly those of the third quarter, although one of the stems bears the date "1666." No pipe stems with this size bore diameter were recovered from the Fort Point Site. Excavations at the Village Center in St. Mary's City, occupied from 1634 until *circa* 1710, yielded 2122 stem fragments of which only 44 (2.1%) have bore diameters of 5/64ths-inch (Miller 1983:75).

Documentary research has identified a John Lewis residing in Maryland by 1666. John Lewis is identified

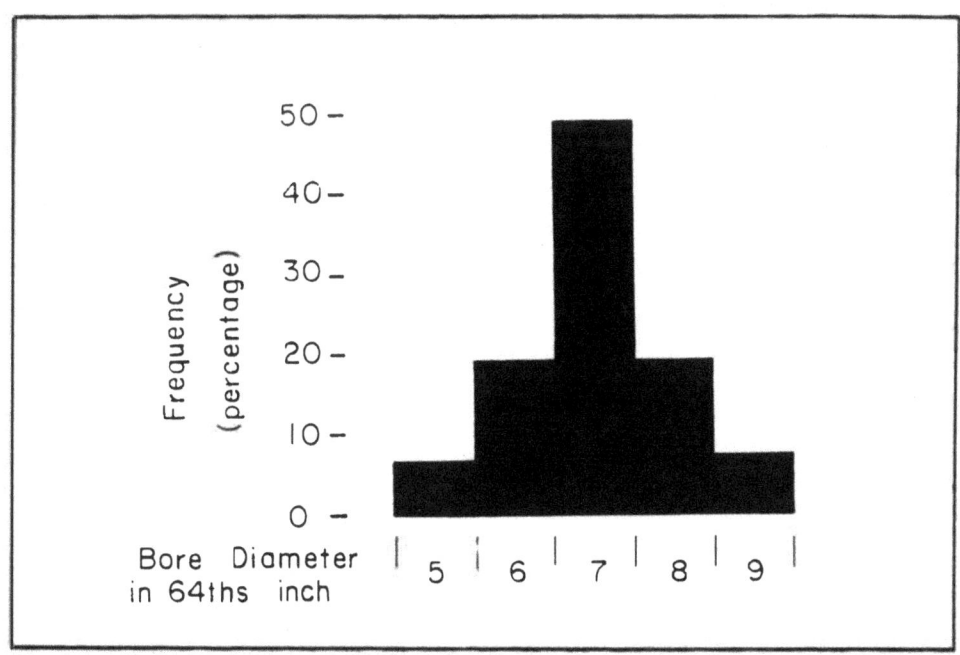

Figure 7: Relative frequency of tobacco pipe bore diameters in the Spence collection.

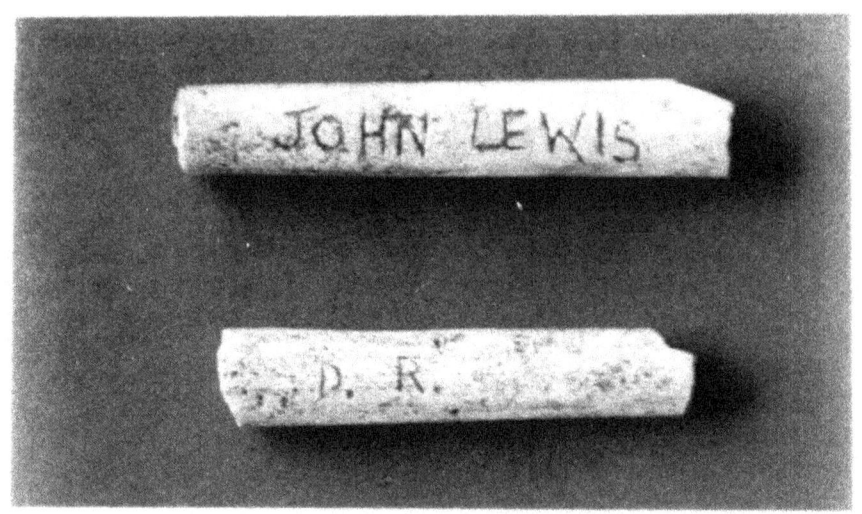

Figure 8: Isolated clay pipe stems, marked "JOHN LEWIS" and "D.R.".

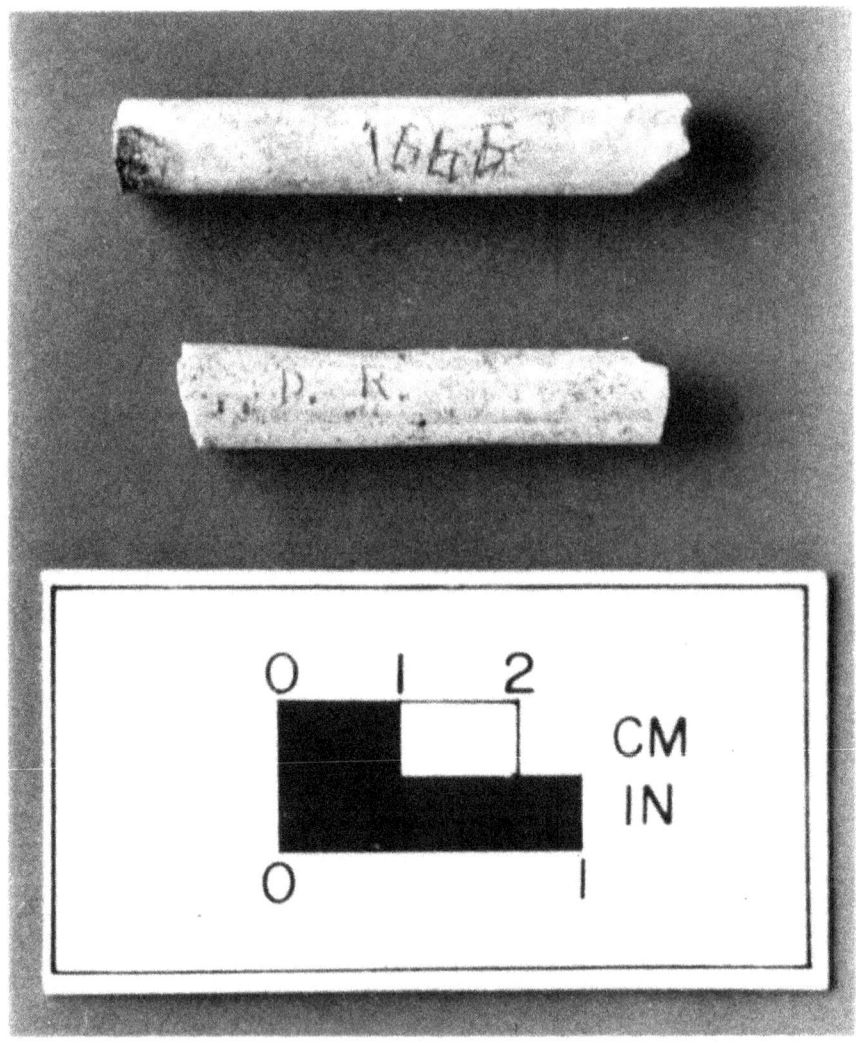

Figure 9: Isolated clay pipe stems, marked "1666" (reverse of "JOHN LEWIS") and "D.R.".

as a planter and householder on nearby St. George's Manor, also owned by the Jesuits. Lewis and his wife, Katherine, immigrated to Maryland from England in 1662 or 1663, and his rights of land were claimed by a Richard Huggins in 1663 (Land Office Patents, Liber, 5:367). Lewis died in 1677 and, when his estate was probated, his belongings included some livestock, pewter tableware, iron cookware and, of special interest, two books (Inv. and Acct., Liber 4:583).

Based on this information, John Lewis of St. George's was probably literate and able to write. Further, he was a tenant on property also owned by the Jesuits, directly across the river from St. Inigoes Manor. In the 17th century, transportation was almost completely water-oriented, and John Lewis could have had ample reason and opportunity to journey to St. Inigoes Manor. His presence in the vicinity of the two tenant sites may be linked to the occupants of the earlier site, dated *circa* 1660-1690. Unfortunately, attempts to identify "D.R." have been unsuccessful.

The unique nature of the find, the lack of associated artifacts, and the small stem bore diameters caused some initial suspicion that the artifacts may have been faked. However, when the stems were shown, unwashed, to professional archaeologists in the region, all were agreed that their outward appearance strongly supported their authenticity. The style of the inscriptions, both letters and numerals, are very similar to styles found in 17th century American documents (Kirkham 1981:34-36). Further, such a hoax would indicate a sophisticated knowledge of the history of St. Inigoes Manor, property now with very restricted access to the public. As for the small bore diameters, the 1666 date may serve simply to demonstrate once more the variation in bore sizes and the limitations of the technique as a relative temporal indicator.

CONCLUSION

The Antenna Field tobacco pipe assemblage, including those recovered from the Fort Point and the Spence Sites and the Spence Collection, contains both identifiable and unidentifiable pipe fragments. While the provenience of these pipes primarily derives from both random and controlled surface collections, the information provided is nonetheless useful for dating the site, as well as for determining origins of tobacco pipes and, by implication, other imported items. The collection is also one of only a few available for the Southern Maryland region outside the more village-like environs of nearby St. Mary's City.

REFERENCES CITED

Alexander, L.T. (1979). Clay pipes from the Buck Site in Maryland. *The archaeology of the clay tobacco pipe, II: the United States of America*. Edited by P.J. Davey, British Archaeological Reports International Series 60:37-61.

Beitzell, E. (1976). *The Jesuit missions of St. Mary's County, Maryland*. Abell, Maryland.

Davey, P.J. *et al.* (1982). The Rainford clay pipe industry: Some archaeological evidence. *The Archaeology of the Clay Tobacco Pipe (VII)*. Edited by P.J. Davey, British Archaeological Reports British Series 100:91-310.

Harrington, J.C. (1954). Dating stem fragments of seventeenth and eighteenth century clay tobacco pipes. *Quarterly Bulletin of the Archaeological Society of Virginia* 9(1):9-13.

International Genealogical Index (n.d.). International genealogical index of the Church of Jesus Christ of Latter Day Saints. Salt Lake City, Utah.

Inventory and Accounts (n.d.). Probate inventory of John Lewis, Liber 4:583. Maryland Hall of Records, Annapolis.

Keeler, R.W. (n.d.) Tobacco Pipes from the St. John's Site, St. Mary's City, Maryland. Ms. on file, Historic St. Mary's City.

King, J.A. (n.d.). Tobacco pipes from the van Sweringen Site, St. Mary's City, Maryland. Ms. on file, Historic St. Mary's City.

King, J.A. and Pogue, D.J. (1987). An unusual pipestem find from St. Inigoes Manor, Maryland. *Historical Archaeology* 21(1):102-104.

King, J.A. and Pogue, D.J. (1985a). St. Inigoes Manor: an archaeological history. *Chronicles of St. Mary's* 34(4):353-359.

King, J.A. and Pogue, D.J. (1985b). *Archaeological investigations at the Antenna Field, St. Inigoes, Maryland*. St. Inigoes, Maryland.

Kirkham, E.K. (1981). *The Handwriting of American records for a period of 300 Years*. Logan, Utah, Everton Publishers.

Land Office Patents (n.d.) Liber 5:367. Maryland Hall of Records, Annapolis.

Miller, H.M. (1983). A search for the "Citty of Saint Maries": report on the 1981 excavations in St Mary's City, Maryland. *St. Maries City Archaeology Series No. 1*.

Oswald, A. (1975). *Clay pipes for the archaeologist*. British Archaeological Reports 14. Oxford, England.

Outlaw, A.C., and others (1989). *The Compton Site, circa 1651-1684*. Louis Berger and Associates, East Orange, New Jersey.

Perogative Court Records (n.d.) Testamentary Proceedings. Liber 5: 116. Maryland Hall of Records, Annapolis.

Smolek, M.A., Lawrence, J.D. and Pepper, S.K. (1983). Archaeological investigations at Fort Point. *Maryland Historical Trust Manuscript Series*, 28.

Walker, I. and Wells, P.K. (1979). Regional varieties of clay tobacco pipe markings in Eastern England. *Archaeology of the Clay Tobacco Pipe I: Britain: the Midlands and Eastern England*. Edited by P.J. Davey, British Archaeological Reports 63.

ACKNOWLEDGEMENTS.

I am grateful to Paul Huey, Mary Owens, Dennis J. Pogue, Alan Spence, and Pat Woodburn for their assistance during the Antenna Field project. The archaeological work was funded by the Naval Electronic Systems Engineering Activity as part of a preconstruction survey. The graphics contained herein were produced by James D. O'Connor.

www.ingramcontent.com/pod-product-compliance
Lightning Source LLC
Chambersburg PA
CBHW041706290426
44108CB00027B/2872

9780860547150